CAMBRIDGE STUDIES IN MUSIC

GENERAL EDITORS: JOHN STEVENS AND PETER LE HURAY

Musical life in Biedermeier Vienna

CAMBRIDGE STUDIES IN MUSIC

GENERAL EDITORS: JOHN STEVENS AND PETER LE HURAY

Volumes in the series include:

Music and poetry in the early Tudor court
JOHN STEVENS

Music and theatre from Poliziano to Monteverdi
NINO PIRROTTA

Music and patronage in sixteenth-century Mantua
IAIN FENLON

Patrons and musicians of the English Renaissance
DAVID PRICE

Music and the Reformation in England 1549–1660
PETER LE HURAY

The music of the English parish church
NICHOLAS TEMPERLEY

The organ music of J. S. Bach
Volume I: Preludes, toccatas, fantasias, fugues, etc.
Volume II: Works based on chorales
Volume III: A background
PETER WILLIAMS

Mendelssohn's musical education
R. LARRY TODD

The musical language of Berlioz
JULIAN RUSHTON

MUSICAL LIFE IN BIEDERMEIER VIENNA

ALICE M. HANSON

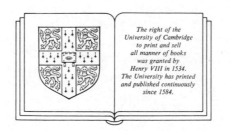

*The right of the
University of Cambridge
to print and sell
all manner of books
was granted by
Henry VIII in 1534.
The University has printed
and published continuously
since 1584.*

CAMBRIDGE UNIVERSITY PRESS

CAMBRIDGE

LONDON   NEW YORK   NEW ROCHELLE

MELBOURNE   SYDNEY

Published by the Press Syndicate of the University of Cambridge
The Pitt Building, Trumpington Street, Cambridge CB2 1RP
32 East 57th Street, New York, NY 10022, USA
10 Stamford Road, Oakleigh, Melbourne 3166, Australia

First published 1985

Printed in Great Britain by
the University Press, Cambridge

Library of Congress catalogue card number: 84–17449

British Library cataloguing in publication data
Hanson, Alice M.
Musical Life in Biedermeier Vienna. –
(Cambridge Studies in Music)
1. Music – Austria – Vienna – History and
criticism – 19th century
I. Title
780'.9436'13   ML246.8.V6

ISBN 0 521 25799 9

UP

CONTENTS

ILLUSTRATIONS

TABLES

ACKNOWLEDGMENTS

Throughout its genesis, from research data to dissertation and book, this work was made possible by the efforts and expertise of many persons to whom I wish to express my appreciation. To my thesis advisor, Professor Herbert Kellman at the University of Illinois, I give special thanks for his guidance and scholarly acumen which gave shape and coherence to my first project. I thank also Professor Cyril Ehrlich at The Queen's University of Belfast for his generous comments and criticism.

I wish to thank collectively the librarians and archivists of the Austrian National Archives, the Viennese City Archives, and the Archives of the Gesellschaft der Musikfreunde for their assistance with manuscript materials. I am indebted also to Hofrat Dr Waissenberg, Director of the Museen der Stadt Wien, for procuring the illustrations. Thanks also to Fern Hyman at the Rice University Library and Connie Gunderson at the St Olaf College Library for their help in locating and lending many uncatalogued treasures.

I am grateful to the Fulbright-Hays Commission and Rice University for the financial aid which made possible my research in Vienna.

For their invaluable assistance in translating many obscure documents and Viennese slang, special thanks are due to William and Carolyn Schildgen. I wish to express appreciation also to Jeffrey Kurtzman, Marcia Citron, and Kirsten Nelson who read and edited my work at its various stages. Thanks also to Rosemary Dooley, Mary Baffoni, and the staff of Cambridge University Press for their patience, recommendations, and aid.

To my parents, family, and friends, I express my deepest gratitude for their humor, love, and encouragement.

AMH

INTRODUCTION

Vienna's rich and enigmatic culture has long fascinated travelers, writers, and scholars, but the period between the Napoleonic wars and the March Revolution (1815–30) is of special interest. For during that era an unprecedented concentration of outstanding musicians, dramatists, writers, and powerful political leaders all lived in the city. Certainly these figures all have been the subject of much critical scrutiny as has Vienna itself. But the broader investigation and correlations between city life and its artists and leaders have been generally ignored. This study aims to fill that gap in part. Its purpose is to examine the impact of certain aspects of Viennese daily life and major institutions on musicians' careers and their compositions, and to consider the character of Viennese life during the first third of the nineteenth century.

The period is known by many names depending upon the writer's interests and bias. Political historians have called the era Restaurationszeit (restoration), referring to the return of the old order of government before Napoleon. Others call the period Stillstand (standstill), implying that little happened until the revolution. Finally, still other historians speak of Vormärz (pre-March), in anticipation of the March revolution in 1848. Personalities have also been used to distinguish the period, such as 'age of Metternich' or 'reign of Franz I'. In the arts, scholars continue to argue about labels of 'classic' and 'romantic' for works created during these years. The term 'Biedermeier' was drawn from a series of satirical articles in the *Fliegende Blätter* of 1855–7, whose hero was a fictional schoolmaster by the name of Gottlieb Biedermeier (literally 'God-loving common man'). The character epitomized the self-confident, smug middle-class man and was soon thereafter applied to the outlook and art of 1815–48 in Germany and Austria. As Carl Dahlhaus has explained, the term is often used in a condescending or derogatory manner and conveys more about social outlook and middle-class institutions than about any distinctive artistic style or form.[1] I have chosen the designation Biedermeier Vienna with no negative connotation but only to take advantage of its period (1815–30) and its broader, more inclusive, social outlook. The term seems appropriate since many Viennese writers, only twenty years distant from the period, refer to those years as Alt Wien (Old Vienna) or the 'Good Old Days' in recognition of their importance and that city life had in some way changed. For music, these years signal a brilliant but abrupt decline in Vienna's international dominance in orchestral art music as well as a change in musical patronage and tastes.

The work begins with a brief summary of the political events, economic conditions, and social fabric of Viennese life at the beginning of the century. An entire chapter is devoted to the various ways the Austrian government and police attempted to regulate music and musicians. Each succeeding chapter then examines individual institutions and genres in which music played an important role: theater, concerts, salons, church, synagogue, and military and popular music. Where possible, I have attempted to correlate factual information about current conditions and events with the lives and careers of musicians in order to offer possible explanations for their actions or to better demonstrate their relation to their contemporaries. The final chapter draws some conclusions about Viennese culture and musical life during the period and offers a brief epilogue describing some of the sweeping changes that occurred in the 1830s.

Such a study necessarily draws upon a wide variety of information. Most of the primary materials were taken from Vienna's national and municipal archives. Another important source was the large body of eyewitness accounts preserved in travel literature, diaries, memoirs and letters. Although such personal records and semi-fictional genres contain obvious bias and literary license, their vivid and often detailed accounts of daily life offer another dimension to a history and understanding of Viennese life.

The great store of scholarship in the diverse aspects of the period provides yet another important area of examination. The monumental scholarly work of Alexander Thayer, Otto Deutsch, Carl Glossy, and Otto Rommel, to name a few, has provided countless avenues of investigation and has raised many intriguing questions. The bibliography at the end of this present book will discuss briefly these and other aspects of the sources.

Because the study repeatedly mentions money, a word about the great variety of currencies then in circulation is warranted. While a full comprehension of the exchange rates of that time is impossible today, a clearer understanding of money's relative worth is imperative before estimating its value. Hence, throughout the work, all moneys are quoted in their original currency and then, in parentheses, converted to florin or Gulden (fl.) in the Conventionsmünze (CM), the standard established after 1811. The distinction is important since, in Vienna, the florin in Wiener Währung (WW) was worth only two-fifths of the former. The following conversion table is provided for the most frequently used moneys around 1820:[2]

	Florin (CM)
1 florin (WW) = 60 Kreuzer (kr.)	24 kr.
1 (Prussian) Reichsthaler (rth.)	1 fl. 30 kr.
= 24 groschen (gr.)	
= 288 Pfennig (pf.)	
1 Spiezthaler (silver) = 32 fr.	2 fl.
1 pound (£) sterling = 20 shillings (s)	10 fl.
= 240 pence (d)	
1 guinea = 21s	10 fl. 30 kr.
1 souverain (gold) = 9 rth.	13 fl. 20 kr.˙
1 louis d'or (gold)	*c.* 11 fl.
1 ducat (gold)	4 fl. 30 kr.
1 dollar ($) = 100 cents (¢)	2 fl. 15 kr.

Throughout, German quotations are presented in English, but they are printed in their original form in the endnotes. Where possible, the translations are taken from published sources. The others are my own.

I

THE CIVIC ENVIRONMENT FOR MUSIC

Much of Vienna's political importance and cultural influence in Europe was attained during the eighteenth century. Hence a brief review of the events and policies of that era is necessary for a better understanding of the city's particular character, outlook, and change during the nineteenth century.

Austria was an unwieldy empire, comprising diverse territories, provinces, and city-states which the Habsburgs had acquired through marriage and war. Not bound by common language, ethnic heritage, or history, Austrian subjects seem to have felt little imperial allegiance, for they continued to identify with their province (e.g. Bohemian), their ethnic group (Magyar or Croat), or with their native city (Neapolitan or Venetian). When subjects moved to Vienna, their regional loyalties and local customs remained strong. Even when German was declared to be the official language of the empire, city residents clung to their native tongues and dialects. In addition, French was spoken in aristocratic society, Italian among artists and musicians, and Latin among clerics and scholars.

Throughout the eighteenth century the primary goal of both Maria Theresia (reigned 1740–80) and Joseph II (1780–90) had been to consolidate and modernize the administration of the empire. Like those of other Habsburg rulers, their reforms asserted the primacy of the state through pragmatic and expedient means. Such policies directly affected many aspects of Viennese life.

Foremost among the reforms was the reorganization of the government and the codification of imperial law. New agencies, managed by professional diplomats and officials, began to carry out the

4

specialized affairs of state. By 1781, a uniform legal code had been compiled, torture abolished, and the death penalty limited to severe crimes. Vienna became the home of foreign dignitaries, lawyers, bureaucrats, and official advisors as well as those seeking work or special favors. The presence of the government had other ramifications in the city, for even the simplest request or business transaction became more bureaucratic, often requiring elaborate procedures and delays. Further, the bureaucracy's slow pace and the low pay of its employees fostered widespread bribery, nepotism and intrigue in both government and business.

To stimulate the economy, Maria Theresia and Joseph II replaced the feudal practices of primogeniture and robot (the service owed a landlord by his serf) with free choice of beneficiaries and a system of land taxes, thereby providing incentives to farmers to buy their own lands and to increase the productivity of their farms. At the same time, the new taxes filled the imperial treasury with needed capital. Although most of the efforts to expand Austria's trade and industry abroad failed during the eighteenth century, the economic reforms led to the introduction of highly profitable silk textiles, sugar refining, and porcelain manufacturing into Vienna.

Social reforms, particularly those of general education, were intended better to equip Austrian subjects for serving the state. By 1774, Maria Theresia had established over five hundred new primary schools. Schools which offered advanced practical skills were also organized. For example, the Theresianum offered military and diplomatic training to the sons of noblemen; the Josephinian gave medical training to military doctors, and the Oriental Academy taught diplomats the languages of the Middle East and Asia. These, with the University, made Vienna a center for learning and a gathering place for some of the empire's most gifted students.

The particular relationship between the Austrian state and the Catholic church also had repercussions in Vienna. Since the end of the Thirty Years' War, Austria had been staunchly Roman Catholic. The familial ties of the Habsburgs to Spain may also explain the degree of religious fervor displayed by the court as well as the zeal with which they persecuted Dissenters and Jews throughout the empire. Such devotion was manifested in Vienna by the great number of religious holidays and ceremonies observed throughout the year and the lengths to which governmental agencies went to regulate public morality. In 1753, for example, Maria Theresia established a Chastity Commission to expose and punish anyone engaged in prostitution or adultery. Similarly, the government fined those caught eating meat in Lent or those who failed to attend confession. These measures laid the foundation for the secret police in the next century.

But, however devout, the Habsburg monarchs repeatedly divested the church of its wealth and temporal power in the empire. In 1773, the Jesuits were expelled, and later many religious orders were dissolved. In Vienna, ecclesiastical courts lost much of their influence, and, in the name of economy, the number of religious holidays was curtailed and the length and grand scale of the Mass were reduced. By 1781, even Protestants and Jews were allowed to worship in public.

The conservative pragmatism of Habsburg policies had varying impact on Vienna's intellectual and artistic climate during the eighteenth century. Dismissed by the state for their impractical and subversive ideas, and condemned by the church for their immorality, the works of the most 'enlightened' were banned by Austrian censors. Some of the literature found its way into a few private salons, but it seemed to make little impression. Hence the work of Austrians in the fields of pure science, philosophy, and literature during the period lacked real distinction. Instead, the greatest achievements were made in theater and music.

The theater was one of Vienna's most popular amusements. Aristocrats staged operas, dramas, and ballets in their salons, while members of the lower classes flocked to comedies performed by traveling companies. Taking advantage of this wide interest in drama, but seeking also to elevate his subject's tastes and to stimulate native writers, Joseph II established a National Theater in Vienna in 1776 and a National Singspiel in 1778. Vienna soon became the capital of classical German drama and Singspiel, renowned for the high quality of its actors and stagecraft. Shortly thereafter, other theaters opened and prospered: Leopoldstadt Theater (1781), Theater an der Wieden (1787), and the Josefstadt Theater (1788).

The civic environment for music

Music was Vienna's other widely cultivated art. Some of Europe's best musicians and composers were employed by the court's chapel and theaters. Vying with them were private orchestras assembled by such aristocrats as the Esterhazy, Kinsky, Schwarzenberg, Liechtenstein, and Grassalkowitz families, which until around 1795 regularly gave private concerts of new music. Likewise, the salons of lesser nobles, wealthy bankers, and bureaucrats held frequent recitals by and for music-loving amateurs. Furthermore, dance musicians, folk singers, and itinerant harpists entertained in Vienna's restaurants and taverns with popular music.

One of the period's greatest innovations was the establishment of regular public concerts. Among these, the concerts of the Tonkünstler Society, begun in 1772, introduced the Viennese to Haydn's *Creation* (1799) and *The Seasons* (1801). The concerts also offered virtuosi such as Mozart (in 1782) and Beethoven (in 1792) the opportunity to perform in public and, thereby, to attract the attention of wealthy patrons and a wider audience.

Vienna's flourishing musical life and the growth of its musical public are reflected in the success of its musical businesses. The piano manufacturers Andreas Streicher (in 1794) and Konrad Graf (in 1804) began to produce fine instruments to meet the demands of dilettante and professional pianists. Similarly, such publishers as Artaria (in 1780), Cappi (in 1796), and Haslinger (in 1801) began to publish music for the home as well as for the theater and concert hall.

But, in spite of the high level of musical activity in the city, life for an independent musician in the eighteenth century was almost impossible without the aid and protection of an aristocrat, as the biographies of Haydn and Mozart testify. Only meager incomes could be made from the sale of compositions; private subscription concerts were both costly and time-consuming for the performer; and private engagements in the homes of even wealthy patrons were often poorly rewarded. Even as a member of a noble household, a musician had difficulties, because, like a servant, he had few rights. A musician was required to compose or perform upon command and he often relinquished all publishing rights of his own music to his employer. In addition, he had to gain permission not only to perform outside of the household, but also in order to marry or change residence. If he displeased his patron, he could expect to be beaten or kicked, as was Mozart, or to be put in jail, like Dittersdorf, for fleeing his post.

News of the French Revolution and, later, Napoleon's rise to power abruptly diverted the attention and energies of the Austrian empire. Music, too, reflected the rising political sentiments. Some music was nationalistic, such as Haydn's song that became the Austrian national anthem and Beethoven's 'Song of farewell to the citizens of Austria' for a regiment of local recruits. Other music was written in a more heroic, possibly revolutionary, vein, such as Wranitsky's Freedom Symphony of 1797 and Beethoven's Eroica or 'Heroic' Symphony no. 3.

The reality of the ensuing wars, however, meant radical change. The Austrians witnessed the official demise of the Holy Roman Empire in 1806 and two French occupations of Vienna in 1806 and 1810. Even their own Princess Marie Louise was given in marriage to their enemy, Napoleon. The long years of battle were devastating also. In Vienna, the population fell by about 46,000 (from 270,000 in 1793 to 224,000 in 1810). Moreover, the money spent to equip and supply the army drained the imperial treasury and the resources of the aristocracy. By 1811, the state had declared bankruptcy and inflation devalued the currency by over 40%. Those whose incomes depended upon fees or wages were reduced to poverty.

With frenzied gaiety, the Viennese celebrated the signing of the peace treaties during the Vienna Congress of 1814–15. Franz I set about rebuilding the empire and reasserting his authority in accordance with past principles. However, the events of the intervening twenty-five years had produced too great a gulf for a full restoration of the old ways. Important political, social, and artistic changes were already underway.

VIENNA IN THE NINETEENTH CENTURY

Vienna began the nineteenth century as the third largest city in Western Europe, after London and Paris. Recovering from the war, the population in 1820 steadily increased at an average annual rate of about 5,500 persons, so that by 1830 it approached 320,000.

Viennese population 1820–30

1821	264,110
1822	267,355
1823	269,368
1824	274,577
1825	278,004
1826	288,809
1827	299,180
1828	306,077
1829	312,974
1830	319,873

(Bammer, 6)

Part of the increase was due to a steady influx of immigrants. Winfried Bammer has demonstrated that in 1810 only 8.25% of all Viennese were foreigners (Fremde). The percentage doubled by 1825 and by 1840 nearly 43% of Viennese residents were foreign born. Many of these people came from the East, including Hungarians, Poles, Bohemians, Czechs, Slovenes, Moravians, Silesians, Serbs, Croats, Armenians, Turks, and Greeks. While the great diversity of nationalities led to problematic conflicts for the government such as ethnic rivalries and separatist movements within Austria, it imparted a richness and color to Viennese culture and art.

Within the heterogeneous population lived the city's musicians, performers, and artists. Unfortunately there is insufficient evidence to estimate their number, for there was no official census and military-conscription records rarely recorded one's occupation. Normann guesses that, in 1827, there were roughly 9,000 businessmen, artists, and academicians living in Vienna, but he does not say in what proportion (xi).

The surnames and birthplaces of well-known Viennese musicians during the first half of the century reflect the diversity of nationality. These foreign musicians were a real boon to the city's musical life because they added their folk culture, their particular type of performance practices, and in some cases their expertise in building musical instruments (see Table 1).

Information about the domiciles of musicians is also scarce, but

Table 1. *Foreign-born musicians in Vienna 1815–30*

Bohemia	Ferdinand Schimon	*Silesia*
Karl Maria von Bocklet	Josef Seipelt	Emanuel A. Förster
Josef Friedlowsky		Franz Gebauer
Jacob Freystädtler	*Germany*	Josef Lincke
Josef Gellinek	Ludwig van Beethoven (Bonn)	Karl Rüger
Franz Gläser	Hermann Neefe (Bonn)	Johann Sedlacek
Adalbert Gyrowetz	Josef Spitzeder (Bonn)	Franz Weiss
Friedrich Hradesky	Conradin Kreutzer (Baden)	
Johann Hummel	Franz Lachner (Bavaria)	*Poland*
Franz Janda	Ignaz Lachner (Bavaria)	Georg Bayr
Leopold Jansa	Friedrich Kalkbrenner (Cassel)	Kaczkowski
Leopold Kozeluch	Ernst Krämer (Dresden)	Johann Vesque
Anton Krafft	J. Peter Pixis (Mannheim)	
Paul Maschek	Josef Preindl (Trier)	*Italy*
Ignaz Moscheles	Jacob Riotte (Trier)	Pietro Rovelli
Franz Pechatschek	Anton Bohrer (Munich)	Anton Salieri
Simon Sechter	Max Bohrer (Munich)	Leon de St Lubin (Turin)
Josef Slawik	George Vogeler (Würzburg)	
Franz Stadler		*Austrian states*
Dionys Weber	*Moravia*	Rafael Dresler (Styria)
Franz Weber	Josef Fischof	Johann Gänsbacher (Tyrol)
Wilhelm Würfel	Johann Horzalka	Anton Halm (Styria)
	Ferdinand Kauer	Joachim Hoffman (Lower
Hungary	Josef Kinsky	Austria)
Josef Böhm	Franz Krommer	Maximilian (Abbé) Stadler
Leopold Böhm	Wenzel Plachy	(Lower Austria)
Stephan Heller	Anton Wrantisky	

studies using sequestration records have allowed some general conclusions. According to Bammer, in the year 1830, of the 42 persons listed in the death certificates as 'musicians', 12 lived within the Inner City and the Leopoldstadt, while the others were evenly scattered in the suburbs (228).

For most people in Vienna, life was harsh. The infant-mortality rate was high, and expectancy of life low. Adolf Schmidl's guidebook states that, during the years 1801–25, the average life span for a Viennese man (he does not specify class) was 36–40 years, and for a woman 41–45 years (16). Thus, if Franz Schubert's lifetime of 32 years could be regarded as a little below average for the city, Beethoven was an old man at 56 years. Many women died in childbirth and it was therefore common for men to remarry or for motherless or orphaned children to be raised by a relative. Again, Franz Schubert's family experience was fairly typical. His father married twice and had 19 children, only 9 of whom survived. His brother Ferdinand also married twice and had 28 children, of whom 12 survived.

British visitors, such as John Russell and John Strang, pointed to Vienna's high illegitimacy rate as proof of the city's immorality. Russell wrote: 'It is not easy to find a city, where dissolute life is so prevalent, where female virtue is less prized, and hence also so sparingly found.'[1] Estimates suggest that some 40% of all births in 1830 were illegitimate, a percentage higher than anywhere in Austria except Graz, and one which continued to rise (Turnbull, 150; Bammer, 10). But figures tell us little about 'morality', for bureaucratic and legal obstacles prevented many couples from qualifying for marriage. As in many parts of Germany and France, priests in Austria were expressly forbidden to marry couples who could not produce evidence testifying to their education, good conduct, loyalty to the government, and sufficient material wealth to support a family. Priests who disregarded the regulation could be held responsible for the support of the children if the couple lacked the means (Turnbull, 152).

Since only about half the Austrians of marriageable age had an education, many couples lived as common-law spouses and thus their children were counted by the state as illegitimate. Such hurdles to marriage may help to explain the large number of bachelors in Austria during the century. Among the Schubert circle alone at least five (Schubert, Jenger, Bauernfeld, Castelli and Grillparzer) never married, and those who did waited until they were at least thirty years old (Kupelweiser at age 30; Max Spaun at 33; Ferdinand Bogner at 39; Karl Enderes at 47; Michael Vogel at 58; and Franz Schober at 60).

Many writers from the period allude to chronic personal illness and express fears about death. The Swedish poet, Per Atterbom, fled Vienna when he learned that a musician he had recently met had died of a lung infection (243); and the diaries of Karl Rosenbaum and the Hartmann brothers record countless colds and illnesses that confined them to their beds. Partly to blame were Vienna's climate, geographical situation, and the current level of medical knowledge. Cold, damp winters and hot, dusty summers with prevailing winds from the Hungarian plains provoked all kinds of ailments. To escape the worst of these, each summer Vienna's wealthy citizens retreated to their summer homes in the country or to popular spas such as Baden (only fourteen miles away), Teplitz, Franzensbrunn, and Marienbad. Musicians often followed the retinues to perform in the resorts' theaters and pavilions or, like Beethoven, they sought a cheaper substitute in the summer houses in the Viennese woods or along the Danube, as in Heiligenstadt. Those forced to remain in the city braved the unhealthy dust, graphically described by an anonymous observer in 1793:

Since the ground is spread with a fine chalk, which through the years has been finely ground, the dust rises easily; the blowing wind leads it along in thick clouds, the air becomes darker with it and people wander like the gods of Olympus – not in an ethereal cloud, but in thick dust which gets into lungs and chest and hurts the eyes...[2]

Thanks to the guidebooks of Schmidl and Pezzl and the travel notes of Wilhelm Horn, a young doctor from Berlin who visited Vienna's hospitals during the summer of 1828, we have more precise information about the variety and incidence of diseases in the city. Immediately striking is the toll taken by periodic epidemics. In 1806, 2,330 persons died from smallpox; in 1822, 565 died from scarlet fever; and, in 1831, 1,953 died from cholera (Schmidl, 16). Horn indicates other ailments common in the population.

Incidence of disease in Vienna (Horn)[3]

| | From records of 1826 | | | | Observed in July 1828 |
| | | | deaths | | |
	men	women	men	women	cases
lung infections	320	213	32	22	32
tuberculosis	384	427	241	155	54
catarrh	672	377	34	8	70
gastric disorders	202	135	5	9	40
dropsy (edema)	169	189	73	79	?
nerve fever	343	139	8	6	70
rheumatic fever	275	403	5	8	57
'Wechsel' fever	343	139	8	6	109
tumors	642	98	6	8	34
chronic gout	186	112	11	4	15

The most common diseases were those affecting the lungs. From 1820 to 1830, recorded deaths from tuberculosis ranged from 400 to 600 (Horn, 190–6; Bammer, 11). By mid-century, some observers labeled it the 'Viennese sickness', contemporary estimates ranging from 4 to 60% of the population (C. J. Weber, 244; Normann, 15). No wonder the slightest cough alarmed mothers and filled most citizens with dread.

Other diseases were caused by impure drinking water. The city's water supply was often contaminated by routine floods of the Danube River and the lack of public sanitation. Horn saw many cases of abdominal typhus and noted that some cases were contagious (213). Some of the guides even warn prospective tourists against drinking the water from the wells of such low-lying districts as Leopoldstadt (Pezzl, *Beschreibung* (1841) 11; Jäck and Heller, 296; Hebenstreit, 66). Unfortunately, physicians could warn of, but not prevent or cure typhus, typhoid fever, hepatitis, and chronic diarrhoea, which were caused by impure water. The diseases brought much suffering and sometimes death – two of the best-known victims of such gastric ailments being Beethoven and Schubert.

Venereal disease was, of course, not openly discussed, but its ravages were of highest concern to Vienna's artists, who tended to live outside conventional sexual mores or who were financially barred from marriage. When the disease itself was not fatal, the treatment (usually mercury) often poisoned or so weakened the patient that he fell victim to other illnesses. Evidently the disease was widespread in the city, in 1828 Horn counting 190 cases under treatment in only one of the hospitals (249). And because the authorities made little attempt to regulate the city's prostitutes, and because many were afraid to report or were ignorant of their infections, the disease spread unchecked.

On the basis of largely circumstantial evidence, recent biographers generally agree that both Beethoven and Schubert had venereal disease at one time in their lives. While it is no longer believed that Beethoven's deafness resulted from that illness, there is some agreement that he was infected at one time.[4] Deutsch contends that Schubert probably contracted the disease around 1823, judging from the veiled allusions of his friends, his choice of doctor, and the treatments which caused him to have his head shaved (*Biography*, 287, 314, 821). But the important point in both cases lies not so much in the fact that the men contracted the disease, which was pandemic in Vienna, but that they suffered its physical side-effects and that they probably shared with their contemporaries in the mental anguish and anxiety about sexual encounters. Such tensions may have had considerable bearing on their friendships with women or even their choice and treatment of texts that deal with love. In a broader sense, perhaps the qualms about such diseases may have contributed to the general repression and displacement of normal sexual expression, discussed at length by Janik and Toulim as characterizing Viennese society at the end of the nineteenth century (46–8).

LIVING STANDARDS

In order to understand more clearly the social position and daily pressures on a musician living in Vienna, one needs a general idea of nineteenth-century living costs and incomes. Taken together, travel literature and letters provide some of the most useful and precise information on these matters.

A common theme is that Viennese housing was expensive and often of poor quality (Pezzl, *Beschreibung* (1841), 24; Jenny, 2,4,; Holmes, 138; Strang, 339). Hotels, in particular, were costly. Hotel rooms between 1808 and 1826 ranged in price from 30 to over 100 fl. a day, according to observers. Comparing them to those of Paris in 1836, Blumenbach found the 'charges for rooms, and everything they provide...extravagantly high' (1, 62). In addition, he noted that many hotels were infested with insects, probably bed-bugs.

Hence, most travellers and single adults were advised to take rooms as lodgers or to rent apartments. But these were not always easy to find or afford, for after 1815, with post-war immigration into the city and the severe lack of capital to build new apartments, Vienna faced housing shortages. Hickmann has shown that, in 1815, an average of 33 persons lived in one Viennese apartment. That average rose to 36 persons in 1825, and by 1830 38 persons occupied the same space (20–1). The crowded quarters may account for the popularity of Viennese neighbourhood restaurants and coffee houses, which served for many musicians and artists as communal and living rooms.

Lodgers usually rented by the day or month (hence Monatzimmer), paying in 1827 from 13 to 14 fl. a year in houses in suburban Liechtenthal or Himmelpfortgrund and from 51 to 86 fl. in the Jägerzeile and Inner City (Banik-Schweitzer and Pircher, Table 7, 160).

Most of the middle-class travelers rented apartments consisting of two (bed chamber, drawing room) to six rooms. Apartment rents also varied according to location, situation, and season. Fashionable districts within the Inner City such as Hohe Markt, Graben, Burgplatz, and am Hof charged more than more distant suburbs such as Rossau or Liechtenthal. Also, rooms on the first two storeys above ground level were preferred to those on the ground or in garrets.

Apartments were rented by the season, bounded by St George's Day (24 April) and St Michael's Day (29 September). So closely associated were these days with payments or rents and moving that in his satire, *Zu Ebener Erde und Erster Stock*, Johann Nestroy named the landlord Georgi-Michaeli Zins (George Michael Rent). The importance of the dates is confirmed in Beethoven's conversation books, for in April and September the pages are full of rental inquiries and calculations. In this Beethoven was not alone, as Pezzl exclaims that during these two months 'half the city changed its residence' (*Skizze*, 67).

When Beethoven sought new rooms in 1824, he recorded the prices and some details about available apartments. That year, apartments within the city with three to five rooms, usually on the second floor, cost between 250 and 600 fl. a year. The Banik-Schweitzer and Pircher demographic study for the year 1827 includes an even wider annual price range – from 112 fl. in the Alsergrund to 441 fl. in the Inner City (160).

Only few could afford to own or rent houses; consequently their price and description are rarely mentioned. About average appear to be the amounts paid for Haydn's home in Gumpendorf in 1810 of 6,840 fl. (CM) and for the Schubert family house in Himmelpfortgrund in 1826 of 6,600 fl. (CM) (Hanson, Table 2). In 1824 Beethoven noted that an apartment house sold for 7,500 fl. and that a house in Döbling cost 7,000 and in Landstrasse 4,000 fl. (CM), and these prices reflect a doubling in cost since 1810, according to Pezzl (*Beschreibung*, 1826, 30).

Food constituted the largest proportion of living expenses, but observers agree that, unlike housing, it was abundant and relatively cheap. In his guidebook for 1823, Pezzl produced an itemized list of food consumed in Vienna. While the statistics are difficult to interpret, they strongly suggest that the typical Viennese diet included meat, fish and eggs (Pezzl, *Beschreibung* (1826), 24–5; Normann, xii–xiii). Many citizens regularly ate at least one meal a day at a restaurant (Trakteur) which offered set menus for variable prices. Pezzl mentions the Blaue Flasche, which in 1790 daily, between 11 a.m. and 3 p.m., served over 350 persons with meals that cost from $4\frac{1}{2}$ kr. to 1 fl. For a mere 8 kr., one received a soup, a serving of meat and vegetables – beer or wine cost extra. He adds that 'The portions are so large that one would have to have a powerfully voracious stomach (Fressmagen) which could eat without ever becoming completely full' (*Beschreibung* 1820, 360–1). In 1824 Beethoven frequented a Trakteur in the Tuchlauben where he dined for only 24 kr. (*Konversationshefte*, IV, 310). Presumably, one could eat for 1 fl. a day in Vienna, but many lived on less. Johann Gänsbacher, future Kapellmeister of St Stephan's cathedral, economized during his student years in Vienna (*c.* 1812) by skipping breakfast and spending only 16 kr. for lunch and 9 kr. for supper – a total of less than half a florin per day (Schmidt, 132).

Food costs also rose during the period. Hickmann's examination of beef prices from 1800 to 1836, for example, shows an expected sharp rise during the war and post-war periods – from 18 to 99 Heller a kilo in 1800 and 1817.[5] Prices stabilized around 1820 to about 35–45 Heller, but generally rose toward 1830 to triple what they had been in 1800.

But even during the Napoleonic Wars when food was expensive and scarce, the Viennese, Caroline Pichler states, could still find food in soup kitchens, on the Wipplingerstrasse. Established by the k.k. Hofkommission für Armenpflege and administered by volunteers from the nobility and middle classes, the kitchens served for 1 kr. a pint (Seidel) of 'Rumford' soup, named after Benjamin Rumford (1753–1814), an American-born English statesman and reformer, who worked in Bavaria to establish better care for the army and the poor. However, Pichler continues, so few people bought the cheap soup that the kitchen closed after only twenty days (25 Jan. to 14 Feb. 1802), possibly an indication that other food was available to the poor even then. She concludes:

...despite the misery of the lower classes and despite the philanthropic complaints of so many charitable souls, who believe their every word and are smitten with sympathy for their need, this deplorable state of affairs, in the great majority of cases, was only a relative one. If real need had been present generally, as in Switzerland and in Hamburg, the soup would have found customers and enthusiasts.[6]

By 1832 Normann maintained that only a few Viennese were unable to afford food and meat, claiming that meat consumption was two to three times greater there than in other large cities in proportion to population (22). Accordingly, Viennese gained the reputation abroad as gluttons. James Holman complained in 1824 that 'at Vienna they do nothing but eat!' (277), and echoing the statements of Russell and Schaden, John Strang surmised, 'But eating – everlasting eating – forms with them the chief charm of existence' (247). While none of the men bothered further to substantiate his observations, the persistence of their charges suggests that the Viennese probably ate better than many of their European contemporaries.

Another necessity was firewood for cooking and heat, which in Vienna was costly (Sandgruber, Table 3). In 1826 Pezzl calls 'expensive' a cord (Klafter) of softwood at 8–10 fl. and of hardwood at 12–15 fl. (1826, 30). In addition, city dwellers paid a service charge for the woodcutters and haulers, which in 1823 amounted to 1 fl. 30 kr. (Beethoven, *Konversationshefte*, IV, 317). Some grand houses reportedly burned a cord of wood a day. In 1824 the Apollosaal, Vienna's largest and most elegant dance hall, burned $1\frac{1}{2}$ cords a night at a cost of 26 fl. 48 kr.[7] Average consumption was surely much less. Pezzl's conservative estimates for 1786 and 1804 place annual fuel costs at 24–40 fl., but these undoubtedly rose after 1815 (1826, 24–5). For example, Beethoven complained in 1823 that he spent 100 fl. on fuel and that that autumn he prepared for winter by paying 13 fl. 48 kr. for three cords of wood with the service charge (Thayer, 865; Beethoven, *Konversationshefte*, IV, 317).

Clothing too was expensive in Vienna, where dress and outward appearances were deemed important. Blumenbach wrote:

Among the middle and lower classes, *dress* is the great and seemingly the only object of variety or ambition. To this passion they sacrifice far more than the Parisian; and nothing strikes the stranger's attention so forcibly, as the richly-dressed population at all places of public resort. (152)

Like other items, clothing soared in price after the wars – between 1790 and 1817 increasing up to six times (Mayr, 221 n.). Shoes rose in cost from 2 to 12 fl., and a pair of boots cost between 6 and 30 fl. If, as Pezzl claims, a man's suit cost between 35 and 42 fl. in 1790, then by 1820 that same suit could easily have cost up to 100 fl. (*Skizze*, 192).

Pezzl's guidebook advises in 1804 that a gentleman should allow 60 fl. for winter clothes, 40 fl. for summer clothes, 80 fl. for formal attire and 45 fl. for additional expenses (*Skizze*, 161). Observers are silent about the cost of women's wardrobes, although they probably cost more since they required more fabric, labor, and variety. An indication of the expense may be the price of fashionable shawls worn by most women, which in 1809 cost second-hand up to 80 ducats (360 fl.), according to Reichardt (224 n.). Writing to the theater director in Hamburg in 1826, the actress Sophie Schröder explained that the cheapest she could have a dress made in Vienna was about 27 fl. (18).

Despite the numerous expenses recorded by eyewitnesses, the actual cost of living comfortably in Vienna is unknown. Pezzl provided figures in 1786 and 1804 for a middle-class gentleman of 'unpretentious life style'. An anonymous writer supplied an estimate for 1793, but without any qualification.[8]

	1786	1793	1804
Room	60 fl.	144 fl.	128 fl. CM
Heat/light	24	30	40
Food	180	365	500
Clothing	160	170	225
Laundry	10	30	30
Miscel.	30	36	44
Total	464 fl.	775 fl.	967 fl. CM

While the figures illustrate the relative cost of food and clothing, their early dates render them unreliable for use in post-war Vienna. Here an incident preserved in Austrian court records offers a better indication of living costs. In 1817 two day-workers (Taglohner) in the court accounting office petitioned the emperor to raise their wages from 2 to 3 fl. a day. One of the men itemized his barest needs:

	Per day	Annual (× 365)
Room (distant suburb)	24 kr.	146 fl.
Food	1 fl. 54 kr.	693 fl. 30 kr.
Clothing/laundry	28 kr.	170 fl. 20 kr.
Total	2 fl. 46 kr.	1,009 fl. 50 kr.

The other man claimed that his minimum subsistence expenses were
3 fl. 10 kr. a day (or 1,155 fl. 50 kr. a year) (Mayr, 220–1). The emperor
replied, calling the men's living standard wretched ('kümmerlich') and
allowed them a token increase. When comparing barest needs of 1,000
fl. in 1817 to Pezzl's 'comfortable' income just a decade before, the
toll of inflation is clear. By 1828 Sealsfield's advice that a gentleman
needed at least 2,000 fl. a year to live well in Vienna, then, must be
no exaggeration (208)!

SALARIES AND INCOMES

Against these expenses must be compared the incomes earned during
the same period. Table 2 has been compiled from archival and personal
records of Viennese residents and more recent scholarly estimates.
Although fragmentary and uneven, the listing of salaries offers a point
of reference and some revelations.

Immediately apparent is the gulf separating the incomes of the
nobility and civil servants as well as the upper military officials from
their lower ranks. Among Viennese performers the range was narrower,
though the state theaters paid their employees better than did the
independent stages in the suburbs. A Kapellmeister ranked about the
same as a court secretary or accountant in a nobleman's employ, while
a performing musician's salary was about that of a school teacher or
lower official.

Among the lower working classes, those in domestic service,
particularly in the homes of aristocrats, could expect to earn more than
lesser military officers or elementary school teachers. The annual
earnings of factory and piece-workers are more difficult to assess
because the workers rarely worked all year round or, like the sedan–chair
bearers, could not work continuously all day. Heavy-machine industries,

Table 2. *Annual incomes in Vienna* (*c.* 1815–37)

	Florin (CM)/year
Nobility	
Fürst	100,000–150,000 fl.
Erzherzog Karl (1811)	103,000
Second son of Prince Schwarzenberg (1820)	91,863
Archbishop of Vienna (1820)	54,000
Wealthy Graf	20,000–80,000
Civil servants	
Staats-Konferenzminister	14,000–20,000
Staatsrat/Konferenzrat	8,000–10,000
Hofrat (senior)	4,000–6,000
Hofrat Kübeck von Kübau (1829)	10,000
Hofrat (junior, 1828)	5,000
Hofrat, NOe Landesregierung	2,500–3,000
Hofsekretär:	
Staatsrat	2,000
Staatsrat (beginners)	800–1,000
NOe Landesregierung	700–1,500
Hoftheater Sekretär (Schreyvogel, 1825)	2,000
Ratsprotokollist, Oberste Justizstelle	1,000–1,500
Regierungsadjunkt (without title)	600–1,200
Hofkonzipist	900–1,000
Konzipist, NOe Landesregierung	500–800
Kanzlist:	
Imperial offices	400–900
Staatbuchhaltung (max.)	500
NOe Landesregierung	300–700
Staatsrat	300–400
Postal employee (average)	400
Letter carrier	250–450
Praktikant (apprentice)	200–400
Servant in Staatsrat	144
Actors and musicians	
Leading actress, Burgtheater (1825)	5,000
Leading actor, Burgtheater	4,476
Leading female singer, Opera (1827)	4,600
Leading male singer, Opera	4,500
Kapellmeister, Opera (1827 after 30 years)	2,400
Kapellmeister, Court Chapel	
10th year	2,000
5th year	1,500
1st year	1,000
Vice-Kapellmeister, Court Chapel	1,200
Kapellmeister, Burgtheater	560

Table 2 (*cont.*)

	Florin (CM)/year
Konzertmeister, Opera (26 years)	1,080
Violin soloist (11 years)	800
Rank-and-file musicians:	
Opera (average, 10 years)	480
Burgtheater	240
Conservatory:	
Singing master	1,000
Violin instructor	700
Singing teacher (female)	600
Woodwind and languages	400
Second court organist	500
Synagogue organist (proposed, 1821)	300
Court Chapel choirboy	280
Instrument maker/mender, Burgtheater	120
Teachers	
Synagogue speaker and teacher (proposed, 1821)	1,500
Mittelschule	450–900
Head of religious school (1821)	700
Second teacher	500
Assistant	300
Normalschule	500–700
Hochschule	250–450
Junior lecturer, university	400
Convent school	400
Governess (noble family, Pest, 1822)	320
Volksschule	120–250
Schubert as assistant	80
Domestic service	
Retainers of Prince Liechtenstein (1836):	
Sekretär	2,225
Inspektor	1,800
Oberbuchhalter	1,700
Gamekeeper	1,100
Amtvorsteher (office manager)	800–900
Architect	840
Librarian	600
Butler	400
Wine steward	244
Hunt apprentice	150
Cook for noble family	300–400
Beethoven's kitchen-maid (1823)	129
housekeeper (1823)	120
Haydn's female servants (1809)	20–30

Table 2 (*cont.*)

	Florin (CM)/year
Military	
Field Marshal	
10th year	20,000
5th year	15,000
1st year	10,000
Oberst (149 fl. 33 kr./month)	1,794*
Oberleutnant (110 fl. 9 kr./month)	1,321
Major (79 fl./month)	948
Sergeant (71 fl. 23 kr./month)	860
Captain (39 fl. 48 kr./month)	473
Lieutenant (26 fl. 48 kr./month)	322
Ensign (19 fl. 42 kr./month)	237
Soldiers:	
Grenadier, artillery (8–10 kr./day)	40–50
Cavalry (7 kr./day)	35
Infantry (6 kr./day)	30
Pensions:	
Officer (lesser rank)	50
Soldier	25
Day- and piece-workers	
Dayworker (Taglohner) (3 fl./day) (max. 1817)	677
Public laborer (20 kr./day)	*c.* 100
Sedan-chair bearer (120–150 fl./day)	*c.* 625–780
Factory workers:	
Men in machine industry (80 kr./day)	320**
Men in silk industry (40–50 kr./day)	160–200
Men in other textiles (20–50 kr./day)	80–200
Women in factories (10–30 kr./day)	40–120
Home weavers (2–5 kr./day)	8–20
Adolescents (7–8 kr./day)	28–30

Sources: Beethoven (Anderson) *Letters*, III, 1083 (Beethoven's servants); Deutsch, *Biography*, xxiii, 933; Gotwals, 346–7, 350 (Haydn's servants); Hanson, 'Incomes', Table 4, 179; Kübeck von Kübau, 584; Mayr, 189–91, 195, 225, 229–30 (teachers, civil servants, laborers); Stekl, 69–79, Appendix VII, VIII (employees of Princes Liechtenstein and Schwarzenberg) Turnbull, 220–2 (military); Wolf, 130 (synagogue workers); HHStA, General Intendanz, Hofoper (1823–5) and Burgtheater 1825; GdMf, Geld Rechnung für das Jahr 1821 (–31) 'Conservatorium'.

* Annual incomes were based on a 50-week year and a 6-day week, although the actual days of service varied.

** Annual incomes were projected on a 40-week year and 6-day week. Water shortages and layoffs closed many textile mills in the summer.

however, paid about twice as much as textile factories, and those working in organized factories made more than home weavers. However meager, the pay earned by women and adolescents in factories undoubtedly contributed much-needed money to many family incomes.

Although interesting and helpful, the salary figures taken alone may be deceiving, for many positions offered additional allowances for housing, allotments of food and fuel plus annual bonuses or pensions. For example, a Hofballmeister in 1826 earned 400 fl. annually in salary. But he also received free lodging, ten cords of wood, and 50% of the Ballhaus' profits.[9]

Employment of musicians

As aristocratic patronage of music declined, professional musicians' income came from four main avenues: employment in state or private institutions such as the theater, church, or military bands; public and private performances; musical composition; and teaching.

The state as employer – A musician seeking employment with any of the court ensembles, state theaters, or with the larger Viennese churches usually applied directly to the Oberstkämmeramt, the ministry in charge of the court's affairs, or he requested letters from influential persons to be sent to that office. One such petition, written by Franz Knoll, a 37-year-old composer and music teacher, in July 1841, is typical. Knoll begins after the fashion of many official documents with effusive thanks to the court for acknowledging his composition based on the Austrian national anthem. He reminds them that in 1826 his piece commemorating the emperor's recovery from illness had been accepted and praised by a Hofrat von Ohns. He then describes his plight. After arriving in Vienna, he could not find work as a composer or music teacher. The sudden death of his wife left him to care for three young children. In desperation, Knoll ends his letter by 'throwing himself at the feet of his monarch' to beg for some work in the government. Knoll's request may not have been granted since the letter is marked 18 August 1841 'Keine Folge gegeben' (no further action taken).[10]

The government was careful to screen its musical applicants, especially when they came from foreign countries and eastern-Austrian provinces. Their concerns are clear from a letter by Count Gallenberg to the Police Office, dated 6 January 1829, concerning the bass, August Fischer, newly hired by the Kärntnerthor Theater. Fischer apparently had been working in Hungary and, for breaking his contract, a Stadthauptmann from Pest tried to 'reclaim' or extradite him. In Fischer's defense, the count carefully explains Fischer's national loyalties, and points out that the claim against the singer was not for a crime but a technicality. He adds that Fischer's sizable income from the Viennese theater would insure that he could settle any future fine or reparation (HHStA, General Intendanz, Hofoper, 1829, K. 71). With such assurances, the letter would allay the police's concerns about the singer's character, political leanings, and financial position – three critical issues in the hiring of state employees.

Sometimes competitions were arranged to fill vacancies in the musical ensembles. Upon the death in 1830 of Ignaz Schuppanzigh, the Court Chamber violinist, seven respected Austrian violinists vied for the position: Josef Stadler, Josef Benesch, Karl Rechsert, Anton Khayl, Franz Grütsch, Johann Hellmesberger, and Franz Rabel. The confidential court reports do not divulge the names of the audition judges, but they indicate that the men were evaluated on the basis of 'moral and religious beliefs' and political opinions as well as their musical ability. For instance, special mention is made of the fact that Benesch was originally from Pressburg and then currently the director of the orchestra in Laibach, since he might have harbored strong national, anti-Austrian sentiments.

One judge criticized Anton Khayl for his 'sarcastic and insupportable sense of humor' and charged that his deformed, lame foot might be upsetting to concert audiences. Curiously, even the eventual victor, Georg Hellmesberger, was subject to criticism. The critical judgment, however, was later crossed out, and the final report contains nothing but praise for the man whom the court commends not only for his virtuosity on the violin, but also for his reputation as a good father with a 'well-ordered household' (VA, Ministerium von Innern, 1151/1830).

The main benefits of employment with state institutions were a moderate but steady income, the protection of the court, and a state pension at the end of service. The salary of Kapellmeister in the Court Chamber Orchestra, for example, was comparable to that of an actor or the court secretary. Members of the opera orchestra received about as much pay as an experienced accountant or bureaucrat. Even the average member of the Burgtheater orchestra earned as much as an official notary or a second lieutenant.

Some of the court financial records shed light on the private lives of Viennese musicians. One of these is a letter from Count Moritz Dietrichstein, the secretary of the Court Theater, written in December 1824 on behalf of Mathias Schmak, a court bassoonist for the opera. The letter recounts Schmak's employment: first hired in 1808 at 250 fl. WW (100 fl. CM) and paid to date 400 fl. WW (160 fl. CM) with 100% *Zuschlag* (a kind of annual bonus). As his health declined, Schmak gave up the bassoon and played less demanding parts on the viola. But, when Barbaja took over the management of the opera, Schmak, like many of the theater's older musicians, lost his job. The court granted him an early pension (133.20 fl. WW with 100% *Zuschlag*), but his family still faced financial problems. During the following winter both Schmak and his wife died, leaving six orphans. Dietrichstein thus ends with an emotional plea for some compensation for the children in recognition of their father's long and faithful service. To its credit, the court later agreed (HHStA, General Intendanz, Hofoper, 10 January 1826).

Other documents reveal that some performers regarded positions in state institutions as too taxing, ill rewarded, and with poor working conditions. Dietrichstein alludes to the perception in a letter to Czernin (11 February 1826) in which he outlines his reasons why he cannot find replacements for the Burgtheater orchestra. Since the reign of Joseph II, he explains, it had been customary for the Court Chamber musicians also to play in the Burgtheater orchestra, since Joseph only held afternoon concerts. But now, under Franz I, the court's frequent evening concerts deprived the theater of its musicians, forcing it to hire costly substitutes. In addition, more numerous royal functions occupied court musicians for days or weeks at a time, further affecting the theater orchestra. He adds that the extra evening duty was especially taxing for elderly court musicians, performing in unheated theaters for up to three hours and returning home at night through all kinds of weather; it damaged their health and often forced them into early retirement.

In the same letter, Dietrichstein points out that some virtuosi declined to play in the theater because the evening duty interfered with private engagements, at which they could earn more than the token salary offered by the theater. A violinist named Feranz alleged further that the position was beneath his ability and that theater service would tarnish his reputation (HHStA, General Intendanz, Burgtheater, 1826, fasc. 16).

Another disadvantage of working in the theater was that the musician's fate rested upon the theater's financial stability, prudent management, and the whim of its director. When Barbaja took over the lease of the Kärntnerthor Theater in 1821, he immediately dismissed many of the older musicians. While the government did its best to absorb some of the players into the Burgtheater orchestra, many received no other compensation. When the theater lease expired in 1826, the new negotiations and reorganization of the theater again threw actors, dancers, and musicians out of work for more than a year. The crisis is reflected in a flurry of petitions to the court requesting aid, alternative employment, or early pensions (HHStA, General Intendanz, Burgtheater, 1826, fasc. 16, January 1826).

The case of Anton Breyman illustrates the vulnerability of even a fine musician. In a letter to Czernin (January 1826), Dietrichstein explains that Breyman, the concert master of the opera orchestra, had faithfully served the theater for sixteen years and that he had been paid a salary of 700 fl. WW (280 fl. CM) with 100% Zuschlag annually. But the closing of the opera house reduced him to poverty. Since he was the sole supporter of four children, one of whom was blind, Dietrichstein urges that he be given a position in the Burgtheater orchestra even though his age (then over 40 years) would normally disqualify him (HHStA, General Intendanz, Burgtheater, 1826). The archives do not tell whether he received the position, but, even if he did, his salary would have been cut by more than half.

Concerts, recitals, benefit performances – Musicians could periodically augment their incomes by participating in special public or private concerts. Touring soloists frequently paid their *ad hoc* orchestra set fees to fill out their recital programs and to accompany their concerti. More lucrative were benefit concerts whose proceeds went to a charitable purpose, often to the soloist. Usually given during a musical tour or just before retirement, benefit concerts rewarded and honored local artists as well as provided vital income for a musician abroad.

Popular virtuosi were sought-after guests in Viennese salons, as the biographies of Beethoven and Paganini attest. While it is not known what musicians earned for such private performances, the rewards must have been good. Beyond any money, jewelry or trinkets given to some performers, introductions to wealthy patrons and prospective music students were no doubt among the intangible benefits. These matters are discussed further in Chapter 5.

Compositions, fees, dedications – Even if not considered 'composers', performers could derive income from composing transcriptions of popular works, dances, or songs. Viennese music publishers constantly sought the new music for their almanacs and Taschenbücher. The custom of exchanging musical gifts and souvenirs around New Year and Carnival further stimulated the market for new, fashionable music. For example, among the Carnival anthologies to which Schubert annually contributed dances are compositions by many other local, unknown musicians (Deutsch, *Biography*, 262–3; 398–9). Similarly, the theme sent out by the Diabelli publishers in 1819 was originally intended to stimulate an attractive, marketable collection of variations by Vienna's famous musicians. Beethoven's response, a series of imaginative, virtuosic, and sublime variations (Op. 120), was an exception.

What composers realistically expected to earn from their music is not known, although the subject of music publishing during the nineteenth century has begun to receive scholarly attention.[11] More readily available are the prices placed by Beethoven and Schubert upon their own works, although admittedly they may not reflect the norm in view of their stature as composers at the time.

Beethoven's correspondence with music publishers and patrons provides a record of some of his commissions and music prices. In 1801, Beethoven suggested to the publisher, A. Hoffmeister in Leipzig, a price of 20 ducats (90 fl.) for his First Symphony and 10 ducats (45

27

fl.) for his Second Piano Concerto (Thayer, 269). Three years later, he raised the price of the symphonic works to George Thomson in England to 30 ducats (135 fl.) (Beethoven, MacArdle and Misch, no. 31, 34). By 1824, he charged Schlesinger 600 fl. for his Ninth Symphony (Beethoven (Anderson), III, no. 1267, 1113). Symphonic overtures also increased in price, from 12 ducats (54 fl.) asked in 1804, to 225 fl. paid by Simrock and Probst in 1823–4 for *Die Weihe des Hauses*. Again, the English offered the highest price, the London Philharmonic Society paying 75 guineas (1,575 fl.) for three overtures (Marek, 532). String quartets, which Beethoven offered for 20 ducats (90 fl.) in 1804, sold for 50 ducats (225 fl.) by Schott in 1821 and by Prince Galitzin in 1827 (Cooper, 41; Thayer, 924).

Beethoven's keyboard music also rose in value. In 1801 he called 'high' the price of 20 ducats (90 fl.) asked for Piano Sonata No. 22 because, he explained, 'this sonata is a first class piece' (Thayer, 269). By 1804, and with no rationale, he asked from Thomson 20 ducats for another, unnamed sonata (Beethoven (MacArdle and Misch), 34); and in 1821 he offered his sonatas Op. 109, 110 and 111 for 40 ducats each (180 fl.) (Cooper, 41). Smaller keyboard works were, of course, cheaper. Beethoven asked Thomson for 8 ducats (36 fl.) for an Adagio or Rondo (possibly for piano solo), and in 1816 his *Six Variations on Scottish and Austrian Airs* brought 50 ducats (225 fl.) (Cooper, 41). By 1823, he offered his Six Bagatelles to Lissner for 20 ducats and the same group to Probst the next year for 30 ducats (Beethoven (Anderson), no. 117, 1035; Beethoven (MacArdle and Misch), no. 382, 440).

Beethoven's songs and folk-song settings earned about 18 to 19 fl. apiece between the years 1804 and 1813, but by 1824 Probst paid 24 ducats (108 fl.) for only three songs (Beethoven (MacArdle and Misch), no. 382, 440).

In comparison, Schubert received far less remuneration. In 1823, Cappi and Diabelli paid only 20 fl. for Schubert's 'Wanderer Fantasy' Op. 15, and in 1826 Artaria paid only 120 fl. for both piano sonatas Op. 53 and 54 – three times less than was paid for one of Beethoven's late sonatas (Deutsch, 'Income', 165–6; Reed, 36). Also, his shorter piano works such as the *Moments Musicaux* sold for only 60 fl.

Between 1822 and 1828, however, Schubert's Lieder averaged about 20 to 25 fl. apiece and larger works 60 fl. (Reed, 35). In 1828 Schott paid 500 fl. for *Die Winterreise*, and Leidesdorf paid 75 fl. for the 'Goethe' songs, Op. 92 (Reed, 36). His popular vocal quartets earned even more, Pennaur paying 90 fl. for Op. 64 and Schott 30 fl. for the quintet Op. 102 (Brown, *Essays*, 262).

Schubert also earned far less for his theater music than Beethoven. For his stage works composed in 1820–1, Schubert earned only 160 fl. (Deutsch, *Biography*, 932) compared to 525 fl. offered to Beethoven for an overture alone (Marek, 532). Just as his numerous contributions to almanachs over the years paid Schubert an estimated 120 fl., Beethoven received 270 fl. in 1813 for a single setting of 15 Scottish airs (Deutsch, *Biography*, 932–3; Beethoven (MacArdle and Misch), no. 119, 108).

Musicians could earn additional money by dedicating their works to influential persons. Beethoven took full advantage of the convention, receiving, for example, from the Empress of Russia 50 ducats (225 fl.) for the dedication of his Polonaise Op. 89. Schubert also received between 16 and 20 ducats (79–90 fl.) for various song dedications (Deutsch, *Biography*, 932). While these honoraria could be substantial – such as the gift of 100 fl. given to Schubert by the Friends of Music – the rewards could also be disappointingly small, as in the dedication of Beethoven's Ninth Symphony, for which the King of Prussia sent an inexpensive ring valued at only about 120 fl.[12]

Sometimes the payments for dedications were delayed and intangible, especially when they were done for the court. For instance, in honor of the emperor's sixtieth birthday, Karl Meisl submitted to the court new commemorative texts to be sung to the national anthem.[13] Although court records do not show whether Meisl was rewarded for the gesture, it is possible that he received other favors later, such as future commissions, or favored status for a court position if a vacancy arose.

Once a composer had established his reputation, he might receive special commissions and monetary incentives. Beethoven, for example, was offered by George Smart in 1816 the sum of 100 guineas (2,100 fl.) – the annual income of a gentleman! – to write an oratorio for England (Marek, 537). And in 1825, Charles Neate offered him 500 pounds (5,000 fl.) to give a concert of his own music in London and 1,000 fl. for a new string quartet (Cooper, 65).

Teaching, coaching – Another source of income was to give music lessons. The great number of musical amateurs in Vienna provided a large market, but eyewitnesses and archival documents suggest that supply outran demand. In 1804, Beethoven cautioned Gottlob Wiedebein, 'You imagine that it would be easy to make your way here. But that would be difficult, for Vienna is swarming with teachers who try to make a living by giving lessons' (Beethoven (Anderson), I, no. 90, 109). Even having acquired students, the musician could find the resulting income easily reduced by cancellations for illness or extended summer vacations or the demands of the busy Carnival season. Thus private lessons were, at best, irregular sources of income.

Famous musicians were able to attract students by their public appearances, private performances, or by referral from their friends. But young and unknown musicians sometimes advertised in the Viennese newspapers to locate students or to offer their skills as accompanists. One such advertisement in the *Wiener Zeitung* (3 February 1820) offered piano and violin instruction. Interested parties were invited to examine the teacher's references in the piano showroom of Stein and Co., to allay any doubts about his qualifications or character (173). In another issue of the same journal, a musician offered keyboard dance music and violin accompaniment for salons in 'respectable homes' only (18 January 1825, 71).

The fees for lessons were probably commensurate with the musician's skill and reputation as well as with the social position of the family who hired him. In 1796, Beethoven arranged for Carl Kübeck to give daily an hourly piano lesson to the daughter of a Venetian aristocrat for 20 fl. a month (Marek, 129–30). Yet even this excellent fee was surpassed by Count Johann Karl Esterhazy, who hired Schubert for the summer of 1818 to give piano lessons to his two daughters for 75 fl. a month (Deutsch, *Biography*, 96). Piano lessons in middle-class homes cost much less. There in 1820 Schubert earned about 2 fl. a lesson, and five years later the *Wiener Zeitung* advertised twelve hours of keyboard instruction for 6 fl. or about 30 kr. per hour (19 January 1825, 71). At that rate, a music teacher would have had to give about two thousand hours (39 hours a week) of lessons to make a modest income of 1,000 fl. a year. In his memoirs, Carl Czerny, a noted pianist and pedagogue, recalled that he gave 11–12 lessons a day from 8 a.m. to 8 p.m., adding, 'This lucrative, but extremely strenuous activity, which taxed my health, lasted more than twenty years, until I gave up teaching entirely in 1836'.[14] Besides giving private lessons, a few musicians taught in the newly organized music schools. The most prestigious was the Conservatory founded by the Friends of Music in 1817. The Society's account books for the years 1821–3 show the high regard for violin and voice teachers, who were paid an annual salary of 600–1,000 fl. The average salary of 400 fl., paid to the other instrumental teachers, equalled that of a junior lecturer at the University or a low-level bureaucrat.

Music schools run by churches and private individuals offered additional opportunities for employment and education. Schmidl's guidebook claims that Vienna had 23 private music schools, naming the k.k. Organ Schule in the St Anne church, run by the 'Organization for the Improvement of Church Music in the Country'. Three other schools were devoted to organ study, singing and figured bass (Sing- und Generalbass- Schule) (236). Pezzl's later guidebook (1841) cites three private singing schools directed by Hr Weinkopf, Joachim Hoffman, and Simon Sechter, all of whom taught music theory, figured bass, and counterpoint (*Beschreibung* (1841), 254). Unfortunately, no other information about the enrollment or the curricula of these schools has survived. Nonetheless, such schools must have performed an important function. After all, not only did Schubert and a friend begin the study of counterpoint with Simon Sechter in November 1828, but in 1832 Franz Grillparzer also took lessons from him (Deutsch, *Biography*, 819).

Thus the net income of Viennese musicians varied greatly. Adalbert Gyrowetz, the Kapellmeister of the Court Chamber Orchestra, earned 2,000 fl. p.a. (after ten years of service) not counting any income he received from compositions, outside performances, or teaching. Many musicians also held more than one salaried position. Josef Merk, for instance, in 1826 served as principal cellist in the opera orchestra (for 480 fl.) and he taught in the Conservatory (for 240 fl.). Anton Hudler played timpani for the Kärntnerthor Theater (480 fl.) and the Burgtheater (280 fl.) (HHStA, General Intendanz, Hofoper 1823–5; GdMf, Geld Rechung, 1824). And in 1826, Therese Grünbaum, one of the highest-paid operatic singers at the Kärntnerthor Theater, earned 4,600 fl. a year. Adding to that the salary of her husband, also a singer, the Grünbaums' income totaled 5,800 fl. – a sizable amount even for two! (HHStA, General Intendanz, Hofoper, 1826 ad. 198).

From the fragmentary evidence about Beethoven's financial affairs, we can assume that his income was comparatively large. His annual annuity from 1811 to his death, even after the bankruptcy of Lobkowitz and the death of Kinsky, totalled 1,360 fl. (Thayer, 611–12). Together with the sale of a single string quartet (*c.* 225 fl.), his income would have provided a comfortable living in Vienna. Yet he still complained of debts. As Solomon has shown, Beethoven had large expenses such as two servants, sometimes two apartments, and the responsibility of Karl's tuition and fees at boarding school (271). But, at his death, Beethoven's estate was appraised at 9,885 fl. 13 kr. (CM) and 600 fl. (WW) – a total of around 10,125 fl. (CM) – an impressive sum compared to other contemporary musicians (Thayer, 1075).

The income of Franz Schubert has recently been re-evaluated by John Reed, who calculates that, between the years 1826 and 1828, Schubert earned an average of 1500 fl. (CM) a year. But, he adds, Schubert's financial position did not improve substantially because the income was irregular and the composer tended to spend money freely when he had it (35–8). Upon his death, Schubert's estate was valued at only 63 fl. (CM). If we include the money received for his music manuscripts sold later to Haslinger in 1828, the estate still totals only 563 fl. (Deutsch, *Biography*, 834, 842–3).

Other documents testify that a great number of musicians lived below the income of a gentleman. Mathias Schmak, the court bassoonist, tried to support his wife and six children on a base salary of only 320 fl., and Joseph Khayl, the court oboist, supported six children on a salary of 480 fl. In 1824, Joseph Lanner received 300 fl. (WW) for an evening's music at the Apollosaal. If his orchestra contained 12–15 musicians (as Sealsfield says in 1828), then each performer received between 15 and 20 fl. for each engagement. At that rate, a dance musician would need to perform at least 65–85 evenings at that prestigious dance hall to earn at least 1,000 fl. a year. Since the conductors undoubtedly received more than the other musicians, the average pay was probably even less. Conductors like Lanner and

Johann Strauss were able to make more money, since they performed at many dance halls in a single night and could command higher pay because of their fame.

Bammer's study of sequestration records from 1830 also supports the claim that most musicians were poor. Of the 42 persons classified by the government as 'musicians', only 15 were deemed Besitzende, or those who possessed anything of value to pass on to their heirs. The other two thirds of the musicians were too poor to leave anything behind (228).

2

MUSICIANS AND THE AUSTRIAN POLICE

Scholars disagree about the severity and effects of Metternich's 'system' of censors and secret police, each citing conflicting documents and eyewitness accounts. The confusion has led to misunderstandings about the relationship between Austria's political institutions and its writers, artists, and musicians. While it is virtually impossible to draw causal relations between the actions of the police and specific works of art, or to determine precisely whether a censor or police agent prevented a work from being created, one can examine the ways in which the police influenced the political climate in Vienna and, in some cases, can explain the manner in which certain works of art were presented.

HISTORY AND GROWTH OF THE POLICE SYSTEM

The Austrian police system of the nineteenth century reflected the personalities of its leaders as well as current events. As a part of Joseph II's plan to centralize the bureaucracy, the police were released from the jurisdiction of the Lower Austrian state government in 1782 (Oberhummer, *Wiener*, I, 88). The project was foiled when Leopold returned to the regional states many of their former powers, but upon Franz II's succession to the throne in 1792, the police system returned to Joseph's model. The intervening French Revolution further convinced Franz of the necessity of a well-organized secret police force. Modeled after the French 'high police', the Polizeihofstelle was established in 1793 and directed by Count Johann Anton von Pergen. Under Pergen's leadership, a network of secret police and domestic spies was organized to prevent and uncover any impending threat to the state.

Ten years later (1803), Baron Franz von Sumerau was named president of police (Fournier, 2–4). During the critical war years and foreign occupations of Vienna (in 1805 and 1809), Sumerau expanded the number and range of duties of the secret police. As their numbers increased, so too grew their distrust of other governmental agents and even of their own petty officers (Oberhummer, *Wiener*, I, 90). By 1806, under the new president, Baron Franz von Hager, the secret police relied not only on highly placed informants but also on scores of coach drivers, valets, waiters, and prostitutes who daily reported their observations and overheard conversations to police authorities (Fournier, 14). Throughout the Congress of Vienna in 1814–15, secret police monitored the activities and messages of most foreign dignitaries and their diplomats. Hager instructed the police to intercept, copy, and relay to him all foreign communications. Even waste baskets and fireplace ashes were scrutinized for political information. Nor were Austrian nobles immune, for archives still contain the intercepted letters of the Empress Maria Ludovica, Marie Luise (Franz's sister and second wife of Napoleon), as well as Field Marshal Prince Schwarzenberg. The extent of the police's activities can best be appreciated by its cost. During his reign, Joseph II allowed 10,000 fl. a year for the secret police. During the Vienna Congress alone, Hager spent 50,000 fl. (Oberhummer, *Wiener*, I, 126–7).

In 1817 Count Joseph Sedlnitsky became president of the Hofstelle. His appointment was controversial since he had originally been summoned to Vienna two years before from Galicia to answer charges of neglect of duty as vice president of the Gubernium. Instead of punishment, however, the emperor awarded him the position of vice president of the police. Viktor Bibl suggests that Franz intentionally chose a weak man to ensure his unfailing loyalty and easy manipulation. Indeed, as president, Sedlnitsky gained the dubious reputation, Hammer-Purgstal says, of being the 'dust on Metternich's soles' or, worse, 'Metternich's poodle' (Bibl, *Polizei*, 324). Under his leadership, Austria's large war-time police system turned its attention inward onto Austrian citizens as well as foreigners. In the shadow of this system, Grillparzer, Raimund, Beethoven, and Schubert created their art.

The police system consisted of two large branches: the public or street police (Oeffentliche- or Gassenpolizei), and the secret or security police (Geheime- or Sicherheitspolizei).

PUBLIC POLICE

Organized under the Polizei-Oberdirektion, the public police was responsible for enforcing city laws, maintaining public order, and controlling the influx of people and goods into and around Vienna. Working in each of the city's twelve police districts, the street police, with their gray uniforms and green collars and cuffs, were a common sight patrolling the streets and marketplaces or directing traffic at the city's gates, bridges and theaters.

Among their many problems in the nineteenth century were the questions of their authority and jurisdiction. Since 1618, a mounted Stadtguardia had shared in the task of defending the city. But not until 1801 were military soldiers (Militär Polizeiwache) included officially as part of the public police. In 1821 a military Wachtmeister, three corporals, and thirty-six regulars, reinforced by a mounted brigade of six hundred men, aided the civilian guard (Zivilwache). By 1848, the soldiers outnumbered civilians by 1,203 to only 120 (Oberhummer, *Wiener* I, 137).

Tensions arose between the two factions of guards. Paid less and required to serve long consecutive hours, soldiers resented and often refused to be disciplined by civilian authorities. Likewise, the civilian policemen criticized the soldiers as being too young, inexperienced, and uneducated to fulfill their duties responsibly. Turnover of military police was as frequent as complaints about their bad behavior to Viennese citizens (Oberhummer, *Wiener*, I, 141–3).

Beyond their internal problems, the public police had insufficient patrolmen to care for the ever-increasing size and population of Vienna. Oberhummer cites the superior numbers and training of the police in Paris and London, pointing out that, around 1840, the ratio of policemen to population in Vienna's suburbs was 1:2000 (*Wiener*, I, 166).

Further problems arose out of the shared duties of the public and secret police. Questions of authority and difference of opinion between the Oberdirektion and Hofstelle sometimes resulted in irregular enforcement of the law. Such anomalies easily account for contradictory statements by eyewitnesses that the Viennese police were extremely severe, often incompetent, and yet too few in number.

Among the primary duties of the public police was to close the city gates each night at nine in the winter and an hour later in the summer (Oberhummer, *Wiener*, I, 146a). Accompanying the closing of the gates, most doors to public buildings, restaurants, and apartments were also locked. Persons leaving or entering thereafter were forced to call the gate keeper or house porter to open the door for a small gratuity. Some observers report that theatergoers often rushed home before the end of a performance just to avoid the porter's fine. In turn, for their services the house porters not only earned extra money but also a place in many Viennese folk comedies as familiar 'little despots' (Langenschwartz, 53; Russell, 248).

Once the gates were secure and sentries were posted, patrols walked the streets arresting drunkards, tavern brawlers and robbers. During the day, the street police enforced fire ordinances, investigated cases of illegal gambling, and tried to keep beggars off the streets. Certain members of the force were given free tickets to the theater and public balls so that they could maintain order and help in any emergency, such as fire or insurgence. Occasionally, they were involved in domestic disagreements. Beethoven, for example, often called upon them to settle his quarrels with his landlords or to intervene in his brother's personal marital problems, even though such matters were probably beyond their jurisdiction.[1]

Another duty of the public police was to inspect travel documents and to uphold customs regulations. While travelers in the nineteenth century expected frequent inspections of their papers and numerous tolls as they crossed the frontiers of states and counties, many describe the Viennese procedure as unusually tedious and thorough. English travelers seem to have been unused to such treatment. In 1829 Mary Novello declared Viennese inspections as 'surely the worst' and Eduard Holmes objected to the 'inquisitional search' and questioning:

Before the last document is delivered to him [the traveler], he must endure a course of frivolous and irrelevant questions, such as his age, religion, whether married or not, object of his journey; and to conclude, he must, by producing a letter on a banker or some responsible person, *show* that he possesses the means of supporting himself there, or be ejected forthwith.[2]

Among the items most carefully screened at the gates were tobacco and wine (taxed as Austrian monopolies) and certain valuables. But most often mentioned by travelers was the regulation of books and written materials with revolutionary or religious subjects. Hebenstreit's guidebook states that Hebrew prayer books printed outside of Austria were forbidden, adding that it was not advisable either to bring in Italian or Slavic works (5–6). The experiences of the author Helmina von Chezy support the claims of the guidebooks, for in 1822, at Vienna's gates, her books and personal writings were confiscated. After examination by the police, they were returned to her the next day (Chezy, II, 252).

Despite severely worded restrictions, however, many exceptions were possible. Peter Turnbull claims that forbidden books legally could be imported for personal use if the traveler secured special permission from the government – a permission, he adds, seldom refused (201). Illegal smuggling of the same goods apparently was common, judging from Glassbrenner's experiences in 1836.[3]

Austrians wishing to leave the country also had to gain the proper documents. According to Turnbull, the government allowed only those trips abroad which had practical purposes; and trips with undetermined stops or travel whose purpose was only to 'satisfy one's curiosity' were usually not granted. Thus, he concludes, bankers, merchants, artists, and members of the upper and monied classes traveled frequently, while lesser nobles and the unemployed rarely left the country (203). Such policies were intended to ensure Austria's domestic security, but they also contributed to the empire's isolation from foreign innovation.

The regulations probably had an effect on the country's performing musicians, because to be eligible for travel they needed to convince the authorities of their good character, talent, and the need to leave. Their petitions not only provide useful biographical information about a musician's travels, but also roughly indicate whether he was in good standing with the government. Still preserved in the state archives is the petition of Louis Drouet, a flute virtuoso and composer, who in 1822 received Metternich's permission and protection to perform in Warsaw, Lemberg, Budapest, and Italy.[4] Similar requests were made in 1823 by Johann Peter Pixis, a professor of violin at the Conservatory, and by Johann Sedlaczek, a flute virtuoso, who planned a concert tour in London in 1825.[5]

Since Austrians were barred from attending foreign universities and trade schools, musicians also needed special permission to attend foreign conservatories. In 1823, Adam Liszt, a steward of Paul Anthony Esterhazy's estate in Raiding and the father of the 12-year-old piano virtuoso, Franz, asked the permission of the government for his son to travel to Munich to give a concert and then to go to Paris to study at the Conservatoire.[6]

In each of the above instances, the government granted the request, but, since all of the musicians were well established or had connections with influential nobles, their cases may have been exceptional. Less fortunate performers presumably emigrated, stayed home, or defied the police. In 1830 young Friedrich Chopin did the latter. Possibly because of his nationality or the political unrest in Warsaw, Chopin encountered difficulties when he applied for a passport to Paris from Vienna. He wrote to his parents of his experiences:

Every day they promise me a passport, and every day I drag myself from Ananias to Caiphas, to recover what I have deposited with the police. Today I learned something new again, namely that my passport has been lost somewhere. In addition to the fact that they won't find it, I must apply for a new one...I am taking Bayer's advice. I'll obtain a passport for England, but I'll go to Paris. (Wierzynski, 139–40)

Such tactics presumably were not uncommon, for Turnbull cites another similar case. Two young Englishmen who were denied permission to travel in Hungary purchased passports to Constantinople instead. When their boat, bound for Turkey, passed through Hungary, they disembarked, traveled freely throughout the country, and then returned to Vienna without further problems (Turnbull, 194). Again, despite their formidable reputation, the Austrian police were unable to keep tight control over international traffic.

SECRET POLICE

The second branch of the police system, the Polizeihofstelle, focused on political and moral (*sittliche*) crimes committed throughout the empire. Like its Austrian predecessors among the Jesuits and Maria Theresia's Chastity Commission or Keuschheitskommission of the seventeenth and eighteenth centuries, and similar contemporary agencies in France, Prussia, and Russia, the Polizeihofstelle directed censorship and the collection of information about foreign or domestic persons engaged in revolutionary, criminal, or immoral activities. The secretive nature of the investigations, together with the draconian punishments for convicted offenders, helped to create an atmosphere of tension and distrust in Viennese public life.

Bureau of Censorship – The subject of censorship in Austria during the first half of the nineteenth century was taken up repeatedly by such writers as Schaden, Langenschwarz, Russell and Strang, who reflected the ideals and romantic sentiments of the new liberal political movement or loyal, monarchist views. However, only a few writers and subsequent historians such as Hans Normann, Adolf Wiesner, Carl Glossy, and Julius Marx have discussed the subject dispassionately or have assessed its implications for Viennese culture.

Censorship was by no means new or unique to Austria in the nineteenth century. Maria Theresia formalized procedures already in practice when she established a Bücherrevisions-Kommission in 1752 (Oberhummer, *Wiener*, I, 188). Joseph II further codified her system which became law in 1795. By 1801, the independent bureau of censorship was incorporated into the Polizeihofstelle. Laws governing censorship were then expanded in 1812 and amended throughout the period from 1820 to 1848.

Austrian censorship was both proscriptive and prescriptive, for official censors not only struck out offensive words, allusions, and illustrations, but in some cases they also added their own thoughts or directed major changes in the plots of dramas or the manner of their presentation. Unlike modern political censors, however, these officials did not specify any particular message or dogma. In addition, not all censorship was exercised by the government. Administrators of the church and city theaters also were allowed to place their own restrictions on materials that were to be used or presented in their respective institutions.

Censorship in Austria was extensive, encompassing not only political and moral subjects, but religious topics as well. As a matter of course, books, plays, libretti, poetry, and newspaper items were closely read and edited in the office of the Polizeihofstelle. But Austrian censors presumably went farther than their counterparts in other countries by scrutinizing professors' lectures before and during their delivery and inspecting printed dedications, engravings, lithographs, portraits, drawings of all kinds, maps and topographical illustrations, playing-cards bearing the portraits of royalty, house signs and super-scriptions, inscriptions on gravestones, medals, and awards. Even music, with its texts and titles, melodies, dedications and illustrations, was not exempt from the censor's pen.

The censors classified their materials with four designations: (1) *imprimatur* or *admittur* meant that the work could be published alone and reprinted in newspapers without restrictions; (2) *transeat*, often given to foreign works, meant that the work was permitted in Austria, but that it could not be reprinted in newspapers nor used in lending libraries; (3) *erga schedam* or *missis deletis* was given to works containing some problematic portions which thus were to be strictly regulated. These usually were allowed to circulate only with the censors' permission among businessmen and scientists; (4) *damnatur* or *non admittur* meant that the work was rejected as dangerous or offensive. Only trusted specialists in certain fields were allowed to have such works and only after gaining permission from the Polizeihofstelle.[7]

Jäck and Heller claim that in 1821 the entire censorship procedure took between five and six months (138–9). Authors had the right to appeal against the final decision of the censors, but both Normann and Turnbull found that such appeals were rarely tried quickly and that they were seldom successful (Normann, 110; Turnbull, 215).

CENSORSHIP IN THE THEATER

Easily apparent are the effects of censorship on Austrian drama. Although records of censored libretti, music, and theatrical playbills date only from 1772, the practice obviously began much earlier (Wiesner, 284–5). The abolition of improvisation was a cardinal and strictly enforced rule, but religious allusions were also historically troublesome for the state. Convinced of its role of public defender of orthodox religious doctrine, the censors banned from Austrian states all mention of Biblical names and stories and the appearance of distinguishable clerical orders and devils. For example, the secular play entitled *Die Geschichte des Hauptmannes von Capernum* was banned in

1825 because of the Biblical town name in the title (Costenoble, 293). In 1821 a play was banned because a hermit's costume too closely resembled the robe of a monk (Glossy, 'Geschichte', 4). To circumvent these regulations, members of the clergy were called 'Uncle' rather than 'Father' or 'Brother', and such words as 'church' or 'God' were replaced with more neutral-sounding words like 'temple' and 'Heavens' (Anschütz, 228).

Political allusions, either visual or verbal, were inspected closely. The words 'constitution', 'liberty' and 'country' were forbidden and the costumes or symbols of the Austrian army or any other contemporary political group were not allowed to appear on the stage.[8] Even theater announcements caused the police concern. In 1813 a report from the provinces near Lemberg alerted the Hofstelle that a number of placards announcing the opera *Kopciuszek* (Cinderella) had been defaced to read 'Kosciuszko', the name of an illustrious Polish patriot who led a rebellion against the Russians in 1794.[9] Especially vulnerable to political censorship were the numerous and popular historical plays, for each was searched for possible reflection on the current government and for historical parallels that might prove embarrassing. For these reasons, the play *Enrico und Bianco* (1825) was banned because certain scenes showed joy over the death of a king and the division of the populace into opposing factions. The play *Der Ueberfall der Perser* (1827) was forbidden because of its analogies to current Persian–Russian affairs; and *O'Connor* by W. Alexis was rejected in 1827 because its statements about love and freedom too closely echoed the slogans of the French Revolution (Glossy, 'Geschichte', 73, 82–3, 88).

The well-known case of Grillparzer's play *König Ottokars Glück und Ende* illustrates the multiple frustrations of the censorship process. Submitted in 1823, the play was detained almost two years before receiving its censorship classification. During this period, the examiners worried about the play's political repercussions, criticizing the portrayal of Ottokar as 'not advisable politically or judicially' because of its obvious parallels with Napoleon (Glossy, 'Geschichte', 49). They charged that Grillparzer belabored the themes of Ottokar's fall from power and his divorce, and they feared the reactions to the work's uncomplimentary references to the Bohemians.[10]

Although other writers were able to overcome the hindrance of the censors to produce masterly literary works, Grillparzer grew despondent and cynical. By the year 1826 he confessed to Beethoven that the censors had destroyed him (Kalischer, IV, 198). Certainly, many historians view the treatment of the play as the model of Habsburg repression, but, in his specialized study of the problem, Julius Marx asserts that the play was neither deliberately delayed nor did the censors intend to provoke the author. On the contrary, many prominent people awaited the play's premiere and even the emperor requested to read the manuscript. Instead, the work appears to have been stalled in the censor's office because the bureau could not efficiently complete its work and its workers were afraid of displeasing the emperor by appearing too lenient (Marx, *Zensur*, 28–9). As a censor told Grillparzer when asked what was considered dangerous in the play, 'Nothing at all, but I thought to myself, one cannot know for sure...' (Bibl, *Polizei*, 290).

Another duty of the censors was to uphold the seemly depiction of class distinction and public morality. The presentation of the upper classes was a sensitive issue, for the censors banned *Die musikalische Akademie* (1822) for its offensive portrayal of the military, *Die fürstliche Jagd* (1827) for its unfavorable depiction of the upper classes, and *Der Stern von Sevilla* (1826) for its characterization of a murderous prince (Glossy, 'Geschichte', 24, 92, 79). Plays which enacted or alluded to murder, suicide, divorce or prostitution were banned also. Restrictions applied even to a play's lovers, for they were never allowed to appear leaving a scene alone together (Bibl, 286). Many celebrated works written outside of Austria did not conform to such restrictions. Goethe's *Claudine von Villa Bella* was banned in 1824 for its presentation of thieves, and Kleist's *Der zerbrochene Krug* was condemned in 1829 for its 'immoral' love scene (Glossy, 'Geschichte', 56, 114). Even Shakespeare's *King Lear* had to be altered because the censors thought its ending too horrifying. When the censors dictated their changes during the play's rehearsal, Heinrich Anschütz, then playing Lear, angrily exclaimed: 'Would that I were not so well paid here in the court theater, so that I might overlook such stupidity, with respect to my future. But I thus must put up with all these inanities because of my family.[11] For his indiscretion, Anschütz received a three-day jail sentence and a warning that another such offense would cost him his position.

Paradoxically, if the censors were inordinately strict with the plays at the court theaters, they tended to be very lenient with the works for the suburban houses, for these stages were famous for their improvised jokes and satirical contemporary allusions. John Strang testifies to the political jokes at the Leopoldstadt Theater, and Glassbrenner mentions as 'shameless' and 'in poor taste' other liberties taken in the folk comedies (Strang, 254; Glassbrenner, 224). Perhaps the authorities believed such actions to be less dangerous when clothed in Viennese dialect and humor, or they felt that such entertainment pacified the lower classes, the major component of the suburban audiences. But even these theaters had their limits of excusable 'excessive behaviour', because, in 1818, the popular actor and play-wright, Ferdinand Raimund, was arrested and sentenced to three days in jail without food for an outburst on stage of jealous rage directed against his mistress, actress Theresa Grünthal. For her part also, Grünthal was reprimanded by the police for an 'immoral lifestyle' (Bibl, *Polizei*, 295–6).

CENSORSHIP OF MUSIC

Although the censorship of music usually involved its written portions such as the libretto or song text, its dedication, accompanying illustrations, some tunes were deemed dangerous. National anthems such as the 'Marseillaise' and Poland's 'Noch ist Polen nicht verloren' were banned. In 1830 Meynert advised travelers that even whistling the 'Marseillaise' in Vienna might provoke the secret police (99). He claims bitterly that the Viennese prefer music in 'church style' to stirring, martial music of the Polacca.[12]

As with plays, opera or song texts were screened for their political implications. As early as 1797, the proceedings of the court Chancery mention a song whose text was unflattering to the King of Prussia. Purportedly written in Silesia and distributed throughout Moravia and Bohemia, the song was condemned by the Austrian authorities and its dissemination was halted. The same records cite a 'Friedensymphonie' in 1797 which was to have been performed by a Viennese musical society. But permission to perform and to publish the work was denied, probably owing to the title's possible revolutionary connotations.[13]

Music from or about Poland continued to be of concern to Austrian censors throughout the first half of the nineteenth century. In 1823, for example, the censor Bretfeld alerted Sedlnitsky about a Polish publication called *Historical Songs*, whose music and illustrations he described as having possible 'disadvantageous tendencies'. Two years later, a case involving a Polish polonaise came before the police. The work was very popular in the eastern provinces and had been played for Czar Alexander of Russia. But when the piece came before the censors in Vienna for permission to be published, a nameless informer reported that the music had originally been a song about Galicia, whose text had been judged politically offensive by censors in Lemberg. Fearing that people would remember or learn the polonaise's former text, Sedlnitsky ordered his bureau to review the work's classification.[14]

Other revolutionary or liberal causes promoted in song were suppressed also. In a note to Metternich dated 6 December 1826, an anonymous writer warned the government about two German Taschenbücher entitled *Arion* and *Orpheus* because they often contained songs written by Philhellenists, a group devoted to the Greek struggle for independence from the Turks.[15]

Music with religious or liturgical texts was examined by both secular and ecclesiastical censors. Judging from the restrictions placed upon similar subjects for the theater, one can surmise from the fragmentary, surviving lists of forbidden works that such songs as 'Hymne auf Gott' (1801) by Kunzen and published in Zürich, 'Pater und Nönnchen' (1840) by Banek in Leipzig, 'Die junge Nonne' (1841) by Mohen in Leipzig, and 'Hymnen auf Pius IX' (1848) anon. were banned for the same reasons. Unfortunately, the censors' comments do not survive.[16]

All composers working in Vienna had dealings with the censors. Usually the process was routine and uneventful, but in May 1824 Beethoven was warned that his concert's program might not be approved because he included selections of the Mass (Missa Solemnis), which, as liturgical music, was banned from secular performance. To appease the officials, Beethoven called the pieces *Hymnen* on the program, but he threatened to cancel the entire concert if they forbade the work – a move that brought considerable pressure on the bureau from Count Lichnowsky.[17]

Franz Schubert's dealings with the censors were far less fortunate. The publication of three songs on texts by Goethe (Op. 19) was delayed for over two years because Austrian law required the written consent of a dedicatee.[18] Because it used an unsanctioned German translation of the Mass, his Deutsche Messe (D. 872) was prevented from being performed as part of the Catholic church service.[19] Even after his death, the censors impeded the publication of selected works. In a letter to the censorship bureau dated 1829, the publisher Joseph Czerny appealed against the ruling of *non admittur* on Schubert's song, 'Der Kampf' (D. 594), based on a poem by Schiller. Guessing that the censors had banned the song because of its text, Czerny pointed out that Schubert had set a text that had already been printed five times in Vienna and once in Graz, each time with the censors' permission.[20]

Most of the censors' resistance was waged against Schubert's operas, however. *Fierabras*, on a libretto by Joseph Kupelweiser, passed the censors in August 1823 with only small deletions in the speeches of the king and servants; *Die Verschworenen* (The Conspirators), on a libretto by Ignaz Castelli, was renamed *Der häusliche Krieg* (The Domestic War) by the censors to avoid the obvious political association; but *Graf von Gleichen*, on a libretto by Eduard Bauernfeld, was banned altogether in October 1826 for its reference to a nobleman's bigamy (Deutsch, *Biography*, 283, 300, 548).

Since Schubert must have been fully aware of the severity of the censors, especially with regard to theatrical works, his choice of such questionable opera libretti is puzzling. Before the censors had even passed the libretto of *Fierabras*, Schubert had already composed more than half of the music; and, despite earlier warnings by his friends about the possibility of a censors' ban, he continued to compose music for *Graf von Gleichen* (Deutsch, *Biography*, 283; Bauernfeld; *Tagebuch*, 1 (August 1826), 34, and (October 1826), 36). Whether Schubert planned to have this opera produced abroad, as Deutsch suggests, or completed the work out of friendship with Bauernfeld, his actions are unusually impetuous, and indicate a possible deliberate defiance of the law – certainly a facet of his character overlooked by his biographers.

But the censors were not always so inimical, for they provided composers and musicians an important service. As employees of court theaters or chapels, performers were protected from hurtful criticism in published journals.[21] The bureau also granted publishing rights that protected a writer or composer from the then common practice of illegal reprinting (pirating) of his works, at least within the borders of Austria. In a sense, they provided Austrian copyright enforced by police confiscation of pirated copies. For instance, in 1829, a Freiherr von Handel wrote to Metternich on behalf of Ferdinand Ries to request the exclusive publishing rights in Austria for the piano reduction of Ries' opera, *Die Räuberbraut*. To support his petition, Handel enclosed a copy of the opera, a copy of the privilege rights already granted the work by the government in Hesse, and a letter from Ries giving his consent. The work was granted not only Austrian publishing rights but also the court's protection from illegal reprintings and sale.[22]

Occasionally the government uncovered pirated materials before they entered Austria. In a letter to Metternich dated December 1830, Sedlnitsky denied a request of a Dr Karl Weitershausen, a teacher at the royal military school in Darmstadt, for Austrian publishing rights for his *Liederbuch für deutsche Krieger und deutsches Volk*. Sedlnitsky had discovered that the work was a mere compilation of songs pirated from other sources and that some of the songs contained unacceptable texts.[23]

Indirectly, the censors performed a beneficial role for the Conservatory of the Friends of Music, for they periodically made large donations of musical exemplars that had been deposited in their offices. An index of the Society's papers from the year 1825 indicates that among the 271 piano, vocal, chamber music and operatic scores sent by the police were Beethoven's *Diabelli Variations*, Kreutzer's *Libussa*, Schubert's *Gruppe aus dem Tartarus*, and Abbé Stadler's oratorio, *Die Befreyung von Jerusalem*. The police probably sent even more music that year, since a letter from the Society's president, Raphael Kiesewetter, thanks the office for 592 musical works received in 1825.[24]

IMPACT OF CENSORSHIP

A common complaint among Austrian writers and composers was that the censors delayed the publication of their works. According to Hans

Normann, the censors could be vindictive by delaying the process for authors they disliked (110). For poet and journalist August Lewald, the endless waiting for even short works brought him to the 'point of despair' (Lewald, 2).

The censors also delayed the distribution of foreign works. In 1824, for instance, Beethoven complained to Schott in Mainz that he had not received their journal *Cäcilia* because it had not yet been approved by the censors (Beethoven (Anderson), III, no. 1290, 1126). Two years later, Johann Nepomuk Hummel had requested Austrian publishing rights for his guide to piano technique, entitled *Ausführliche theoretisch-praktische Anweisung zum Spielen des Pianofortes*. But, because he wanted to inspect the work personally, Sedlnitsky delayed.[25] Such delays could have been injurious to popular works since they would have allowed pirated copies or unauthorized transcriptions to be made and circulated before the police could prevent their sale.

Beyond causing delays in publication, the alterations of a work by the censors was resented. Carl Herloss particularly objected to the treatment of poetry. Not only did corrections often lack the unity and tone of the original, but the newly concocted verses frequently discredited the whole work (Forstmann, 173). Hans Normann ridiculed the pedantry of the censors as well, claiming that they treated writers' work as a teacher might correct a schoolchild's homework. In some cases, he contended, no one could justify the changes. Not even the legislative part of the government had the power to force an author to adopt and to undersign its opinions as did the censors (113)! Thus, the censors came to embody the insufferable pedantry and inflexibility of the whole Austrian state.

An immediate result of the process was the exodus of many talented authors or the publication of their works abroad. In 1827 Forstmann explained that it was expensive to do the latter, but an author was rewarded by having his works published without the interference of Austrian censors (Forstmann, 172). The practice officially was forbidden without the approval of the government, but, as Normann relates, authors found many opportunities to smuggle their works out of the country without detection. Moreover, a work published abroad anonymously or under an assumed name often created a greater stir and market value in Vienna than if it had been published in Austria (114).

Other victims of the censorship procedure were newspapers and journals. Wilhelm Chezy stated from personal experience that it was difficult to establish new periodicals in Vienna, since articles could easily be detained for months by the censors. Sometimes they struck out installments, thereby rendering long works incomprehensible.[26] Many newspapers flourished during the period, but their contents tended to feature non-topical subjects, escapist stories or a potpourri of short pieces reprinted from other journals.[27]

Censorship also affected the profits of Viennese booksellers and music dealers. Since these never knew which foreign books or music would be permitted, they had difficulties in ordering new works, and they often lost money on works that were prohibited suddenly from sale.[28] For them, as for the newspaper publishers, it was probably safer and easier to deal with homegrown works that were neither controversial nor suggestive.

Summing up the many irritations faced by Austrian writers, Sealsfield declared in 1828:

A more fettered being than an Austrian author surely never existed. A writer in Austria must not offend against any Government, nor against any minister; nor against any hierarchy, if its members be influential; nor against aristocracy. He must not be liberal – nor philosophical – nor humorous – in short, he must be nothing at all. Under the catalogues of offenses are comprehended not only satires, and witticism; – nay, he must not explain things at all because they might lead to serious thoughts. (Sealsfield, *Austria*, 209–10)

Austria gained the reputation as an empire isolated from the mainstream of European ideas and literary trends. The travelers Jäck and Heller claimed that in 1821 the Viennese desire to read was no longer as strong as in Germany, and Andlaw's memoirs recall that lending libraries and art galleries stood empty (Jäck and Heller, 146; Andlaw, 202).

Enforcement of censorship laws – According to Herloss and Normann, authors and publishers could be punished for not submitting works to the censors, or for printing forbidden materials, by fines of up to 100 ducats (450 fl.), loss of employment, a possible lifetime censure, or arrest

(Forstmann, 172; Normann, 116). But witnesses claim that such drastic measures were rarely imposed and that within the bureau itself there were numerous contradictions and inconsistencies. For example, works once permitted under Joseph II, but forbidden under Franz, were often reprinted abroad and then imported back into Austria under pseudonyms. Works banned one week by one censor might be allowed the next by another man, owing to error or a difference of opinion (Forstmann, 172–3). On the other hand, works that had already appeared in print might be forbidden when they were set to music.

Even expressly forbidden works were available to certain persons with the government's knowledge. Indeed, in 1828 Postl heard many political discussions and saw numerous foreign newspapers and forbidden books among certain aristocratic and financier circles (Sealsfield, 197). The situation continued at least another six years, according to an anonymous writer, although in such gatherings only trusted friends were allowed to participate.[29]

The assertion that the Viennese knew nothing about current events or about new literary works is challenged further by the observations of eyewitnesses. In 1827 Herloss judged that Austrians actually read more than people in Germany and that Viennese coffee houses competed with each other for the greatest number of foreign journals they carried. Again, in 1838 an anonymous observer stated that the politically stirring letters of Börne were read more widely in Austria than anywhere else in Europe, even though Austrian bookdealers and their patrons took some risk in obtaining them. Such testimony is also borne out by Rudolf Till's examination of the library of Johann Hoheisel, a school director who lived in Vienna until 1841. Analyzing the scope, size and variety of Hoheisel's collection, which contained numerous 'forbidden' works from France, Switzerland, and Germany, Till concludes that Austria simply could not have been the proverbial 'walled China' of Europe.[30]

The diametrically opposed statements of eyewitnesses together with the fragmentary and often contradictory surviving evidence preclude an easy, definitive understanding of Austria's censorship at the beginning of the nineteenth century. At the very least, the discrepancy between the law and its enforcement challenges the wholly negative picture painted by many liberal writers then and now, as well as the recent attempts to disregard Vienna's censors entirely. It would be more accurate to say that exceptions under the law were made for members of the nobility, the wealthy, and the intelligentsia, while the brunt of regulation seemed to fall upon students, bureaucrats, and Bürger, since the real threat of revolution, it was perceived, lay with them.

Secret intelligence – To complement the control of printed materials, the secret police directed a network of spies and agents to gather confidential reports about the actions and conversations of selected persons both in Austrian lands and abroad. These were the informers whose descriptions evoked fearful images of betrayal, interrogation, and imprisonment.[31] The actual number of spies is unknown, but contemporaries judged it to be large. In 1822 Adolf von Schaden accused the government of spending great sums for its 'army of spies' (85), and six years later Postl maintained that, since 1811, the government had paid one Gulden a week to over 10,000 laborers, servants, and prostitutes for information:

Every footman in a public house is a salaried spie [sic]: there are spies paid to visit the taverns and hotels, who take their dinners at the *table d'hote*. Others will be seen in the Imperial library for the same purpose, or in the bookseller's shop, to inquire into the purchases made by different persons. (Sealsfield, *Austria*, 85–6)

By 1834, an anonymous writer claimed that secret police had infiltrated the entire nation, guessing that there were over six thousand officials and countless more secret agents (*Seufzer*, 85).

Perhaps no one group in Vienna felt more harassed by secret police than the English. In 1825 John Russell cited an example of a well-to-do Englishman in Vienna whose papers were seized by the police without warning or provocation (338). Martha Wilmot also noted in her letters: 'The police of Vienna equals that of Paris...I suppose that we never cough, sneeze, nor turn a child into the Nursery to *blow its nose* without the event being reported to Government' (38). She writes that she sent her confidential mail by courier only because regular post was opened by the police. The practice of intercepting and inspecting mail continued into the 1820s because other writers mention that their letters from abroad were opened routinely (Schaden, 100).

Thus, as with censorship, Austria gained a sinister reputation abroad. Hans Normann vividly describes the police in 1833:

One compares this institution to the Spanish Inquisition, and tells the most horrible tales about it, cries about spiritual infibulation, and considers all these men, who are at the head of this institution, and likewise those who live and function in its pay (so says the wicked world), to be blood thirsty tyrants, cannibals, and monsters.[32]

But, disclaiming his own characterization, Normann, as does Boas, asserts that the secret police were not as evil as their reputation. In fact, Normann defends them, maintaining that spies were used only for apprehending thieves and smugglers. Boas asserts that anyone in Vienna could speak freely, so long as he spoke quietly, reasonably, and without intending to incite a riot (Normann, 120–1; Boas, 171).

This more moderate view of the secret police is further confirmed by Herloss, who wrote: 'Of liberal talk, however, no notice is taken by the police because they well know they have nothing to fear from the rabble, and believe they only have to keep an eye on a few hotheads. After all, the German remains quiet until only the most pressing need shakes him from his lethargy.'[33] Others point out that the Austrian police were far more lenient than police in Prussia, Bavaria, and Russia and that, even within the empire, the Viennese usually were treated better than those living in the provinces (Charles, 29; Meynert, 101). Glassbrenner best portrays the discrepancy between Vienna's reputation and the reality, as he saw it in 1836:

And coming to Vienna, one is treated in the friendliest and most polite manner by all of the higher officials, one finds even among the lower officials only a few blockheads; one hears everywhere candid political discussions and everyday new *bon mots* touching on the crown and nobility; one finds forbidden books among all families; subscribes to the circle of forbidden journals; sees everyone smoking forbidden tobacco in places where smoking is prohibited; one buys goods everywhere which would have to be much more expensive had they not come to Vienna through illegal channels; one drinks forbidden wines everywhere, and finds forbidden girls everywhere! Where is the secret police; what is it doing? One seldom hears that anyone suffered a fine, the Viennese themselves point out a spy to you here and there, but if one should ask whether in years a Viennese has been inconvenienced by these spies, one receives a decisive no for an answer. Really![34]

As late as 1840, Turnbull also defended the Austrian police, finding fault only with a few, over-zealous, ambitious subordinate officials who misused their power by enforcing even simple regulations to the letter (200). Like the censors, the secret police agents arbitrarily enforced the law, and only in cases of grave crimes or cases involving government employees, members of secret societies, or students were they consistently severe. These particular targets of police concern deserve closer attention because, at the beginning of the nineteenth century, many of Vienna's greatest intellectuals and artists were among them.

Student associations and the secret police – Student associations, called 'Burschenschaften', flourished in German university towns throughout the eighteenth century. Each fraternity had its own traditions and regalia, but they all were notorious for their duelling, drinking bouts, and pranks. The associations became the focal point for German nationalism and some even fought together in regiments against Napoleon. After the wars, they continued to espouse the cause of German unity by wearing medieval German costumes and by pledging oaths of loyalty in speeches and songs. The fervor of this movement reached a climax at the Wartburg Festival in 1819, at which the student Karl Ludwig Sand murdered August Kotzebue, a Prussian diplomat and writer.[35] Immediately, representatives from the German and Austrian governments met to curb further student protest. Their resolutions, largely influenced by Metternich, were compiled in the Carlsbad Decrees.

Because Austrian fraternities had been established much later than their German counterparts, they had fewer members and much less influence. Nonetheless, the government had been suspicious and intolerant of their political activities from the beginning. The Kotzebue murder gave the emperor and Metternich an excuse to strip Austrian professors of most of their academic freedoms, to ban student associations, and to remove student dissidents by forcing them to enlist for long terms in the army.[36]

Censors helped to carry out Metternich's edicts by screening all imported collections of student songs. Their duties were made difficult by the common practice among students of turning innocuous songs into witty, but lewd, parodies. An example of the transformation can be seen in the song, 'Gaudemaus igitur', whose original text can be traced to a thirteenth-century penitential song. Throughout the eighteenth and nineteenth centuries, however, it had many interpolations, especially among its philosophical and *vivat* verses. Predictably, the strophes about women survive in at least four manuscripts. Usually, only the last two pious versions appear in print:

Jena 1745/reprinted	Vivant omnes virgines
Wittenberg 1899	Faciles accessu,
	Floreat virginitas
	Difficilis ingressu.
Keil, 1776	Vivant omnes virgines
Studentenlieder	Faciles accessu,
	Vivant et mulieres
	Faciles aggressu!
Kindleben, 1781	Vivant omnes virgines
Studentenlieder	Faciles, formosae
	Vivant et mulieres
	Bonae, laboriosae!
Melzer, 1808	Vivant omnes virgines
Burschenlieder	Faciles, formosae
	Vivant et mulieres
	Fidelesque conjuges
	Boni laboriosi.[37]

Perhaps more odious to Austrian censors, and easier to eliminate, were the political movements celebrated in the student songs. In the 1820s, songs lionized the Greeks in their war for independence. In the 1830s, songs applauded the revolution in France and the Polish resistance against the Russians. The last verse of Karl Simrock's poem, 'Drei Tage und drei Farben' (1830) illustrates the inflammatory tone of many songs:

> Grosse Dinge hat die Zeit geboren
> Gross und wundertätig ist die Zeit,
> In drei Tagen ward ein Thron verloren,
> In drei Tagen ward ein Reich befreit.[38]

The poem cost Simrock his entire academic career.

Hence, it is not surprising that a number of student songs were included on the censors' list of restricted works. In 1843 alone, two collections are cited: *Liederbuch für Studenten mit Melodien*. Hrg. Gustav Braun. Berlin (*erga schedam*); *Alte und neue Studentenlieder mit Bildern u. Singweisen*. Hrg. Kuhter und Marschner. Leipzig (*damnatur*).[39]

Informers served the police by reporting the activities of students both in the classroom and at local coffee houses. Of particular interest for the history of Austrian literature and music is the action taken against Johann Senn and his circle of friends.

Around 1816 a number of young Austrian students began to meet regularly at the Schwan on the Landstrasse. Within three years the group included such later notable men as Johann Senn, a native of Tyrol and a talented poet, Josef Scheiger, a future Polizeidirektor in Graz, Johann Mayerhofer, a writer and future censor, and his room-mate, Franz Schubert. The memoirs of Franz Bruchmann, a classmate of Schubert at the Konvikt, recalls this circle of friends and their admiration of Senn, whom they recognized to be the 'most mature and gifted' among them (Bruchmann, 128–9). But, for the reward of 100 fl., someone told the police of the group's alleged illegal activities.

The morning after a 'wild' farewell party for Alois Fischer on 20 January 1820, the police arrested a number of students and searched their belongings for incriminating evidence. Named in one police report were Franz Schubert, 'the school assistant from the Rossau', Joseph Streinsburg, a law student and the son of a court secretary, Zechenter, and Franz Bruchmann (Deutsch, *Biography*, 128; Doblinger, 51). According to Doblinger's research, others were jailed and their rooms searched. The police did find remnants of Burschenschaft-type regalia including some songs and a shillelagh (Ziegenhainer) with the carved letters E(hre) F(reiheit) V(aterland), or Honor, Freedom, Fatherland, and below, a symbol of crossed swords and names of students.[40]

Implicated by these papers, Johann Senn was arrested two months later. Through the fourteen months of his custody and interrogation, Senn's behavior was described as 'insulting and stormy', and, when he was forced to write down his philosophical and political beliefs, he filled ninety-two pages. Senn's academic career, however, was ruined. Barred from tutoring in Vienna (his main source of income), he travelled to Innsbruck where he finally gave up his studies to become a soldier (Bruchmann, 129–30). Two other close friends of Senn also suffered similar exile. Stegmayer returned to Galicia, where he later became a governmental official; but Gerhardi killed himself in Prague (Doblinger, 57). Bruchmann writes that the other students cited in the police report received only reprimands, but even such mild punishment was serious enough to warrant his own departure from Vienna to study biology at home. He did not return to the city until May the next year (129).

Although the surviving accounts reveal nothing about the consequences of the arrest for Franz Schubert, we can speculate that it may have accounted for his change of lodgings soon thereafter.[41] But more damaging might have been the records of the incident kept in police files. Since most petitions to the government required official affidavits of good character (Leumundzeugnis), past trouble with the police theoretically could have prevented a musician from gaining employment in any of the imperial musical institutions or from being allowed to travel or publish abroad.

Secret societies and the police – Soon after the Napoleonic Wars, a number of secret societies espousing free-thinking, nationalistic movements, or the overthrow of the monarchy sprang up throughout Europe. Treating such groups, like student associations, as a threat to the state, the Austrian government passed laws which explicitly stated that any Austrian belonging to, supporting, corresponding with, or offering assistance to any secret society was liable to arrest for a period of from one to three months. Foreigners engaging in similar activities were subject to a sentence of three to six months in jail. Furthermore, if an organization was discovered, its papers, letters, money and equipment became property of the state, and anyone implicated by its papers was also liable to arrest.[42] The sentences were made even more frightening because political prisoners were often sent to the Spielberg prison – one of the most inhumane and formidable prisons of the nineteenth century.[43]

On the whole, Metternich's tactics were highly successful. Student activity was minimal compared to that in German lands and few political societies seriously challenged the Austrian state until the revolution in 1848, which, incidentally, failed to unseat the emperor. But, exactly in its zeal to prevent such plots, the secret police made some spectacular errors and, consequently, new enemies. The investigation and dissolution of the Ludlamshöhle is a prime example. Well publicized because its membership included some of Vienna's most eminent writers, actors, musicians, and businessmen, the case became the model of the police's arbitrary and miscalculated enforcement of the law.

From the lively accounts left by the former members, Ignaz Castelli, Karl Rosenbaum, Heinrich Anschütz, and Franz Grillparzer, we know that the group began as a Stammtisch — a close circle of friends who met regularly at the same restaurant for dinner.[44] Around 1817 the group settled at the Haidvogel inn and adopted the name, Ludlamshöhle, after the play of the same name by Adam Oehlenschläger, a visiting Danish dramatist.[45] The name may have been connected with the restaurant's smoky, dark rooms, which resembled the caverns in the play, but Castelli claims that the name merely commemorated the topic of conversation that led to the club's creation (Sauer, 24; Castelli (1969), 101–2).

Throughout its brief history, the Ludlamshöhle boasted the fellowship of Vienna's brightest artists, performers, and businessmen as well as prominent foreigners. So popular were the club's meetings that in 1822 the *Wiener Zeitung* claimed that, whenever visitors asked the police about the whereabouts of certain Viennese personalities, they were directed to the Ludlamshöhle (Castelli (1969), 115–16).

Although Rosenbaum's diary suggests that women occasionally joined their husbands if the group met in his garden, the Ludlamshöhle primarily was a men's organization characterized by smoking, drinking, coarse jokes, and ribald songs. Much like a modern lodge, the group developed an elaborate set of rules and initiation rites. However, all of its ceremonies were humorous parodies and only those persons with a quick wit became true members or 'Bodies', while the rest remained 'Shadows' (Rosenbaum, 28 April 1824, 127v). Each new Body was then granted a new, humorous name that reflected his occupation or accomplishments. Grillparzer was called 'Saphokles der Istrianer' after his play *Sappho;* Carl Maria von Weber was dubbed 'Agathe der Zieltreffer' in honor of his opera *Der Freischütz;* and actor Heinrich Anschütz was called 'Lear der Neuwieder' for his role of King Lear and his home in the suburb of Neu-Wieden (Castelli (1969), 115–16).

Throughout their lives, the members of the Ludlamshöhle denied that the group was political in any way. They claimed it was intended only to provide entertainment and good dinner companionship.[46] The group normally met after the theater three or more times a week. Over dinner, members read poetry, told jokes, or performed impromptu sketches. The wittiest of their creations were published in handwritten newspapers entitled *Die Trattnerhof Zeitung, Der Kellersitzer, Der Wächter* and *Die Wische*.[47]

Some of the traveling artists were offended by the group's madcap pranks. Per Atterbom, a visiting Swedish author, was repelled by the club's prevailing tone and conversations, which often ended in senseless, off-color stories or gossip. But, he wrote, 'What else was there to do?' (224–5). Carl Maria von Weber had similar first impressions: 'It must have been the devil that thrust me into that wasps' nest. Were it not for the necessity of keeping well with the critics who wallow in such filth, Satan himself could never drag me there again' (Weber, 316). After a few visits, however, he too enjoyed the company and became a member.

One night in April 1826, thirty-two policemen broke into the club's meeting rooms where they confiscated the newspapers, songs and money box.[48] Zedlitz, Grillparzer, Schwarz and Schlechta were awakened before dawn and placed under house-arrest. In their haste to uncover a dangerous political plot, the investigators made some ludicrous mistakes. A packet of letters containing 'coded' messages turned out to be harmless greetings of a Jewish mother written in Hebrew to her son in Nikolsburg. A mysterious-looking powder taken from Castelli's house was not poison but cough medicine (Zausmer, 100–1)! The next day Ignaz Jeitteles, Sichrofsky, Haussareck, and Fischof were interrogated. According to Anschütz and Castelli, the police made fools of themselves by requiring the men to explain the true import of Ludlam's jokes, symbols and traditions (Anschütz, 321–4; Castelli (1969), 135).

But, contrary to bitter accounts written long after the actual event, Zausmer contends that the police behaved well throughout the inquiry ('Ludlamshöhle', 105). Rosenbaum, too, called his interrogator a 'polite, young man', adding that his questioning lasted only one half hour (12r). Sentimental memories of the Ludlamshöhle by Castelli and Anschütz imply that the group never reassembled; but reports by the police indicate otherwise. Their records, for example, chronicled a meeting of some Ludlamites in May 1826, at which Schwarz presided as Caliph, Castelli told some pointed jokes, and three men sang Ludlam songs late into the night (Glossy, 'Grillparzer', 254).

The trial of the Ludlamites did not reach the Lower Austrian Landesregierung until November — eight months after the initial police action. The only account of the trial, recorded at second hand by Rosenbaum, indicates that the case was judged inappropriate for that body and therefore was sent back to the police office (Glossy, 'Geschichte', 255; Rosenbaum, 31r). Piering, the spokesman for the police, ignored the protests of the defendants and sentenced them to forty-eight hours in jail. The government workers among them received house arrests, but the others served their sentences in jail. 'How unjust', exclaimed Rosenbaum about the whole proceeding.

A number of intriguing theories have arisen about the reasons for the police action. Those advanced by the persons involved and liberals writing long after the fact usually blame the police.[49] But perhaps the police do not deserve the harsh judgement for, in retrospect, they may have had some legitimate cause for alarm. In 1826, the political activity of the Carbonari had increased, and in the same year in St Petersburg a conspiracy against the czar had been uncovered.[50] Anschütz's diary recorded: 'Since the discovery of the Carbonari conspiracy in Italy, a basis of only a few facts was necessary for the Viennese police of the time to enter forcefully into the life of society.'[51] Is it any wonder that the meetings of the Ludlamshöhle in secluded back rooms of the Haidvogel caught the eye of the police?

In addition, the Ludlamshöhle used many symbols, passwords, and cryptic names for the days of the week and its members. The club's colors were red and black — the same as those of the Carbonari. Also, the phrase used in jest by the club, 'Rot ist schwarz, und schwarz rot', had the ring of Carbonari passwords.[52]

Even if the police had cause to break into the club's meeting rooms, their investigation should quickly have indicated their blunder. Certainly, their dogged tenacity in searching the houses of the members and taking testimony and the nature of the sentences they imposed did not fit the crime. In fact, when final judgements were made, the Ludlamites' crimes seem to have been not so much their involvement in a 'secret society' as their subsequent cavalier behavior toward the police during the investigation. Since the police, and not the court, gave out the sentences, they no doubt felt the need to punish the men who had caused them such public embarrassment throughout Vienna.

After 1830, the case became for writers urging revolution a prime example of police incompetence. Even moderate onlookers grew cynical when they saw that the police, who failed to solve the city's more serious problems, still took time to pursue pointless investigations of innocent artists and writers. The case also revealed the arbitrary nature of Austrian justice, since many individuals had been known to joke about the government in beerhouses and restaurants without fear, but only these few Ludlamites were punished. Ironically, in this way, the police defeated their own ends, for some of the apolitical Ludlamites who were unjustly punished in the 1820s became the vanguard of the revolutionary movement twenty years later.

3

MUSIC IN THE THEATER

Public spectacle and dramatic productions were a celebrated part of Viennese life as early as the sixteenth century, but just after the Napoleonic Wars the city witnessed an unprecedented concentration of outstanding dramatists, actors, dancers, and operatic singers. Theatrical entertainment rose to unparalleled popularity. This era has provided fertile ground for extensive research into each of the five Viennese theaters, the leading dramatists and theatrical genres, yet often overlooked is the role of the theater in Viennese society and its impact on the city's musicians.[1]

VIENNA'S MAJOR THEATERS

Vienna supported five theaters: the Burgtheater and Kärntherthor Theater, located in the inner city, and three suburban theaters – the Theater an der Wien, Leopoldstadt Theater and Josefstadt Theater. Illustration 1 indicates their location in 1833.

The Burgtheater, owned and run by the court, was one of the few theaters in Europe to offer classical German drama. Despite its architecture in 1838 called by Frances Trollope 'dingy, ugly and inconvenient in form' (I, 319), the theater boasted a company of international acclaim, including Heinrich Anschütz, Carl Costenoble, Sophie Schröder, and Julie Löwe.[2] The Viennese held the theater in high regard, according to Adolf Glassbrenner, who facetiously suggested that it was thought to be 'holier than God', and 'whoever did not praise it was cursed'.[3] Table 3's listing of theater ticket prices reveals that the Burgtheater charged moderate prices for its plays and that most of its seats were unreserved.

The Kärnthernthor Theater, also a court theater, specialized in opera and ballet. Prized for its elegant interior, the theater, nonetheless, was

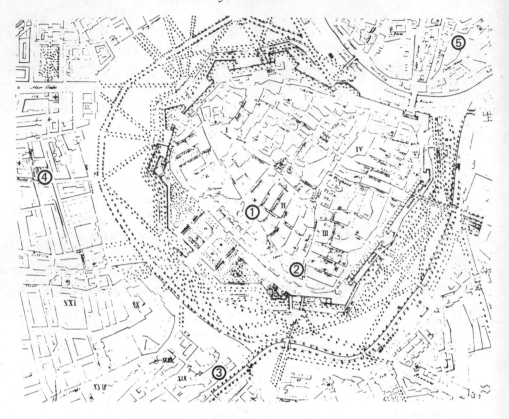

1 Location of Vienna's five major theaters 1815–30
  1. Nationaltheater nächst der k.k. Burg (Burgtheater)
  2. K.k. Hoftheater nächst dem Kärntnerthor (Kärntnerthor Theater)
  3. Theater an der Wien
  4. Theater in der Josefstadt
  5. Theater in der Leopoldstadt
  (Schmidl, *Wien wie es ist*, 1833)

usually cramped, stuffy, and hot – 'tropical' by Helmina von Chezy's standards (255). Among its notable musical premieres were Beethoven's *Fidelio* (final version) in 1814, his Ninth Symphony in 1824, and Weber's *Euryanthe* in 1823. But, in its day, the theater was equally famous for its operatic idols: Isabella Colbran, Josephine Fodor-Mainville, Caroline Unger, Henriette Sontag, Giovanni David, and Andrea Nozzari – all specialists in Italian virtuoso singing.

The theater's resident ballet troupe also excelled, successfully vying

Table 3. *Ticket prices in Vienna's five major theaters (c. 1833)*

	Burg-theater	Kärntnerthor Theater Ital.	Germ.	Theater an der Wien	Leopoldst. Theater	Josefst. Theater
Box Seat	5·00*	20·00	8·00	5·00*	3·12	4·24*
1st Parterre						
Reserved	1·24	2·20	1·24	0·48*	0·36	0·36
Unreserved	1·00	—	1·00	0·30	0·24	0·24
2nd Parterre						
Reserved	—	—	1·00	0·20	—	—
Unreserved	0·30	—	—	—	—	—
1st Gallery						
Reserved	—	2·20	1·36	0·48	0·36	0·36
Unreserved	—	1·20	1·00	0·30	0·24	0·24
2nd Gallery						
Reserved	—	—	—	0·36	0·24	0·24
Unreserved	0·30	—	0·40	0·20	0·15*	0·15
3rd Gallery						
Reserved	0·48	2·00	1·00	—	—	—
Unreserved	0·36	1·20	—	0·16	0·07*	0·07
4th Gallery						
Reserved	—	1·10	0·45	—	—	—
Unreserved	0·20	0·40	0·24	0·08	—	—
5th Gallery	—	0·24	0·15	—	—	—

The ticket prices were taken from the following travel guides:
  Schmidl, 209–211; Pezzl, *Beschreibung* (1841) 458–9.
The figures marked with (*) indicate variants quoted by Normann, 69, 74, 82–3. Normann cites:
  Burgtheater Box 8.00 fl.
  T. an d. W. Box 6.00 fl.; 1st Parterre Res. 0·42.
  Leopoldst. 2nd Gallery 0·12; 3rd Gallery 0·80.
  Josefst. Box 1.48 fl.; Res. (parterre?) 1·00.

with Parisian companies with its impeccable technique and original choreography. Two celebrated pioneers in the interpretation of romantic ballet, Marie Taglioni and Fanny Elssler, began their careers on the stage of the Kärntnerthor Theater.[4]

Ticket prices varied widely. For Italian opera ticket prices almost doubled, but for German works and ballets the prices were comparable to those at the Burgtheater. Table 3 also indicates that this theater had more tiers or galleries than any of the other local theaters.

The suburban theaters offered a wider range of drama. The Theater an der Wien, remembered today for its premiere of Mozart's *Magic Flute* in 1801, was billed by contemporaries as the city's 'largest and most beautiful theater' (Schmidl, 23). Possessing complicated machinery and a stage that allegedly supported 500 persons and 50 horses, the theater produced great spectacles, melodramas, and Zauberstücke (light dramas with music that featured 'magical' stage effects and scenic transformations). Compared to those charged by the other two suburban theaters, the tickets at the Theater an der Wien were expensive, but they were considerably below the cost of those at either court theater.

Productions at the Leopoldstadt Theater were much smaller and less lavish than on the other suburban stages. George Smart, the principal conductor of London's Philharmonic Society, wrote disparagingly of the theater's 'small and dirty' stage and scenery (99). But in the eyes of its contemporary playwrights, the theater surpassed all others in its presentation of Viennese folk comedies. Ignaz Castelli extolls the theater's comedians LaRoche (in the role of Kasperl), Anton Hasenhut (as Thaddädl), Ignaz Schuster (as Staberl), Ferdinand Raimund, and Josef Korntheuer, and comediennes Johanna Huber and Therese Krones, whom he calls the epitome of Austrian clowns (Castelli (1969), 77–80). The relatively low price of tickets, together with the appeal of the comedies helped to make the Leopoldstadt Theater a favorite among members of the working classes.

The Josefstadt Theater received governmental permission to present opera, ballet, drama, melodrama, and pantomime. But despite its wide offerings, the theater attracted only a few good actors and continually suffered from financial difficulties. As a result, it lived in the shadow of the other theaters (Castelli (1969), 9). Not until the 1830s did the theater revive its prestige when it presented Wenzel Scholz, a talented comedian, and gave debuts to Weber's *Oberon* (in German) in 1827, Kreutzer's *Das Nachtlager in Granada* in 1834, Raimund's *Der Verschwender* in 1834, and Lortzing's *Zar und Zimmermann* in 1837 (Rommel, *Volkskomödie*, 425).

MUSIC IN THE THEATER

Opera – Music was intimately linked to all theatrical genres, but the most important of these was opera. Operatic music permeated Viennese daily life. Arias were not only known and repeated in theaters, salons, and concert halls, but they also formed the basis of innumerable variations and transcriptions for home use as well as the repertory of street organs and music boxes (Schmidl, 23). Well-known singers and opera plots provided the subjects for parodies in the folk theaters. For example, Adolf Bäuerle's *Die falsche Primadonna* (1818) referred to the celebrated Italian soprano, Angelica Catalani. Josef Gleich parodied Boieldieu's opera *La dame blanche* (The Lady in White) with his own *Die schwarzen Frauen* (The Ladies in Black) in 1827. Karl Meisl poked fun at Spontini's *La vestale* in his *Julerl, die Putzmächerin* (Julerl, the Cleaningwoman) in 1828 and Auber's *La muette di Portici* in his *Die geschwätzige Stumme von Nussdorf* (The Loquacious Mute of Nussdorf) in 1830.[5]

During the 1820s, the rivalry between proponents of Italian and German opera grew heated and hostile. In Vienna, Italian opera had the advantage because of its long tradition of Italian productions and because the director of both the Kärntnerthor Theater and the Theater an der Wien was Domenico Barbaja, a Neapolitan casino and theater entrepreneur who concurrently managed the opera houses in Milan and Naples. Barbaja brought to Vienna internationally recognized singers such as Isabella Colbran (1789–1870), considered to be the *prima assoluta* of all Europe between 1806 and 1815; Josephine Fodor-Mainville (1789–1870), Rossini's intended Rosina for his *Il barbiere di Siviglia*; as well as Andrea Nozzari (1775–1832), Giovanni David (d. 1851), and Antonio Ambrogi (1786–?), all handpicked interpreters of Rossini operas.[6] He also introduced the Italian system of opera subscriptions, and he imported the new Italian vocal virtuosity from Naples. Consequently, the Kärntherthor's Italian opera company, with its outstanding vocalists and polished, popular repertory, far surpassed the theater's German troupe, whose singers and repertory were less refined.

Despite his obvious Italian bias, Barbaja commissioned Carl Maria von Weber to write *Euryanthe*, a German romantic opera, for the Kärntnerthor Theater in 1823. But Barbaja likely was motivated by his business sense rather than artistic impulses, for he knew that the presence of Weber and Rossini together in Vienna would surely ignite the passions of their respective factions – an ideal means of selling tickets.

Italian opera easily won out. The Rossini craze had reached overwhelming proportions when Rossini first arrived in 1822. Anton Schindler, Beethoven's biographer, used the words 'intoxication', 'frenzy', and 'fanaticism' to describe the city's reception (Schindler, 271). A reporter for the *Allgemeine musikalische Zeitung* in Leipzig recorded the tumult: 'It was really enough, more than enough. The entire performance was like an idolatrous orgy; everyone there acted as if he had been bitten by a tarantula; the shouting, crying, yelling of "viva" and "fora" went on and on' (Schindler, 271).

German and English writers tended to be critical of Rossini's success. German intellectuals and nationalists deplored the 'empty virtuosity' and lack of serious subject matter. In his 'Aufruf an deutsche Komponisten' (July 1823), composer Louis Spohr detected in all German audiences save in Vienna a dissatisfaction with the overly sweet melodies, the senseless plots, and the lack of artistic unity in Italian operas; and he appealed to German composers to abandon foreign musical models to create a new, German opera ('Aufruf', 457–64). Spohr's dislike of Viennese audiences, however, probably stems from the failure earlier (1821) there of his opera *Zemire und Azor*, which he attributed to errors in assigning the roles, inadequate rehearsal, and Viennese prejudice against foreign German works.

Not all Viennese condoned the adulation of Italian opera, judging from a satirical lament (purported to have been written by Ignaz Castelli) that was submitted to the police in July 1822 by an anonymous informer from Baden. The lament on the departure of the Italian company was written in Viennese dialect and was to be sung to the popular tune 'Es reiten drei Schneider zum Thor hinaus'. Italian bravura, insipid plots, and the exorbitant ticket prices were among the targets for ridicule:

> The Italians are going out to the gate, Ade!
> With all roulades and trills at an end, Au weh
> Even if one cupped his ears ever so much,
> Such beautiful songs one will hear no more
> Au weh, au weh, au weh.

Forsaken and poor is great Vienna, Au weh
Where will we now take our three Gulden, O je
We took bread from our mouths, and spent it on our ears
Au weh, au weh, au weh.

Who will now go to the opera, Au weh
And perhaps listen to moaning by C. W. Gluck, O je
We have been robbed of our greatest happiness
All we Germans are incapable of anything
Hehe, hehe, hehe.

When German operas are performed, O je
There one can hear even talking, Au weh
We, however, do not go to the theater to hear what is happening inside
Ne, ne ne.

Long life to Rossini, you great man, Ade!
You have done so much for us, O je
If you did not exist, you heavenly composer,
From where would we take something to hum
O je, O je, O je.

(VA, P.H. 6739/1822. The complete original in Appendix A)

The vogue of Italian opera continued well into the decade. In 1826 Johann Hecke, a traveler from Berlin, mentioned that the operas of Rossini with their 'trilling mannerism' and endless repetition were still popular in Vienna (Hecke, 72–3). Two years later, Edward Holmes complained:

From the specimens of the musical performances I have met with, there is scarcely a corner of Europe in which the taste of the operatic community can be worse. It has been said that the people of Vienna are Rossini mad, but they are mad not only for him, but mad for his worst imitators: with good ears they tolerate the worst of music. They out herod Herod in their noisy and vociferous applause of their favourites; this is the system now pursued towards a lady who is in the good graces of the audience: she receives a loud greeting on her entrance, is interrupted with bravos in the middle of her song, there is more applause, she is regularly called back to make her obeisance and to hear fresh acclamations. (116–17)

While it is virtually impossible to substantiate the observers' comments about the quality of the operas in Vienna, the modern reader can begin to appreciate the criticism of it by examining a list of operas produced in the year 1824 (Table 4). Of the twenty-six recorded operas that year, almost half were Italian or adaptations of French operas. And,

Table 4. *Operas performed in Vienna during 1824*

Date	Title	Composer	Dramatist	Theater
Jan. 19	*Das Faustrecht in Thüringa*	Kauer	Hensler	Jo
Jan. 24	*Der Taucher*	Kreutzer	—	Ka
Feb. 11	*Zwei Wörter*	Dalayrac	Marsollier	Jo
Feb. 12	*Witwentrauer*	Generali	Foppa	Ka
			Grünbaum	
Feb. 18	*Der Brief an sich selbst*	Gläser	Meisl	Jo
Mar. 9	*Graf Armand (Der Wasserträger)*	Cherubini	Bouilty	Jo
Mar. 18	*Das Schloss Lowinski*	Seyfried	Stunz	TaW
Mar. 19	*Der Schnee*	Auber	Scribe	Ka
Mar. 27	*Sauertöpfchen*	Gläser	Meisl	Jo
Apr. 1	*Gabriella di Vergy*	Carafa	Tottola	Ka
Apr. 8	*Johann von Paris*	Boieldieu	Just	Jo
		Seyfried		
May 4	*Edoardo e Cristina*	Rossini	Schmidt	Ka
Jun. 19	*Der Kieffhäuserberg*	Marschner	Kotzebue	Jo
Jun. 27	*Der gebesserte Lorenz*	Eulenstein	Gewey	Ka
Jul. 10	*Elisa e Claudio*	Mercadante	Romanelli	Ka
Aug. 21	*Die blaue Katze*	Roser	—	Jo
Sep. 1	*Das Schloss von Montenero*	Dalayrac	Ihlée	Jo
Sep. 18	*Doralice*	Mercadante	—	Jo
Oct. 6	*Mosè in Egitto*	Rossini	Tottola	Ka
Nov. 5	*Le nozze di Telemaco ed Antiope*	Mercadante	Bassi	Ka
Nov. 20	*Il podestà di Bourgos*	Mercadante	Bassi	Ka
Nov. 20	*Der Feuervogel*	Drechsler	Gleich	Jo
Dec. 2	*Die erfüllte Hoffnung*	Kreutzer	—	TaW
	(Command Performance)			
Dec. 6	*Das Zauberhorn*	Lubin	Vogel	Jo
Dec. 13	*Die kürzeren Mäntel*	Gläser	Meisl	Jo
uncert.	*König Waldemar*	Weigl.	—	—?

Taken from Anton Bauer, *Oper und Operetten* for the year 1824 (Graz, Herman Böhlaus, 1955). See also: Franz Steiger, *Opernlexicon* (Tutzing: Hans Schneider, 1978).

as Hecke and Holmes claimed, works by Rossini and his imitators, such as Mercadante, were numerous. Further, the titles of the works such as *The Blue Cat*, *Little Sourpot* and *The Magic Horn* suggest that some plots may well have been trivial. Very few of the works presented that year remained in the operatic repertory, and of those – Cherubini's *Graf Armand* (*Les deux journées*), Rossini's *Mosè in Egitto*, Boieldieu's *Johann von Paris* (*Jean de Paris*), Mercadante's *Elisa e Claudio*, and Carafa's *Gabriella di Vergy* – none was German.

Incidental music — In folk comedies of the suburban theaters, simple, strophic songs containing satirical or topical allusions were used to summarize the plot or to moralize on its outcome. In 1827, Eduard Forstmann observed that these pleasing, melodious tunes quickly circulated among the lower classes and that they were performed on many street corners (159). Sometimes mistaken for authentic folksongs, a few of these theater songs survive today. The lyrics from Adolf Bäuerle's *Aline* or *Wien in einem anderen Weltteile* (1822), for example, are quoted in modern Viennese travel brochures: 'es gibt nur a Kaiserstadt,'s gibt nur a Wean' ('there is only one imperial city, there is only one Vienna' (Rommel, 114–15; see Appendix B for two examples of theater songs).

Beyond folk comedies, music was essential to a variety of other genres such as melodrama, parody, Singspiel, Lustspiel, and Zauberspiel. Repertory studies of Viennese theater fare during the years 1825–6 reveal the wide range — from serious romantic opera (*Die weisse Frau*, *Der Freischütz*, *Leicester*) to provocative novelties entitled *Joko, the Brazilian Ape*, *The Dog from Gottshardsberg*, and *The Journey through the Air*. Many of the titles suggest the popularity of magic and fairytales: *The Magic Rose*, *The Magic Lake*, *The Miraculous Spectacles in the Magic Woods*, *The Fall of the Fairy Kingdom*, *The Fairy in France*, *The Fairy in Krähwinkel*. Perhaps the music masked the noises of the elaborate stage machinery as it produced the many scenic effects and characteristic stage transformations.

Closer examination of the repertory lists from those years also indicates that the creators of most of the German works were resident conductors at the local theaters (see Appendix C). Wenzel Müller and Franz Volkert, for instance, conducted at the Leopoldstadt Theater. Phillip Riotte was a conductor at the Theater an der Wien, and Franz Gläser worked at the Josefstadt Theater. Even though these men wrote much theater music, both they and their creations are largely forgotten today.

Classical drama also utilized music in orchestral overtures, *entr'acte* music, and finales.[7] Usually a pastiche from opera and symphonies, the incidental music introduced and accompanied a play, although not always with direct dramatic connection. A record of certain musical choices was kept by Ignaz Mosel, deputy director of the Burgtheater from

1818 to 1829. For his production of Schiller's *Wilhelm Tell*, he fashioned an overture from those of Haydn, composed rustic Swiss dances and goatherd songs, and borrowed from the finale of Cherubini's *Lodoiska* and Handel's Pastorale. For Shakespeare's *Hamlet*, he chose music of Ludwig Persius; for *Henry IV*, he chose music by Beethoven; and, for *Othello*, he combined selections by Cherubini, Beethoven, Johann Vogel, and Josef Haydn.[8]

Composing music for theater could be lucrative. Beethoven took advantage of the opportunities in Vienna by writing the overture, *Die Weihe des Hauses*, for the festive reopening of the Josefstadt Theater (after its renovation) in 1822; he also contributed incidental music for Goethe's play *Egmont* and Kotzebue's *Die Ruinen von Athen* and *Coriolan*. Schubert, too, aspired to success in the theater, and his early attempts, overtures to *Die Zauberharfe* and *Der Teufel als Hydraulicus*, received good reviews. The overture and choruses from *Rosamunde* of 1823 were applauded, even encored according to eyewitnesses, yet certain critics called the music 'original, but eccentric'. Troubles with the dramatic plot and the performers further contributed to the play's failure (Deutsch, *Biography*, 313–14). Unfortunately, Schubert's operas fared worse and generally were ignored.

THEATER IN VIENNESE SOCIETY

Many nineteenth-century chroniclers affirm that Viennese social life revolved around the theater. Men and women paid social calls or attended teas before a performance, which began around 6 or 7 p.m., and they met for supper or dancing afterwards, at 10–11 p.m. (Klingemann, II, 181; Strang, 332). Street traffic ebbed and flowed with theater hours. From 1 to 3 p.m., while people ate dinner, the streets stood deserted, but late in the afternoon there was always a rush to the theaters (Dibdin, 342).

The theaters served as a public meeting place where tradespeople discussed current affairs and business, women paraded their newest finery, foreigners made their first social contacts, and courtesans attracted new lovers. The latter activity, a sore point with the police and 'respectable' theatergoers, was painfully conspicuous in the parterre of the Leopoldstadt Theater and apparently contributed to that theater's special character (Klingemann, II, 117; Glossy, 'Geschichte',

2 'In the gallery of the Leopoldstadt Theater', by Josef Lanzedelly (*c.* 1820)
(Historisches Museum der Stadt Wien, Inv. Nr. 61.974)

41). Such social activities angered the actors, for, as Heinrich Anschütz (one of the principal Shakespearian actors at the Burgtheater) lamented, the audiences were more concerned with their conversations than with the drama, which they ignored altogether (240) (see Illus. 2).

As a central gathering place, the theater assumed other functions. Except for religious or state ceremonies, only at the theater were groups of people permitted to assemble. In addition, the theaters brought together upper- and working-class people for the single social activity in which they jointly participated. Certainly the exclusive, private boxes and reserved seats in the choice galleries preserved class distinctions, but, as J. F. Reichardt noticed in 1810 in Vienna,

...all the great public diversions and amusements are enjoyed by all classes without any abrupt divisions or offending distinctions – in these respects, Vienna is again quite along among the great cities of Europe...In London, an ordinary citizen does not venture into the parterre of the great Italian opera – the drama of the nobility and the great rich world – without having at least marked himself as an elegant and wealthy gentleman by some outward sign – a fine expensive ring, or something of the sort...Reichardt (Strunk, 730)

The theater provided the main topic of polite conversation – a testimony to its social importance. At least five Viennese journals reviewed new productions and announced the arrival and departures of celebrities. Of the journals, the most durable were the *Wiener Hoftheater-Almanach* (pub. 1804–16), the *Wiener Theaterzeitung* (1806–45) and *Das Theatralische Taschenbuch von k.k. priv. Theater in der Leopoldstadt* (1814–64).[9] Viennese literary salons, like that of Caroline Pichler, regularly met to read aloud and discuss plays, while more informal circles like the Ludlamshöhle met after a performance to review and parody drama (Pichler, 1, 408–9; Castelli (1969), 101).

Conversation about the theater invariably turned to gossip about the personal affairs of the actors or theater managers. Glassbrenner claims that Viennese audiences eagerly pursued each new scandal:

In no other city in the world does the theater audience take part in so many cabals and intrigues as in Vienna; there is no play on the boards that, in this respect, could compete with it. If an actress has given into the passionate desires of a cavalier, she will be showered with applause until she also gives into the passionate desires of others.[10]

But theater intrigues could also turn against a performer. When Therese Krones, a popular actress from the Leopoldstadt Theater, became implicated indirectly in a sordid murder of a priest by her lover, her audiences whistled her off the stage.[11]

Finally the theater seemed to provide a socially acceptable outlet for the communal release of violent emotions for a society whose political regulation and etiquette did not tolerate personal excess. Foreigners continually express bewilderment over the wild behavior of Viennese audiences. In 1824, John Russell ranked the Viennese first among Europeans in the 'exaggerated passion' for the theater (209). Twenty years later, Friedrich Hurter assessed the same hysteria as a 'symptom of a deeper social ill' and noted:

What at other times was observed as a means of recreation and respectable amusement is now seen by many as, if not a business, then as a serious part of life; and it continues to be treated with deference and importance, as if the theater were the institution which superseded everything except basic needs in the area of making demands upon the time and attention of the public.[12]

Glassbrenner offers the most vivid account of Viennese passions during a performance of Italian opera in 1836:

Mothers leaned against Fathers and gave vent to their feelings, youths fainted from bliss and fell into the laps of young girls, officials forgot suddenly that they would have nothing to do tomorrow, and even the police watchman, who must stand every night behind the curtains, had a tear, a half-inch in diameter, falling down his cheeks. I also clapped furiously, because I feared I would be thrown out if I did not.[13]

Although such anecdotes are exaggerated, the central observation may contain some truth, for even prosaic police reports express repeated concern about violent outbursts among the city's theater audiences.[14]

VIENNESE TASTES IN DRAMA

A common assertion about Viennese audiences is that they were extremely demanding and fickle. Indeed, both the actress Sophie Schröder and the writer Frances Trollope compared Viennese theatrical tastes to 'fits of fashion' (Schröder, 21; Trollope, 1, 372). But, while keeping abreast of new trends, favorite actors were expected to produce flawless performances and were allowed to deliver pointed satire only so long as it remained within certain boundaries of good taste:

The Viennese shows the same zeal in the theater. The favorite actor in the Burg, at whose appearance even children and old people give enthusiastic applause, is hissed if he makes a slip of the tongue; the singer in the Kärntnerthor, at whose notes people sway their heads from side to side and in whose melodies they seem to bathe, receives no uncertain demonstrations of displeasure as soon as his throat commits a blunder, and the most revered comedian in the Theater an der Wien of the Leopoldstadt momentarily falls into disgrace, if, with his joke, he oversteps the boundaries, which are certainly extended far enough.[15]

Paradoxically, while modern writers praise the accomplishments of the Viennese theaters of that period, surviving eyewitness accounts contain few compliments. Partly responsible were the writers' expectations, since many were well-educated foreigners who came to Vienna hoping to hear German works by Mozart and Beethoven. Instead, they were disappointed by more fashionable Italian and French pieces. In 1819 the dramatist Adam Oehlenschläger declared that in Vienna 'the musical taste is, in my opinion, no longer good, and Mozart's spirit has not taken root in the mind and soul of the listeners. Mozart's works have been offered at such length and so often that they have grown tired of them and have again returned to dull Italian opera seria' (39). Similarly, the English observers Edward Holmes and Frances Trollope deplored the disparity between the city's reputation abroad and the current level of performance. Trollope recorded, 'My notion of a Vienna opera had something very exalted in it: something in which visions of Mozart, Haydn and Weber were joined with ideas of execution as national and as perfect as their compositions. But the reality is otherwise' (I, 368). Native Austrians, like Anton Schmidl, joined the chorus of criticism, but for different reasons. For him, the overwhelming popularity of Italian opera reflected a decadence of taste that corrupted all Austria (272). Again, in the 1830s other writers mention the decline. In 1834 an anonymous German traveler observed:

But all Viennese complain that it [the theater] is far from matching the earlier splendor which it had around ten years ago, when the greatest talents were here united, when LaBlache and Fodor, Ambrosi and the unsurpassed Rubini shone and when the ballet competed with the Parisian [companies]. Now the Italian opera has perished, the ballet is not distinguished and the German opera is not extraordinary.[16]

Speculation about the reasons for the theater's supposed decline provides valuable social criticism. Wolfgang Menzel, a Swiss writer, blamed a 'prevailing philistine spirit' in the 1830s for the lack of original drama (276). The actor Anschütz, however, blamed Austrian censors for banning or emasculating excellent plays while leaving untouched silly, meaningless pieces (227). Naturally, he reasoned, Viennese dramatic tastes had sunken to mere 'naive frivolity or frivolous naiveté' (228).

Writers with republican views interpreted the popularity of the comic theater as a plot by the government to keep its citizens from more intellectual pursuits. Sealsfield, one of the most outspoken writers on this issue, blamed Metternich in 1828 for having intentionally suppressed serious entertainments among the middle classes, leaving them trivial pastimes as the 'only objects of their thoughts and desires' (195). Three years later, John Strang concurred, explaining,

You may easily imagine, that under so jealous a despotism as that of Austria, the legitimate drama does not flourish in proportion to farce and spectacle. The reason is obvious. It lies in the dread of liberal opinions, which find no place in the latter, while the former is filled with them because they excite no jealousy, are freely patronised by the Government; but it is altogether different with the productions of Schiller and Shakespeare, which speak to the intellectual sympathies of human nature, and teach the glorious lesson to be free. (255)

The suspicions of both men were well founded, for, as a police report from 1824 reveals, the state recognized the far-reaching influence of the theater:

...the maintenance of the Kärntnerthor Theater is very desirable, beyond [being] a responsibility of the police, for the police authorities must be concerned with increasing rather than hindering the decent amusements of its citizens; in order, on the one hand, to restrain these activities endangering morality and public order and security, and, on the other hand, to bring variety to daily conversation and supply for the latter material that is as abundant as it is harmless.[17]

REGULATION OF THE THEATER

The above-mentioned accusations against the Austrian government raise questions about the extent to which the state participated in theatrical affairs. Documents from the archives of the court theaters and police offices testify to certain activities controlled by the state.

The distribution of free tickets and theater subscriptions occasionally came under governmental supervision. In view of the theater's popularity, the acquisition of tickets was usually difficult. Most tickets for box and reserved seats were sold by subscription a year in advance. Some boxes, reserved for nobility and the very rich, were even passed on as a part of the owner's estate. Glassbrenner humorously describes the plight of certain 'cavaliers' who tried to secure box seats at the Burgtheater because it was fashionable. They often spent large sums of money and were forced to wait up to five years before they succeeded and could thereafter be 'comfortably bored' (178).

The government usually awarded free theater subscriptions or tickets *ex officio* to certain government employees. In 1826, a report to the Oberkämmeramt lists the names of those who were to receive this privilege. The chief of police, the city's commandant, and the theater's doctor were placed in special reserved seats, while tickets for general admission went to certain military officers, court councilors, Hofagent Sonnleithner (*ex testamento* of Kaiser Josef II), dramatists (Grillparzer, Zedlitz, Vogel, Herzenkron), music critics (Bernard, Bäuerle, Seyfried, Schick, Felix Joel, and Halirsch), and the court printer (Wallishauser).[18]

A similar, although less complete, list of free passes to the opera for the year 1824 indicates that the two court Kapellmeisters (Salieri and Eybler), the official theater composer (Mosel), theater secretary (Moritz von Dietrichstein), censor (Bretfeld), watchman (von Sieber) and others, notable among whom were Schreyvogel, Sedlnitsky, and Sonnleithner, received free tickets.[19] In this way the government rewarded its artists and gave them the opportunity to learn from others' creations.

Since the majority of tickets available to the general public were for unreserved seats, it was customary to send someone ahead to save seats so that the ticket-holder could arrive later in comfort and fashion.[20] This duty could have been harrowing, for, as theater historians report, as early as 1780 nobles sent only their strongest sedan-chair bearers or servants for this purpose.[21] Sending strong men for the task becomes understandable when one reads Castelli's account of crowds waiting to enter the Leopoldstadt Theater. There a 'thick crowd of people herded together', pushing, shoving to get a good seat (Castelli (1969), 76). Sometimes the crowd turned violent, for the government of Lower Austria declared in 1800 that no child under the age of sixteen could be sent to the theater to secure seats.[22] (see Illus. 3).

The police occasionally became personally involved with a theater's internal affairs. In 1820, they investigated allegations of illegal ticket distribution. The corresponding report describes the current abuse of ticket privileges as 'monstrous', citing a case where over 800 persons – whole families and almost every member of the Court Chamber – entered the theater almost free, because the box office had illegally reduced prices or given tickets away. As a result, the theater was overcrowded, but it made no profit.[23] Another complaint, filed in 1829, describes the case of a retired army officer who tricked the theater cashier into believing he was dressed in full uniform, in order to receive the military discount.[24]

Because the police also took responsibility for public safety before and after each performance, many theater regulations refer to carriage traffic and parking.[25] In addition, a policeman was always on duty behind the theater curtain to watch for fire and to help people escape in the event of an emergency. Fire was a real hazard in the theater,

3 'The theater-lovers in front of the Leopoldstadt Theater', by Joseph Lanzedelly (*c.* 1820). (Historisches Museum der Stadt Wien, Inv. Nr. 61.961)

where open flames or theater lanterns were used for illuminating highly flammable backdrops and curtains. The disastrous fire at the Hoftheater in Munich in January 1823 as well as the Ringtheater fire in Vienna in 1890 demonstrate the wisdom of the police watch.

Other laws and police memoranda document the state's fear of public disorder in the theater. These fears were not unwarranted in view of the riotous demonstrations that broke out in Paris during the revolution and the uproar sparked by the last act of Auber's *La muette di Portici* in 1830 in Belgium. Hence, as early as 1800, officials passed rules outlining public decorum in the theaters.[26] As well as barring dogs from the theater and requiring men to remove their hats, the regulations attempted to limit applause by preventing the audience from requesting encores and by not allowing a performer to appear before the curtain to bow or speak. Only artists making their debuts or those visiting from other theaters were permitted to take curtain calls (*Sammlung der Gesetze*, 1817, 87–8).

Such rules do not appear to have been strictly enforced, for eyewitnesses repeatedly testify to tumultuous applause, whistling, hissing, stamping, and shouting among the audiences. Admitting a problem in 1824, the police reminded the managers of the Kärntnerthor Theater that such practices were forbidden (Glossy, 'Geschichte', 51). But the situation persisted since Glassbrenner reports in 1835 that, during a performance of three Italian divas, the audiences clapped until their hands were sore, the balconies shook from the tumult, and the singers repeated their arias up to twenty times.[27]

Only the government's bureaucrats seem to have been subject to all regulations. For example, when *Zauberspiel, Die Schaunacht im Felsentale* was performed in December 1822, and the author, Josef Gleich, was called out, he did not appear because he was a government official. Even when his supporters formally requested his appearance on the stage, the police refused permission (Glossy, 'Geschichte', 34). In the same way, Franz Grillparzer could not acknowledge the applause for his *König Ottokars Glück und Ende* in 1825 because he was an official of the Court Chamber (Costenoble, 341; Pichler, II, 184).

But in its role as censor, the state actively participated in the theater's administration. Not only were its dramas, printed handbills, advertisements, and songs subject to its censorship (see Chapter 2), but costumes also came under the scrutiny of the police. A memorandum from the chief of police, dated 11 December 1826, directed all police to renew their guard against indecent costumes and 'shocking nudity' on the city's stages (Glossy, 'Geschichte', 86). Another notice from March 1829, written by an inspector of the Kärntnerthor Theater, reports that the skirts of the ballet dancers offended the 'general welfare and morality' of the audience. He proposed that the dancers eliminate the starch from their underskirts, that authorities inspect the length of each costume before a performance, and that dancers use flesh-colored leggings whenever they wore very short skirts (VA, P.H. 1701/1830, 'Theater Kleidung').

But again, in contrast to the strict rules for the court theaters, rules for suburban theaters apparently were more permissive. English writers, of course, were shocked by the tight-fitting and revealing costumes worn by the women. Holmes confessed, 'My English proprieties were somewhat scandalized at finding a number of young ladies introduced on the stage here in short tight jackets without tail, silk breeches, and stockings equally as tight (137). Trollope was shocked by the 'brevity of draperies' worn by the corps de ballet (I, 369). Other visitors apparently were more blasé for they are silent on this matter.

The police also investigated charges of misconduct among its theater employees. A letter from Kaiser Franz to his theater secretary, Count Wrbna, dated February 1809, underlines his concern about the theater.

It is with great displeasure that I have learned that immorality at the two court theaters and at the one an der Wien among the employed actors, dancers, etc. has run rampant, much to the scandal of the public, and the most prominent perpetrators of this behavior are supposed to be several cavaliers of the direction staff.

Since this moral turpitude cannot in the least be allowed among the staffs of the public stage, which should be the school of good manners [according to] its definition, and never can be such, as long as the persons of same will not have a good public reputation; so you have the duty to inform the theater administration of my displeasure and to add the warning that I personally want to be able to hold myself apart from the evil moral reputation of the stage, and to observe truly that the cavaliers of the theater administration will restrain themselves all the more certainly from seducing certain persons to immorality; or otherwise I will be forced to take stricter measures.

Also I hold you responsible, dear Count Wrbna, to the most conscientious duty of assuring yourself of the public reputation of the persons in the theater as much as possible, to have the necessary reminders presented to the theater direction, and if these should prove fruitless, to bring the matter to my attention. (HHStA, General Intendanz, Burgtheater, 1822, 'Verzeichnis und Index über die Theater Akten von 1809–1822', II no. 37, 4 Feb. 1809)

Accordingly, many secret observers informed the police of questionable behavior by those connected with the theater. A surviving remnant of one such report, dated October 26 1812, discusses the conduct of an actor, Schilbach, formerly employed at the Theater an der Wien, but at the time a member of the Josefstadt Theater. Apparently a spendthrift, Schilbach was deeply in debt, had severely maltreated his wife and abandoned his children. But, in this case, the anonymous writer urges the court's sympathy for the children in view of their mother's recent death and Schilbach's former service to the theater (VA, P.H., 941/1813, 'Theater Censur', 26 October 1812).

In another report to the police, dated November 1822, an informer complains that the singers (presumably of the Kärntnerthor Theater) periodically refused to sing the *da capo* portions of their arias. Other singers appeared on stage intoxicated and disrupted entire scenes (Glossy, 'Geschichte', 33–4). In October 1828, another letter names certain actors and singers who regularly engaged in gambling in particular coffee houses. So great was their skill that they attracted crowds, among whom were their fellow-performers from the court theaters (VA, P.H., 1405/1829, 'Neuigkeiten in Wien').

But, in other circumstances, the police actually aided performers by silencing their critics. In 1813, Prince Lobkowitz complained to the censors on behalf of the singers Pauline Milder, Antonia Lachner, Siboni, and Johann Vogel about a highly critical review that appeared in the journal *Thalia*. He entreated the police to be more diligent in preventing such 'slanderous writings' from being published (VA, P.H., 941/1813, Oper, 25 April 1813). By April 1817, a royal decree gave the censors the power to ban reviews of concerts of other public entertainments if the reviews contained unreasonable reproach of the performers. In May 1823, the decree was renewed with the added provision that the police should forbid articles that criticized virtuosi or that insulted the theater (Wiesner, 314, 340).

While contemporary writings deplore censorship in the Austrian theaters, it should be noted that Austria was not alone in such censorship, for censors in Germany and Italy also struck out offending political, religious, and ethical materials from their operas and dramas. In fact, Julius Marx asserts that, compared to other German censors, the Austrian censors were not overly severe. Rather, he claims, they received undue notoriety through travel reports written by uninformed foreigners and by inaccurate memoirs written by political liberals. Furthermore, the lack of comparable information about censorship in other countries during the nineteenth century makes the Austrian system appear disproportionately oppressive (Marx, *Zensur*, 57).

Taking into account the statements of eyewitnesses and Marx's theories, a third assessment of censorship's impact can be made. Like other official duties such as customs inspections, the issuance of travel documents, and censorship, the control of the theater depended upon stringent rules and heavy fines. Yet, as with other laws, their enforcement was often irregular and arbitrary. In fact, it appears that the government rigorously enforced the law only in cases of obvious abuse, political emergency, and where its own institutions and employees were involved. Unfortunately for Vienna's musicians, performers, and writers, the state still controlled the best theaters. Thus, to be successful, artists not only had to compromise their work in accordance with the whims of their audiences and the limitations of the various theaters, but they were also forced to submit to the fears of a paranoid government.

4

PUBLIC CONCERTS

Vienna's rich musical life attracted the attention of performers and music lovers throughout the nineteenth century. In 1812, composer Louis Spohr exclaimed: 'Artistic performances in Vienna were measured by the highest standards and to succeed there was to qualify as a master' (*Journeys*, 81). Ten years later, Carl Maria von Weber voiced similar sentiments:

And so it came that Vienna was established as the Areopagus where alone musical art was to be judged, where artists were to stand before the judgement-seat, where laurels were to be given or withheld, where verdicts were to be delivered and reputations made; and Vienna, although blinded now and then by the dazzle of false glitter, or led astray by fashion's fancies, deserved its honours. (II, 271)

And yet, in spite of these acclamations, little is actually known about the city's public concerts, the conventions of performance, or the audiences. Still a novelty, public concerts left few formal records and music, because of its ephemeral nature, seems to have defied description by those who attended. Moreover, the few surviving concert programs – representing only a fraction of the musical activity – the irregularly reported and vaguely worded newspaper reviews, and a few diary entries about certain performances are not likely to yield definitive, new conclusions. A broad investigation, however, may shed some light on new aspects of concert life.

THE ROLE OF CONCERTS IN VIENNESE
SOCIAL LIFE

Accounts left by travelers and residents suggest that much of Vienna's social activities revolved around the performance of music at home and in public halls. Accordingly, the number of concerts was large. During her research, Hilde Fischbach-Stojan counted 75 major concerts during the year 1824 alone; and, for the period 1826–7, William Weber found mention of 111 concerts, as compared to 125 in London and 78 in Paris.[1]

The public-concert season, like the theater season, began in autumn and lasted until early summer. Concerts were most numerous on Normatagen, days set aside as religious or state holidays when theaters were forbidden to present drama. Thus, Sundays and the spring Lenten season were closely associated with music making. On one particular Sunday in 1836, Wenzel Blumenbach counted no less than twenty-five placards announcing balls and concerts for the day – apparently not an unusual number for Vienna (vol. 1, 121).

Public concerts usually began around midday. The rules governing the practice had political overtones, for it was in the government's interest to thwart entertainments that competed with its own court theaters in the evening (Loewe, 332; Holman, 282). Moreover, as Herman Ullrich suggests, the government may have been wary about allowing large groups of people to gather in the city at night. The police could better control the crowds during the day ('Konzertsälen', p. 121). The early hour, however, did not seem to deter music lovers from attending concerts. On Sundays and holidays, afternoon concerts were accessible to people from all classes; but even on weekdays the usual concert times fell during the normal dinner hour between 1 and 3 p.m., thus allowing even city officials and bureaucrats to attend if they wished (*Sketches of Germany*, II, 173).

There were a few exceptions to daytime concerts. Interspersed between acts of operas, plays, or ballets, *entr'acte* concerts were presented, consisting of one to three musical numbers. Carl Loewe cites the concerts of Milanollos which began after the theater's evening program at 11 p.m., and Eduard Holmes recalls attending a summer concert outdoors next to St Stephan's cathedral at midnight (Loewe, 332; Holmes, 122). But both men intimate that these performances were unusual events.

Throughout the century, concerts served many purposes. For musicians, concerts which raised money for themselves or needy colleagues were a financial necessity. Many of the large benefit concerts for musicians and other charitable organizations thus became permanent fixtures on Vienna's social calendar. Examples of these include the concerts of the Tonkünstler Societät (for retired musicians and their families) and of the Institute for the Blind. Every year on St Stephen's Day (26 December) the emperor sponsored a benefit concert for the Bürgerspital.

In an age without insurance, concerts were often the sole means of raising relief money for victims of sudden catastrophes and natural disasters. During the Napoleonic Wars, a group of eminent Austrian noblewomen called the Damen-Verein organized public concerts to raise money for a hospital.[2] In March of 1830, after a sudden flooding of the Danube River which killed seventy persons and left scores of citizens homeless, a flurry of charity concerts was arranged. Of these, the most spectacular featured a number of works of Rossini, played by the orchestra of the Friends of Music; but the main attraction was Rossini's overture to *Semiramide*, arranged by Carl Czerny for 16 pianists (8 piano duets) and performed by members of the Austrian aristocracy, including Countess Antonia Esterhazy, Princess Therese von Lobkowitz, Prince Windischgrätz, and Counts Gyorg and Amade. The overwhelming success of the concert was reflected in its huge profit of 2,800 fl. (CM) (Pohl, 19; Hanslick, 1, 184).

Special musical events accompanied occasions of national import-ance. Birthdays, namedays, coronations, and weddings of the royal family were always observed in Austrian theaters by singing the national anthem, 'Gott erhalte Franz den Kaiser', but additional poems, songs, or special music could also be performed to mark the day.[3] On 11 February 1822, the students of the Theresianum Akademie, the prestigious Viennese secondary school for sons of the nobility, presented a special concert for the emperor's birthday which featured a patriotic poem by one of the students and concluded with a chorus written by Deinhardstein and Franz Schubert.[4] Similarly, when the emperor recovered from a near-fatal illness in 1826, the Viennese sang patriotic songs in the streets and attended special masses. A cantata, entitled *Des Kaisers Genesung*, was written by Johann Mikan and set to music by Adalbert Gyrowetz, and was performed on 1 May 1826 to commemorate the event.[5]

Other concerts marked the anniversary of important personalities and events. For example, in 1825 Ignaz Seyfried organized a concert to observe the anniversary of Mozart's death; and three years later Josef

4 'Origin of the folk-festival in the Brigittenau in Vienna *c.* 1645' (note the musician and dancers) (Historisches Museum der Stadt Wien, Inv. Nr. 57.818)

Lincke gave a similar concert after Beethoven's death.[6] In addition, music ceremoniously accompanied the signing of treaties and the opening of new city bridges and buildings. For example, the Kettenbrücke (suspension bridge) prompted the composition of the Kettenbrücke waltzes by Johann Strauss Sr (Op. 4 and 19).

Certain concerts were seasonal or associated with holidays. On May Day, for instance, the Viennese celebrated the beginning of summer by donning their best clothes, promenading in the city's parks, and attending a traditional, early morning (9 a.m.) concert in the Augarten.[7] On the first Sunday after the full moon in July, the Viennese observed Brigittenkirchtag (see Illus. 4). Despite its original religious connotations, the day was celebrated by citizens of all ranks with picnics, dancing, and informal concerts.[8] During this festival in 1830, one particular restaurant advertised its special fantastic decorations with fountains, tableaux of the Colossus of Rhodes, temples and grottos. Along with dance music, an informal concert by the regimental trumpet corps of Count Auersperg was featured.[9]

Carnival season (from 7 January to Ash Wednesday) was a period devoted mainly to balls and theater, but also some concerts reflected the gaiety of the season. A family tradition of the Hochenadel household, for example, was to organize home concerts of humorous music on the last Sunday in Carnival. During one such concert, Leopold Sonnleithner recalled having heard Haydn's 'Toy Symphony', a 'sung-symphony', Generali's aria on a single note, and choruses from various comic operas (Sonnleithner, 740).

THE ORGANIZATION AND MANAGEMENT
OF CONCERTS

Arranging a public concert was both expensive and complicated. Without the aid of modern concert managers or professional orchestras, performing musicians were forced to find their own concert halls, assemble competent musicians, and attract an audience large enough to cover the concert expenses. Friends and personal acquaintances played an important role in the success of any concert. But failure and deficits were always a possibility.

Securing a concert hall in Vienna was no easy task. Few of the theaters could be used for concerts either because they were occupied by dramatic companies, or because they were too expensive to rent. Even during Normatagen, some theaters were reserved exclusively for annual benefit concerts.[10] Since Vienna had no official concert hall before 1830, musicians turned to churches, the Aula of the University, the chambers of the county government (Landeshaus), restaurants, dance halls or private homes to perform their music. It is not surprising that the showrooms of the city's piano manufacturers and music publishers gained prominence as recital halls since they offered young or foreign musicians an opportunity to perform in public at no cost.[11] The performers demonstrated the instruments or newly published pieces, while displaying their own talents and making all-important contacts with well-established musicians and patrons.

One of the first expenses for a concert-giver was the rental of the concert hall. The fee for Vienna's court theaters was considerable. In May 1824, for instance, Beethoven was to have paid 1,000 fl. for the use of the Kärntnerthor Theater and its orchestra (Thayer, 902). In 1828, Paganini was charged 60 fl. for the daytime use and 200 fl. for evening rent of the same theater.[12] As a result of these large fees, musicians and directors of dance troupes often shared an evening in a court theater in order to divide the rent (Ullrich, 118). Smaller halls cost less. The rooms in the Tuchlauben, owned by the Friends of Music, cost only 5 fl. per evening, and that fee could be waived if members of the Society were participants or sponsors of the event.[13]

Other major concert expenses included the cost of heating, lighting, fees for various inspectors, guards and carpenters as well as the musical scores, programs, tickets, and handbills. In London, Louis Spohr was forced to spend ten pounds sterling on refreshments also (*Journeys*, 216–17)! A more precise indication of concert expenses is available in the account books of the Friends of Music. Table 5 lists the expenses incurred by that Society during its four annual concerts during the period from 1821 to 1830. The consistently high price of candles suggests the advantage of daytime performances with the availability of natural sunlight. The notable absence of money paid for heat may also indicate that the concert halls were unheated – another practical advantage to concerts held during the day and in the spring.

Some concert-givers faced the additional obstacle of intrigues against them. Unknown native or foreign musicians generally had difficulties in Vienna because of what Hanslick describes as a prevailing suspicion that most musicians were immoral charlatans who would cheat their audiences through fraud or would flee the city before paying their bills (Hanslick, II, 855–6; Loesser, 177–9). National bias could interfere with the concert preparations and performance. Spohr's travel journals cite many incidences of local intrigues, but he suggests that the practice could be found in most major cities. In January 1821, he wrote of certain musical circles in Paris: 'It is always a risky business for a foreign violinist to appear in Paris, as the Parisians are possessed with the mad conceit that they have the best violinists in the world, and regard it as a sort of arrogance when a stranger considers himself qualified to compete with them' (*Journeys*, 240). As a result, it was customary for newly arrived performers first to create good will and

Table 5. *Society concert expenses 1821–30 in fl. (CM)*

	1821	1822	1823	1824	1825	1826	1827	1828	1829	1830
1. Book printing and binding	—	89·51	129·00	—	150·38	71·18	72·21	59·00	74·36	68·52
2. Advertising	17·24	25·00	21·48	22·00	23·00	24·00	23·00	24·00	23·00	24·00
3. Copying of parts	128·36	271·18	140·18	144·12	213·54	148·22	156·51	221·36	193·21	225·42
4. Sale of parts from the composer	120·00	160·00	10·48	—	—	—	—	11·30	16·30	4·00
5. Preparation of the orchestra	120·00	480·00	260·00	240·00	360·00	240·00	142·00	176·48	235·00	294·00
6. Transportation of instruments	50·36	41·36	36·48	37·12	28·00	24·00	26·48	29·12	28·54	33·48
7. Lighting	237·12	224·00	278·50	299·55	298·17	277·33	276·54	261·40	271·14	268·45
8. Heat	—	—	—	—	0·24	—	—	—	—	—
9. Watchman	14·05	13·46	15·22	13·55	17·45	20·09	17·36	19·04	20·32	20·32
10. Cashiers and ticket-takers	2·00	8·00	8·00	8·00	8·00	8·00	8·48	9·36	8·48	8·00
11. Fees and piano tuning	263·04	282·48	291·12	239·36	181·36	126·24	175·36	217·12	250·24	278·48
12. Preparation of hall	52·00	40·00	28·00	31·36	26·48	36·24	26·48	16·36	32·12	22·00
13. Miscel. (taxes, costumes, newspapers, etc.)	66·06	42·18	5·00	52·04	19·01	21·48	19·48	41·19	29·41	82·17
Total	1,071·05	1,678·37	1,270·06	1,088·30	1,327·23	997·58	940·30	1,087·33	1,184·12	1,330·44

Taken from GdMf, Geld Rechnungen für die Jahre 1821–1830

to establish their reputations by seeking out the city's amateur musical organizations and performing or composing for them for free or at nominal cost. Having once gained public attention and the esteem of his colleagues, the performer could then use the organization's facilities and the services of its orchestra for his own benefit concert (Loesser, *Pianos*, 174–5). In Vienna, where competition was stiff, expenses high, and music critics particularly harsh, half a year might pass before a musician could afford to risk giving a full concert (Loewe, 323; Klingemann, 192).

Thus, the concert-giver needed to be a shrewd businessman and careful judge of his orchestra and potential audience in order to make a profit from a concert. Again, it is the travel journal of Louis Spohr which records the usual process. In March 1816, Spohr wished to arrange a concert in Strassburg. He first ingratiated himself with the director of the city's musical society. He carefully noted the capabilities of the amateur orchestra as well as the various taxes and fees he would be expected to pay. Only after judging his popularity did Spohr risk giving a second concert at his own expense (*Journeys*, 131–2).

As expected, established artists had fewer problems arranging their concerts, but they too needed to strike bargains with theater owners and orchestra directors in order to make a profit. In 1823, Barbaja offered Ignaz Moscheles, a widely known pianist, the use of the Kärntnerthor Theater for an unlimited number of concerts as long as he agreed to share one-half of all his profits (Moscheles, 84). Spohr mentions similar arrangements in Venice in 1816, where the proprietor of the Santa Lucia theater offered him the use of the theater in return for two-thirds of the proceeds received from certain expensive box seats (157–8).

To further keep down the expense of a public concert, performers heavily relied on their family and friends to participate without pay in the program. For example, Spohr, a violinist, usually appeared with his wife, a harpist; and Paganini often shared his concert with his mistress, Antonia Bianchi, an operatic singer. Spohr indicates that some musicians donated their services out of respect for the soloist, recalling that the violinists in Florence, not usually known for their generosity, performed gratis for his concert there in 1816.

In Vienna, established artists often used the orchestras of the court theaters or the Friends of Music. But, in some cases, musicians were recruited directly. Announcements were posted around the city which asked musicians who were interested in participating in a particular concert to contact the concert-giver.[14] Concert organizers also probably visited local coffee houses and taverns where musicians regularly congregated. Matschaker Hof, an inn in the Seilergasse, was such a haunt, according to Holmes who described it in 1828 as the 'headquarters of the musicians of the city, at which they generally assemble to lounge over the gossip of their art...here Beethoven, before his last illness, was frequently to be found' (125–6).

If a concert was to present a new work or to employ a large orchestra, additional parts were often needed. A number of companies in Vienna satisfied such needs with loaned scores or copying services. Pezzl's guidebook names Friedrich Mainzer's sel. Witwe, located near the Kärntnerthor Theater, and Franz X. Ascher's Musik Leih- und Copier Anstalt which, in 1840, loaned music for 36 kr. a month and a 4 fl. (CM) deposit. Concert-givers could also rent musical instruments from such local dealers as Michael Leiternay's Leihanstalt in der Alservorstadt, or from Franz Rzehaczek, as Beethoven did for his concert in 1824 (Pezzl, *Beschreibung* (1836), 205; Schmidl, 237).

Legal obligations were imposed on all public concerts also. First, the law required that the municipal police be informed of the concert's location, date, and program. Next, music impost taxes were charged for each performance. Finally, censors inspected the proposed program, its handbills, and tickets. Although the process seems to have been more a formality than a real hindrance for a performer, from time to time there were problems. In 1780, for instance, the censors banned the performance of a 'Friedensymphonie' for a possible revolutionary connotation. And in 1812, just before the first performance of his oratorio in Vienna, Spohr learned that the censors forbade the names of 'Jesus' and 'Mary' from appearing in print, either in the cast of characters or in the printed libretto (*Journeys*, 84).

Even after a performer had secured a concert hall, gathered an orchestra, and satisfied the government, he had other worries. Eyewitness accounts suggest that the level of musical performance throughout Europe was generally low. Few cities, including Vienna, had professional orchestras, and amateurs could not always execute difficult scores. Hence a performer needed to be careful about selecting works within the capabilities of his orchestra. Regional performance practices also had to be considered. Spohr records that in Rome in 1816 orchestral players rendered his works unrecognizable by freely ornamenting their parts even when they played together in large ensembles.[15] Another factor responsible for poor performances may have been the lack of adequate rehearsal.

As in other large cities, in Vienna rehearsals generally consisted of one Generalprobe, which seems to have been more a simple run-through than a session to correct faulty passages or to polish musical nuance. Large works with chorus received more rehearsal, but instrumentalists still performed after only a few playings. Probably typical of many concerts is the rehearsal schedule attached to the announcement of Spohr's cantata, *Das befreyte Deutschland*, in 1819. The singers, all amateurs and members of the Friends of Music, rehearsed at noon twice a week for two weeks (4 rehearsals); the solo quartet and part of the orchestra met for only one sectional rehearsal; the ensemble combined for the first time in a Grossprobe on a Thursday, which was followed by the Generalprobe on Saturday in the concert hall (Grosser Redoutensal). The performance took place the next day. In all, the chorus had six rehearsals and the orchestra had only two.[16]

Except for a few passing remarks or reports about serious conflicts, little information survives about rehearsal procedure in the early part of the century. One can infer from descriptions, which call 'novel' the practices of keeping time with a baton and interrupting players to make corrections, that many musicians were unused to rigorous, disciplined ensemble playing or were unwilling to obey a conductor – an invention of the mid-century (Spohr, *Journeys*, 206). Further, familiar stories of orchestra members reading scores whose ink was still wet or scores which were unlocked and distributed only briefly for a performance in order to avoid music pirating, suggest that sight reading, and not rehearsing, was a necessary musical skill.

CONCERT SERIES AND MUSICAL TASTE

Just as the procedures for arranging a concert and preparing the musicians were ill defined, so too concert programs lacked 'standard repertory'. At the beginning of the century, one might have heard a potpourri of solos and ensembles, popular and 'art' music. But with the founding of musical societies, a conservatory, and musical journals, musical tastes began to divide into distinct camps.

One faction, generally those from musical societies, music schools, and journalists, championed the cause of serious art music by 'classical' composers of the recent past. They tended to condemn modern, virtuosic music and concerts which merely entertained. For, to them, a concert was to be an intellectually stimulating, elevating experience and music was to conform to what they believed to be artistic laws – a philosophy in keeping with their middle-class education and values. An outspoken advocate from this camp was Beethoven, whose statements Johann Strumpff recorded in his memoirs in 1824: 'And now he unbosomed himself on the subject of music which had been degraded and made a plaything of vulgar and impudent passions. "True music", he said, "found little recognition in this age of Rossini and his consorts"' (Thayer, 920). Again, five years later, Mary Novello, the wife of the English music publisher, recorded a conversation on the subject with Adalbert Gyrowetz, the then Kapellmeister of the Court Chapel. Like Beethoven, he rues the neglect of the good 'old' music:

On my expressing regret at hearing so little of the music of Mozart and Haydn, either operas, masses, quartets, quintets, he shook his head and said that the age of good music was gone by. He pointed to a large quantity of waltzes, airs with variations, dances, marches and trifling pieces that were lying spread out in the music shop upon the counter, and said (with a laugh of just contempt) that that was the kind of music that was now the fashion in Germany... (183).

In keeping with such ideals were the concerts offered by the Friends of Music and the Concerts Spirituels.

SOCIETY FOR THE FRIENDS OF MUSIC

In 1814 the charter of the Friends of Music declared its primary goal to be the 'elevation of all branches of music'. It intended to establish a conservatory, promote works of 'classical' music, set standards by which to judge modern music, and publish a musical journal – all essentially didactic activities. Numbering almost one thousand members (participating and supporting members) in 1825, the Friends of Music sponsored each season one large Musikfest (1812–16 only), four Society Concerts, and about sixteen smaller Abendunterhaltungen. The concerts were presented and attended by the group's members, a mixture of amateur and professional musicians (Hanslick, I, 148–9; Pohl, 4).

The Musikfeste, which flourished for five years, presented oratorios much like its predecessors, the Liebhaber Concerts at the beginning of the century. The huge musical forces of singers and instrumentalists required the use of the k.k. Winterreitschule in the imperial palace, which could accommodate about 1,500 persons (Klein, 293–4; Ullrich, 112). The lack of lighting fixtures and heat in this, the largest hall in the city, probably accounts for the scheduling of the large concerts during the day. The festivals specialized in the works of Handel (*Timotheus*, 1812, 1813; *Samson*, 1814; *Messiah*, 1815) and Abbé Stadler's *Die Befreyung von Jerusalem*, 1816.

The Society Concerts resembled private, commercial concerts in their size and diverse repertory; however, there were distinct differences. First, their soloists and orchestral conductors were rotated in order to give valuable, non-competitive experience to their amateur performers. The concert programs also featured serious music of the past generation by such composers as Mozart, Cherubini, Spontini, Méhul, and Beethoven. Table 6 lists twelve of the most frequently performed orchestral works during the period 1815 to 1830. Noticeably lacking are the sensational overtures of Rossini and contemporary virtuosi. The attention given to whole or almost entire symphonies was also a rarity. The same table points out that, during that same period, all nine of Beethoven's symphonies were presented. Of these, the First, Third and Seventh appear to have been most popular, while the Ninth Symphony was not yet performed in its entirety. Of note is the frequency of Mozart's symphonies also. But closer investigation indicates that, apart from the 'Haffner' Symphony, only the three late works (Nos. 39, 40, 41) were well known. Haydn's works in the same genre, however, were almost never performed by the Society during the same period (Hanslick, 126–60).

The Society also offered works for solo instruments (with orchestral accompaniment) usually performed by their composers, such as

Table 6. *Concerts of the Friends of Music*
Orchestral works 1815–30

			Total no. times
Twelve most frequently performed orchestral works			
Beethoven	Egmont Overture	1815, 1822, 1823, 1829	4
Mozart	Symphony in D	1815, 1824, 1826, 1830	4
Mozart	Symphony in C	1817, 1822, 1824, 1828	4
Cherubini	Faniska Overture	1815, 1823, 1826, 1829	4
Krommer	Symphony in C	1823, 1827, 1829	3
Mozart	Symphony in G	1816, 1826, 1830	3
Mozart	Symphony in E♭	1818, 1825, 1830	3
Beethoven	Coriolanus Overture	1818, 1830	2
Cherubini	Medea Overture	1822, 1829	2
Cherubini	*Tage der Gefahr*	1819, 1829	2
Spontini	*Ferdinand Cortez*	1817, 1827	2
Méhul	Ariodante Overture	1815, 1825	2

		Total no. times
Performance of Beethoven Symphonies		
Symphony No. 1	1815, 1819, 1822, 1827, 1829	5
Symphony No. 2	1815, 1823, 1826	3
Symphony No. 3	1820, 1825, 1829, 1830	4
Symphony No. 4	1821, 1825, 1829	3
Symphony No. 5	1820, 1822, 1828	3
Symphony No. 6	1827, 1830	2
Symphony No. 7	1817, 1821, 1826, 1829	4
Symphony No. 8	1820, 1824, 1828	3
Symphony No. 9	1827 (I, II only)	I

Taken from Richard Perger, *Geschichte der k.k. Gesellschaft der Musikfreunde in Wien* (Vienna: Adolf Holzhausen, k.k. Hof- und Universitäts-Buchdrucker, 1912), I, 285–91; Hanslick, I, 156–60; Concert Programs in NB, Musiksammlung, and WStB, Concert Program Collection.

Mayseder (violin), Romberg (cello), and Bogner (flute) (Hanslick, I, 154). But the concerts avoided works for the piano. At the beginning of the century, only three concerti (by Dussek, Kalkbrenner, and Thalberg), a few concert variations, and a single Adagio e rondo are listed in the concert programs. In each case, the Society seemed to discourage displays of pianistic virtuosity and improvisation – essential elements of commercial concerts.[17]

Vocal music played an important role in the concerts. Much of the

Table 6 (*cont.*)
Vocal Music 1815–30

	Solo	Ensemble	Total no. times
Italian vocal music			
Rossini	1817, 1823, 1824, 1826, 1827, 1829	1820, 1822	8
Mayr	1820, 1828	1817, 1818, 1821, 1827	6
Mozart	1817, 1822	1816(2), 1817	5
Paer	1824	1816(2), 1818, 1821	5
Pacini	1827, 1829, 1830	1823	4
Mercadante	1824	1825	2
Bellini	1828, 1829	—	2

German vocal music			
Haydn	'Der Sturm'	1830	
Beethoven	'Opferlied'	1824	
Schubert	Vocal Quartets	1821, 1822	
Mosel	'Danklied'	1829	
Weigl	from *Gli Orazi*	1819	
Spohr	from *Faust*	1821	
Gyrowetz	Aria	1821	

		Total no. times
Choral music (for massed choirs)		
Stadler	1817(2), 1818, 1819, 1820, 1821(5), 1829	11
Handel*	1812(2), 1813, 1814, 1815(2), 1816, 1817, 1820(2)	10
Haydn	1819, 1820, 1821, 1825, 1827, 1828	6
Mozart	1823, 1824(3), 1827, 1826	6
Salieri	1815, 1816(2), 1818(2)	5
Mosel	1817, 1820(2), 1821, 1822	5
Preindl	1817, 1818(3)	4

Taken from Perger, *Geschichte*, I, 285–91; Hanslick, 156–60; Concert Programs in NB, Musik-sammlung and Theatersammlung, GdMf, and WStB, Concert Program Collection.
* The Society's first successful concerts were performances of Handel's oratorios *Timotheus* (1812, 1813) and *Samson* (1814). Despite frequent performances of his works, only these two plus the *Messiah* were performed.

choral music, derived from oratorios, sacred cantatas, psalms or hymns, was sung in Latin or German and was composed by Viennese residents, many of whom were local Kapellmeisters or court musicians, such as Stadler, Preindl, Weigl, Salieri, Mosel, Mozart, and Haydn (see Table 6). Vocal solos consisted of cavatinas, arias, and scenes taken from Italian operas by Rossini, Paer, Mayr, Mercadante, and Mozart. The practice further fueled the debate between the proponents of Italian and German opera in the city. Typical of the rhetoric is an article appearing in the *Wiener Zeitschrift* in 1817 which asked about the choice of concert pieces, 'Why always from Italian arias?' (Hanslick, 1, 153).

At first the Society Concerts were presented in the small Redoutensaal in 1815 and 1816. But the growing number of members required the larger quarters of the great Redoutensaal in March 1816. There the concerts remained until 1847 and again from 1851 to 1869 (Klein, 291–2). The great hall accommodated about one thousand persons.

The Society's smaller Thursday evening concerts, called Abend-unterhaltungen, were founded in 1818. As Otto Biba's recent research has shown, the number of concerts varied from year to year, averaging about 13 to 16 a season during the period from 1820–30 (Biba, 'Abendunterhaltungen', 9–10). More like a musical salon than a public concert, the Abendunterhaltungen were held in intimate surroundings, first in the home of Johann Baptist Lang in the house, Zum roten Apfel, then (1819) in the art gallery Müllerschen Kunstsaal, (1820) in the Gundelhof, and finally (1822) in the rooms of the Roten Igel in the Tuchlauben or the chambers of the County Hall (Landeshaus). These subscription concerts for Society members cost 3 fl. a month for approximately three concerts (Biba, 'Abendunterhaltungen', 9; Pohl, 11–12).

Also resembling salon fare were the musical programs which contained at least one string quartet or quintet, a solo instrumental piece, and a vocal solo. Common to many programs were vocal ensembles, either a choral work or light quartet sung by students of the Conservatory (Hanslick, 1, 160–1). Indeed, prominent on many programs were the Lieder and vocal ensembles of Franz Schubert. Most of the music performed in public during his own lifetime was first presented at the Abendunterhaltungen.

As with the Society Concerts, the size of the chamber concerts' audiences cannot be determined precisely. Judging from reports about the various concert halls, however, if an Abendunterhaltung was well attended, the audience could have exceeded one hundred persons. More interesting is the as yet unexplained sudden decline in the concerts after 1836, from thirteen or more a year to no more than nine until 1841, when they ceased but for a final series in 1856.[18]

Public concerts

The Society for the Friends of Music also sponsored annual concerts which featured the students of the Conservatory. The first of these Prüfungs- or Examination Concerts took place in the County Hall in August 1823. Occasionally the concerts were moved to larger halls such as the Kärntnerthor Theater in 1825, 'so that the greater public could be convinced of the institute's progress' (Hanslick, I, 163).

Most of the Zögling or student concerts began with a Prologue which demonstrated the students' proficiency in Italian. Next followed an examination of the underclassmen in the 'elements of music and the art of singing'. The musical portion then began. Typical of most concerts was the program presented in August 1824. The orchestra opened with Beethoven's Prometheus Overture, followed by a number of vocal ensembles, single movements of concerti for violin, clarinet, and oboe, and a Polonaise for solo cello. The concert ended with a rousing performance of the 'Hallelujah Chorus' by Handel, performed by the entire student body (GdMf, Concert Program, 19 August 1824).

CONCERTS SPIRITUELS

Another amateur group to cultivate serious art music was established in 1819 by Franz Xavier Gebauer, choir director of the St Augustine church. The concerts produced by this group were called Concerts Spirituels, modeled after the French concerts of the same name. The series consisted of eighteen bi-monthly concerts held on Friday afternoons (4–6 p.m.). At first given in the church, the concerts soon moved to various small, secular locations (Mehlgrube and the County Hall after 1824). The cost for the entire series was minimal, only 8 fl. (CM) for eighteen performances (Hanslick, I, 186–7).

Under the leadership of Gebauer (until 1822) and thereafter Piringer and Geissler, the Concerts Spirituels specialized in the performance of sacred choral music and symphonies. Like the Society Concerts, these concerts presented whole symphonies, but, unlike the former, Gebauer's group carefully avoided any music with bravura. Solo concerti were excluded from all programs until the 1830s, and popular Italian vocal music was passed over in favor of works by German or Austrian composers, many of whom were members of the organization. Typical of most concert programs was the one from 19 May 1820 – the last concert of that season, held in the County Hall and performed by a combined choir and orchestra of one hundred musicians (GdMf, Concert Program, 19 May 1820, 4 o'clock):

Pastoral Symphony – Beethoven
Offertorium for double choir – Salieri
63rd Psalm – Stadler
'Hallelujah Chorus' – Handel (orchestration Mosel)
Overture to *Das befreyte Jerusalem* – Persius
Hymn – Mosel
'Meeresstille' – Goethe/Beethoven
Chorus and Finale from the cantata *Heiliger,*
    sieh gnädig by Mozart

According to a number of contemporaries, the quality of the performances was often low, because the orchestra of amateurs was expected to perform works at sight or with a single rehearsal just before the concert (Hanslick, 1, 186). Even with the addition of some professional musicians, usually in the brass section, the reviews continued to be negative. In 1821, for example, Beethoven referred to the concerts as 'hedge music': 'I am requesting Geh'bauer to let me have a few tickets (two), for some of my friends want to go to this hole-and-corner musical performance – Perhaps you yourselves have some of those lavatory tickets. If so, send me one or two – Your amicus, Beethoven.'[19]

COMMERCIAL CONCERTS

The opposing faction of concert-goers espoused the new virtuosic music, which came primarily from Italy. Drawn from the upper and lower classes, this group was impressed by the sensual appeal of music. Carried away by demonstrations of virtuosity or novelty, it tended to regard public concerts as an entertaining means of escape.

Benefits, Akademien, virtuoso concerts and some *entr'acte* performances constituted the public commercial concerts. The inherent profit motive of these productions is reflected in their diverse and popular offerings, which featured virtuosi, dramatic recitations, and demonstrations of new or exotic instruments. Because large audiences were actively sought and usually eager to attend, the commercial concerts were held in Vienna's largest halls`–` the great Redoutensaal, the Kärntnerthor Theater, and the Theater an der Wien. Each of these halls could hold more than one thousand people (Klein, 296–8; Ullrich, 114).

Like the serious art music concerts, commercial concerts also opened with orchestral music. Overtures by Cherubini, Beethoven (especially those to *Prometheus* and *Fidelio*), Mozart, Méhul, and Weber were popular. In fact, the overtures to Weber's operas *Euryanthe* and *Oberon* almost became fixtures at the concerts of the Kärntnerthor Theater in the year 1827.[20] But the repetition of the works may reflect more about the theater orchestra's capabilities than about contemporary musical tastes, because the orchestra, often a combination of amateurs and substitutes, may have been unwilling or unable to undertake new music night after night.

Surprisingly, in view of his unprecedented success in Viennese opera houses, Rossini's orchestral music appeared infrequently on concert programs. Indeed, surviving concert programs list only three overtures by Rossini performed in the years 1821, 1823, and 1827. But the city's public concerts generally did not include overtures from any of the more current Italian operas. Again, the absence may be explained by the theater's inability to pay for new scores, a lack of time to rehearse new works, or the prohibitive difficulty of the increasingly brilliant orchestral scores.

Symphonies generally were excluded also from commercial concerts. Instead, the orchestra's primary responsibility was to accompany the soloists. But, as if to compensate the audience for the lack of orchestral music, most commercial concerts featured solos for a wide variety of instruments, including guitar, mandolin, Waldhorn, harp, harmonium, and even czakan (a musical walking stick), in addition to more traditional string and woodwind instruments.

In a virtuoso's concert, the featured performer appeared only two or three times. After the overture, the soloist would usually perform a movement from a concerto. The second piece, separated from the first by a vocal ensemble or solo, was often in a lighter vein, such as a set of variations on a popular melody. Most of the brilliant or popular pieces were reserved for the end. Characteristic of the virtuoso concert was the program presented by 11-year-old Franz Liszt in the small

Redoutensaal on 13 April 1823. Beginning at 12.30 in the afternoon, the concert lasted about one-and-a-half hours and cost a modest 1 fl. 12 kr. (CM). After a movement from a symphony by Mozart, Liszt played Johann Hummel's Grand Concerto in B minor. Although most virtuosi played their own compositions at that time, Liszt, still a young student, probably flattered his Viennese hosts by performing their works. Four singers from the Theater an der Wien then presented a quartet by Konrad Kreutzer, after which Liszt concluded with a 'free fantasy' based on a theme submitted by someone in the audience – a gesture obviously intended to please the crowd (WStB, Concert Program, 13 April 1823).

In Vienna since the time of Mozart, piano works were an important staple of commercial concerts. Prominent in the concert repertory between the years 1815 and 1830 were popular 'potpourris', variations, and polonaises. The darlings of Viennese audiences were the pianists Johann Hummel, Ignaz Moscheles, and Carl Czerny (Novello, 183). Most of the virtuosic showpieces no longer survive, but a few of the travelers commented on the men's improvisational talents. Louis Spohr, for example, described Hummel's technique in 1814 at a private musicale in Vienna. Hummel had been asked to provide dance music for some young people, but, as he noticed a group of music connoisseurs gathering around the piano, he began to elaborate the basic dance rhythm and tune:

No sooner had Hummel noticed this new audience than he began to improvise freely, holding, however, to the steady waltz rhythm in order not to disturb the dancers. He took the most striking themes and figures from my own compositions and those of others that had been played in the course of the evening's program and wove them into his waltzes, varying them more fancifully with each repetition. Finally he worked them into a fugue, giving full reign to his contrapuntal wizardry, without even disturbing the pleasure of the dancers. Then he returned to the gallant style and ended with a bravura which was extraordinary even for him, still exploiting the themes he had originally selected, so that the whole extravaganza had the character of a fully rounded composition. (*Journeys*, 109–10)

Besides displaying unusual technical ability or compositional ingenuity, many performers resorted to well-publicized tricks and showmanship to impress their audiences. During his Akademie in 1826, Jacques-Fereol Mazas, a Parisian violinist, ended his program with a

Fantasy and Variations played entirely on the violin's G string – a feat that Paganini popularized two years later (NB, Musiksammlung: Concert Program, 13 September 1826). In March of 1824, Carl von Gaertner, a guitarist, ended with a Grosse Fantasie played 'partly without the use of his right hand and in a new manner of harmonic tones' (GdMf, Concert Programs, 19 March 1824).

The public's fascination with virtuosity led also to affection for child performers. During the previous century, Mozart and his sister were only two of countless prodigies who toured throughout Europe; and until 1824 Vienna supported a highly successful ballet company that featured very young dancers. Hence, concert organizers were eager to place children on their programs and to cite (sometimes falsified) the ages of young performers to engage an audience's sympathy. In Vienna during the year 1822 alone, Franz Liszt made his debut at 9 years of age; the brothers Carl and Anton Ebner (aged 9 and 10) from Pest gave violin concerts; and Fanny Salomon (aged 12 and a student of Carl Czerny) gave a private piano recital. Several children from the same family often appeared together, as did three members of the Holzmann family (aged 7, 8, and 13). In November 1830, in the Viennese suburb of Rennweg, the children performed a Kinderoperette (WStB, Concert Program, 9 November 1830).

Equally intriguing to Viennese audiences were musical novelties. Czerny's arrangement of Rossini's overture for sixteen performers has already been mentioned, and similar 'monster' works were relatively common. In 1802, the family of Basilius Bohdanowicz gave a concert entitled 'Nine Questions'.[21] Combining the allurements of their young age and number (eight children) as well as musical novelties, three of the girls sang the same aria – each time in a different language. The second half of the concert, called 'Rareté extraordinaire de la Musique', contained an Andantino with four variations for one piano and four performers. The concert announcement describes the piece as 'for 8 hands or 40 fingers, which will be performed by the dear sisters of the Bohdanowicz family for the second time' (WStB, Concert Program, 8 April 1802). The announcement clearly demonstrates the showmanship, exaggerated language, and direct appeal to the audience characteristic of so many commercial concerts.

Some concerts were used to demonstrate technically improved or altogether new instruments. While the invention of the pedal harp and valve horn and the improved construction of pianos were accepted eventually, many of the new instruments soon became obsolete. Of these was the 'Organon-Pan-Harmonica' devised by Joseph Friderici, an organ builder from Hildesheim. In a concert in November 1828, the instrument, which could imitate over 450 instruments including flutes, oboes, clarinets, and bassoons, performed a full program of opera overtures, arias, and dance music. Similar were the 'accoustical experiments' demonstrated five years before by E. F. Chladni on his Euphon in the Jahnische Saal for an admission price of 2 fl.[22]

Thus, while the Society Concerts and other didactic musical series sought to improve the musical tastes of their audiences by preserving and performing the music of the past, the commercial concerts' appeal lay in entertainment and novelty. Where the Society's Concert programs were orderly and somewhat unvarying, the virtuoso concerts brought together serious and frivolous pieces performed by traditional and new instruments. Whereas the musical institutions tended to revere music as a serious and sacred art, commercial concerts treated music as a kind of consumer commodity, calculated to make the greatest momentary appeal.

BEETHOVEN AND PAGANINI — COMPARISON OF CONCERTS

Two musical events during the first decades of the nineteenth century stand out as extraordinary and historically significant: Beethoven's last Akademie in 1824 and Paganini's Viennese concert tour in 1828, both of which marked a high point for their respective musical publics.

Throughout his 35-year residence in Vienna, Beethoven had arranged only nine public benefit concerts for himself, five having taken place in 1814.[23] After his last concert in 1814, ten years passed before he arranged another Akademie, persuaded by a letter from a number of influential nobles and high-ranking bureaucrats. Dated February 1824, the letter expressed dissatisfaction with the current musical tastes in Vienna and appealed to Beethoven's patriotism as a German to uphold serious music:

Need we assure you that at a time when all glances were hopefully turned towards you, all perceived with sorrow that the man whom all of us are compelled to acknowledge as foremost among living men in his domain looked on in silence as foreign art took possession of German soil, the seat of honor of the German muse, while German works gave pleasure only by echoing the favorite tunes of foreigners and, where the most excellent had lived and labored, a second childhood of taste threatens to follow the Golden Age of Art?... from you the native Art Society and the German Opera expect new blossoms, rejuvenated life and a new sovereignty of the true and beautiful over the domain to which the prevalent spirit of fashion wishes to subject even the eternal laws of art. (Thayer, 902)

Beethoven's supporters urged him to prepare a concert and to act quickly, for it was soon Lent, the height of the concert season.[24] Through Schindler and Count Palffy, Beethoven negotiated for a concert hall. As in his dealings with music publishers, Beethoven bargained with the theater directors, threatening to move to other halls if his terms were not met. The original choice for the concert was 8 April in the great Redoutensaal; but the authorities refused to give their permission.

Count Palffy, director of the Theater an der Wien, then offered Beethoven the use of his theater for two concerts, unlimited rehearsals, plus lighting and fees, for a total cost of 1,200 fl. Learning that the composer was making inquiries with Louis Duport, the director of the Kärntnerthor Theater, Palffy lowered his price to 1,000 fl., asking only for expenses and that he be allowed to repeat the concert a third time. In addition, he offered free use of the theater's orchestra, with a fixed admission price of 2 fl. for the parterre and gallery, and 3 fl. for all other seats. He assured Beethoven that gross receipts would reach 4,000 fl., with profits ranging between 2,000 and 3,000 fl. from the first two performances (Thayer, 902–3).

Beethoven's friends assumed the duties of assembling and rehearsing the orchestra and chorus. Piringer, director of the Concerts Spirituels, selected some of Vienna's best amateur instrumentalists; Sonnleithner rehearsed the singers; and Blahetka arranged for concert announcements and handbills (Thayer, 900). One of these announcements was posted to request the services of additional instrumentalists:

The undersigned hereby most politely invites all gentlemen amateurs to assist him at his concert which is to take place at the Theater an der Wien on 22 April. Those who will be so good as to take part therein are kindly requested to affix their signature below. Ludwig van Beethoven[25]

The concert program reveals Beethoven's uncompromising demands upon both orchestra and audience, for he was emphatic that no pianist and no vocal or instrumental soloist should appear in the performance (Thayer, 905). Instead, he submitted to the municipal authorities and censors a program consisting of the overture 'Weihe des Hauses' (Op. 124), three movements from the Missa Solemnis (Kyrie, Credo and Agnus Dei – Op. 123), and the Ninth Symphony (Op. 125).

Beethoven's concert encountered its first serious problem with the censors, who would not allow portions of the Mass to be performed in a secular public concert. Despite a letter to the censor, Sartorius, in which he offered to call the selections 'Hymnen', and his threat to abandon the whole concert if the works were not included, the censors refused to allow the program. Only after Count Lichnowsky personally intervened with a special appeal to Sedlnitsky, the president of the police, was the program approved (Beethoven (Anderson), III, 1120; Thayer, 905).

By late April, the works were in rehearsal under Dirka and Schuppanzigh when the second serious problem arose. Beethoven had chosen his friend, Ignaz Schuppanzigh as concert master to direct the orchestra's string section. This action, however, supplanted the theater's regular concert master, Franz Clement. Even though he was requested to apologize for the seeming affront to Clement, Beethoven evidently delayed. The theater orchestra sided with their regular director and refused to play. This mutiny, along with pressure exerted by close friends to force him to make immediate decisions on various aspects of the concert, led Beethoven to rebel by canceling the concert at the Theater an der Wien and threatening to move the performance to the small County Hall (Thayer, 905).

Some time later, an agreement was reached with Duport. Beethoven was allowed to use the Kärntnerthor Theater, the theater's orchestra, chorus and lighting for two concerts at a fee of 400 fl., but he was limited to three rehearsals in the hall and he was barred from raising the ordinary admission price (Thayer, 906). The latter point was a major obstacle for, although the rent was lower than the agreement with Palffy, the prices were too low to make a profit. After six weeks of discussion and appeals even to the police, Beethoven again was denied the right to raise the ticket prices.

The concert was finally presented on Friday, 7 May 1824, at 7 p.m. Unfortunately, the delays meant that the regular concert season had ended and Vienna's high society, including the court, had begun to leave for their summer estates or foreign travel. Hence, the emperor and his wife were absent from the premiere, as was Archduke Rudolph, Beethoven's student and friend. The concert, however, was attended and applauded by Beethoven's close friends and many admirers. Observers present at the concert reported that, during the second movement of the symphony, the audience burst into wild applause and cries of 'Vivat' – legally inadmissible in the court theater. At the fifth interruption, the police commissioner demanded silence (Thayer, 909).

Overall, the concert was more a tribute to Beethoven personally than to his latest music, since the works had little success subsequent to the concert. The performance was probably not an artistic success either, for reports of the rehearsals stated that the chorus' female voices, comprised mostly of young girls, were too weak and immature; the soloists had difficulties with their parts; and the score contained numerous errors. Certainly the concert reaped few financial rewards. Gross receipts reached only 2,200 fl. WW (880 fl. CM) while the copying costs and other expenses were high. After all his efforts and setbacks with theater directors, censors, soloists, and copyists, Beethoven earned only 420 fl. WW (178 fl. CM) from the concert.[26] No wonder he felt cheated after Palffy had predicted such great profits!

Beethoven must have been discouraged by the small returns, for he passively allowed Duport to make radical changes in the program for the next performance. To broaden the appeal, Duport added Beethoven's trio 'Tremate, empi, tremate' (which he fraudulently called a 'new' work); he cut all but the Kyrie from the Mass; he inserted the aria 'Tanti palpiti' from Rossini's opera *Tancredi*, but he left the overture and symphony. The second performance began at 12.30 on Sunday 23 May 1824, but, this time, the theater was only half full. According to Thayer, the good weather had diverted the public's attention, but the very late date of the concert and the previous attendance of Beethoven's friends at the first performance may have contributed to the dismal turn-out.[27] Luckily, by previous arrangement, Beethoven received a guaranteed sum of 500 fl. (CM) and 50% of all profits from the second concert. Duport suffered a loss of 800 fl. (Thayer, 912).

The experience further reinforced Beethoven's low opinion of Viennese musical establishments. He had, in fact, expressed such sentiments ten years before when he heartily agreed with Johann Tomaschek who said that, 'there is nothing more aggravating and vexatious than preparing for a concert'. Beethoven replied: 'You are certainly right. So many blunders are made that one cannot get on with things. And the money one has to spend!...the devil take it' (Sonneck, 103–4).

In striking contrast, Paganini's concerts of 1828 were the most popular and financially lucrative of all commercial concerts in Vienna up to that time. While not the first foreign virtuoso to so conquer the Viennese public, Paganini was one of the first musicians to appeal to both music connoisseurs and music lovers.[28]

The Paganini concerts began inauspiciously to a half-empty great Redoutensaal on Saturday, 29 March 1828. After all, Paganini was unknown in the city, the hall was large, and the admission cost was unusually high (between 2 and 4 fl. CM). But, as Hanslick points out, the first concert created such a stir that the audiences, refusing to go home, stood afterward in the streets discussing the concert. Thereafter, Paganini played to full houses (I, 243).

A wild Paganini-craze quickly swept over the city. Food, articles of clothing, and theater parodies were suddenly named after Paganini and his tremendous violin technique. Even the city's five-florin notes (in WW), the admission cost of his concerts, were temporarily called 'Paganinerls'.

An unpublished diary of Mathias Perth, a generally prosaic court bureaucrat, reveals how deeply Paganini's concerts touched even uninterested Viennese. In an entry dated Saturday, 29 March 1828, Perth records his amazement about the rumors of Paganini's profits (possibly 7,000–8,000 fl.), but he says nothing about the violinist's artistic achievements. Two weeks later Perth reports that the concert audiences reacted with 'stormy applause' and that scores of people had fainted and had to be carried out. By the ninth concert, Perth decided to see for himself if the rumors were true. He describes his experience on 6 June 1828:

It cost me a lot of money, I was dripping with sweat, but I heard him, and in order to get an idea of his playing, one must hear him. The effect of the tones he coaxes from the violin on each listener is indescribable. We have great, accomplished violinists in Vienna: Mayseder, Böhm, Clement, Hellmesberger, Lubin, Jansa, Fradl, etc.; but Paganini is not only the greatest, the first, [he] not only surpasses everyone, but offers proof of how backward all are, in comparison with his astonishing art. If now he affects us intensely, moves us to melancholy and almost draws tears from us with his soft melting tones, he also knows how to put us immediately into the happiest of moods; we can hardly believe the strength which is at his command, like a tyrant, [playing] his instrument in such a way that one imagines he will destroy it again under his hands.

Perth concludes his enthusiastic account:

I can make no comparison between him and other violinists, and yet I would like so much to do so – but with whom shall I compare him? I would like to say: Paganini is among violinists what Napoleon, at his height, was among the generals of Europe.[29]

Police reports corroborate Perth's observations. Responsible for the control and protection of the audiences, the police investigated the rumors that many had fainted in the theater. After consulting with the policeman on duty in the theater and with the theater's house doctor, Aloys Persa, the Hofrat of police, decided that the incident was of minor significance. However, he chided the police for under-estimating the size of the concert crowd and for allowing the theater possibly to oversell the tickets (VA, P.H., 3557/1828, Hofstelle Censur).

The reports of the doctor and other eyewitnesses describe briefly the conditions during the performances. The Burgtheater's ventilation was notoriously poor and the crowds produced suffocating heat. Many people stood in line for hours to get good seats. As a result, many fainted, and doctors had difficulty in aiding them because people blocked all the aisles (VA, P.H., 3557/1828, Beilage, I, II).

Paganini's concert tickets were expensive at the Burgtheater, ranging from 10 fl. (CM) for a loge to 30 kr. for an unreserved place on the fourth floor. When the concerts moved to the larger Kärntnerthor Theater, the prices rose again, from 12 fl. (CM) for a first-floor loge to 30 kr. for a fifth-floor, unreserved place.[30]

The high ticket prices together with large attendances reaped big profits. Court account books show that for a single concert on 13 May 1828, the theater collected 1,998.20 fl. (CM). After deducting the expenses of the hall, musicians, and other incidental costs, Paganini made a profit of 990.21 fl. (HHStA, General Intendanz, Hofoper, Carton 71, Oper 1828, no. 114). By the time he finished his last concert in Vienna, Paganini's earnings reportedly totaled over 30,000 fl. (Deutsch, *Biography*, 757 n.)!

From a musical standpoint, Paganini's concerts were unconventional also. At first they did not include overtures, they presented only two artists (Paganini and Antonia Bianchi), and they contained unaccompanied violin works. By June of 1828, when his popularity was well established, Paganini incorporated into his programs serious orchestral music, such as Beethoven's symphonies, in addition to 'crowd-pleasing' pieces played on a G string, a Cantabile for double-stops, and variations on the Austrian national anthem.[31]

That Paganini's concerts succeeded where Beethoven's had failed is the result of more than Beethoven's problems with concert arrangements. And the patrons of serious art music were no less discriminating in 1828 than they were in 1824. Rather, the make-up of the various concert publics was changing. The small, influential cadre of music lovers that had championed Beethoven and who continued to see that his works appeared on Society Concerts were increasingly outnumbered by the ranks of the newly affluent, whose desire for musical entertainment was recognized and exploited by concert organizers. By 1824 many of the nobles who supported Beethoven had lost their wealth or had died. Many of the theaters, now financially unsound, were managed by businessmen instead of aristocrats, who realized that the democratization of concert programs was the only way to turn a profit.

Beethoven's refusal to make substantial compromises in his music or his programming was not inconsistent with his past behavior. But in 1824 his actions no longer achieved for him the notoriety or monetary rewards of the past. The optimism and humanistic sentiments expressed by the Ninth Symphony did not accord with the pessimistic resignation of the times. Instead, the majority of Viennese demanded musical diversion and entertainment provided by a Paganini or Johann Strauss, men who not only knew how to play the violin or to write a good waltz, but also knew how to attract and take advantage of an audience.

5

MUSIC IN THE SALON

During the nineteenth century, the Viennese home, and particularly its parlor, was the focus of family, social and intellectual life. Modeled on those of French aristocratic circles of the previous century, domestic Viennese salons helped to determine the city's overall cultural tone. For music, the salons are of special importance because they reflect the general shift of musical patronage by the aristocracy to a monied middle class. Unfortunately, however, since salon gatherings were commonplace events among close friends and relatives, their very nature precluded formal record keeping. Thus, the best surviving information comes from travel notes of visitors, who managed to record something of their social engagements. But because many of the travelers were of the middle class, they rarely came into contact with aristocratic salons, and, because many were foreigners, they may have been excluded from many of Vienna's close-knit social circles.

Salon activities, like much of Vienna's social life, flourished in the fall and winter months, but were especially profuse during Carnival season. Guests usually gathered for late afternoon tea (4–6 p.m.) or in the early evening (6–9 p.m.) and stayed until 10 or 12 midnight (*Seufzer*, 106; Normann, 105). Depending upon the ages and interests of the group, the salon host offered a variety of entertainments. Among the most common of these were polite conversation, card games or readings of poetry and prose; music ranked next in popularity. Salon recitals or Hauskonzerte often required the participation of all the guests, regardless of age or expertise. Such music-making not only supported Vienna's piano-manufacturing and music-publishing industries, but also indirectly left behind some hints about the character and quality of musical performance among the various social classes.

ARISTOCRATIC SALONS

The costly Napoleonic Wars contributed to the economic ruin of many Austrian aristocrats. And, as the government increasingly turned to middle-class financiers and industrialists for credit and goods, aristocrats began to lose political influence and probably something of their former grandeur. Such social changes directly affected musical patronage, for many nobles no longer could afford to maintain private orchestras or to commission new works. For example, the famed Esterhazy orchestra disbanded in 1809, Prince Lobkowitz went bankrupt in 1811, and in 1816 Rasumofsky's palace and priceless music collection were destroyed by fire (Thayer, 154–5; Marek, 436, 481).

Contemporaries were keenly aware of the change. The memoirs of Leopold Sonnleithner speak of the effect on the arts:

But since the last decades of the eighteenth century this situation has gradually changed in essence, yes almost reversed itself. The rulers (with honorable exceptions) regard the patronage of the arts almost solely as an unavoidable burden; these 'great' gentlemen who are next in line have, for the most part, given up their splendid buildings, their galleries, their orchestras, and have turned to other muses. In the nineteenth century, the high-ranking patrons of art have, for the most part, disappeared and the muses have taken refuge under the protection of the unpretentious middle class.[1]

As if to compensate for their losses in political and artistic leadership, Austrian nobles generally excluded members of the middle class from their homes. A journalist for the *Oesterreichische Rundschau* wrote in 1817, 'No minister anymore has an open house. Thirty years ago Vienna was a most beloved capital, because everyday a house stood open to anyone, [there] were dinners and assemblies, but in the years 1816 and 1817, as a rule, all houses are closed...[2]

Of course, aristocrats still gathered with their friends in their opulent salons and, according to a few eyewitnesses, continued to entertain on a grand scale. For them a soirée might include over a hundred guests, with performances by professional musicians of recitals or dramas.

The memoirs of Countess Louise (Lulu) Thürheim, sister-in-law of Count Rasumofsky, briefly recount the salon in the home of Prince Esterhazy both in Vienna and Eisenstadt during the first decades of the nineteenth century:

Nehmt weg die Fürstenkron', den Adel altersgrau,
So bleibt sie doch noch immer: die riegelsamste Frau.

5 The carriage and trappings of a noblewoman in Vienna
(Schliemann, *Schattenbilder*, 113–14)

Several times during that winter one played at the home of Princess Lubomirska
and Countess Esterhazy, née Marquise Roisin. The house of the latter was among
the most agreeable in Vienna. No one possessed as much talent as she and her husband
for inventing and arranging small festivals, there were live marionettes, burlesque,
masquerades, live charades, Chinese shadow pictures, chess – and whist parties where
on the playing cards members of the party were represented.[3]

The *Rundschau* observer reported on other celebrated aristocratic
salons in Vienna. During the winter months of 1817, Count Czernin
entertained up to sixty dinner guests each evening. In April the same
year, Count Bellegarde held a Sunday soirée at which the crowned
princes and princesses presented tableaux and proverbs before a grand
ball. At the home of Zichy-Ferrara, the Countess Bombelles of
Dresden presented charades and displayed her musical and acting talents
(Glossy, *Studien*, 64, 67).

After the Vienna Congress, the home of Clemens Metternich,
Austria's secretary of foreign affairs, was the gathering place for
internationally distinguished dignitaries and artists. Each Sunday
soirées were held that presented music and the opportunity for
conversation. According to Blumenbach, the guests met in small

groups of twos and threes to talk on diverse subjects. Metternich generally only spoke with ambassadors and high-ranking officials, while his wife entertained the women and other guests (I, 143).

The diplomat Franz Andlaw called the Metternich home the 'showplace of festivities of every kind' and remarked about the importance given to music. On Metternich's birthday in 1828, for instance, Antoinette (née Leykam), Metternich's wife, arranged a special concert which featured the renowned piano virtuoso Sigmund Thalberg and the violinist Niccolo Paganini – his only private appearance during his wildly successful tour in Vienna (1828). On another occasion, German and Italian singers competed with Viennese celebrities, and sometimes the Metternichs presented fully costumed opera scenes.

The diary of Anton Prokesch, another diplomat, indicates that some of Metternich's soirées were gala affairs of state. At one gathering in March 1830, among the over eighty guests were the ranking officials from Sweden, Saxony, Baden, and Constantinople; at another soirée in 1832 over one hundred persons, including members of the imperial family, were present (176).

Another vestige of the brilliant aristocratic salon in Vienna after 1820 was the home of Moritz Dietrichstein, secretary to the Court Theater. There, according to the memoirs of Hugo von Weckbecker, a distinguished array of playwrights, actors and scholars met regularly. Among the musicians present was his relative, Sigmund Thalberg (the natural son of Franz Josef Dietrichstein) (134).

Other families specialized in private theatrical performances. Around 1804 a Bavarian traveler attended a performance at the Fries home. The Countess Fries had built a small stage in her salon where she, her daughter, and the Countess Schönburg presented full-length Singspiele lasting up to three hours (83–5). Whether or not these productions continued after the wars is not known, but archive records from the Schwarzenberg family indicate that they continued the practice in the 1830s (Stekl, 142–3).

Throughout the 1830s the salon of Prince Josef II von Schwarzenberg, under the direction of his sister Eleonore, set the standard for Vienna's highest society. Here musicians, actors, and artists provided most of the entertainment and only those listed on the *Rangliste* (society's 'crème') were admitted (Stekl, 137). On 3 April 1830,

Prokesch witnessed a concert which featured Sigmund Thalberg, Therese Grünbaum singing Beethoven's *Adelaide*, and a dramatic recitation by Heinrich Anschütz (24).

Additional allusions to domestic music-making suggest that other aristocrats maintained less lavish, but equally active, musical salons. Sonnleithner states, for example, that Graf von Apponyi favored music for the violin and chorus in his home, while the Baroness Buffendorf preferred the performance of choral fugues and choruses from sacred music (Sonnleithner, 737–8).

Some of Vienna's nobility arranged concerts and dramas in their hunting lodges outside the city. When Prince Johann (I) Liechtenstein went hunting in the fall each year, his household and up to eighty guests moved to his castle in Felburg. There, in the evenings, he arranged concerts and dramas for the theater he had installed (Stekl, 137). In such a setting, the concerts may have featured music that described the hunt — a popular subject of chamber music.

But by 1820, many observers claim that the salons of the aristocrats were neither intellectually stimulating nor centers for art. Instead, Andlaw called them dull and superficial.

If I were to characterize briefly the tone of society at that time, I would want to call it just harmless: the conversation moved, without political cabals, in a fairly uniform circle and great importance was placed on essentially insignificant things, about which one himself often later smiled. It was a struggle for [who should be accorded] superiority in elegance; one argued in all seriousness over the question of who belonged to the 'crème' of society, and it was not always beauty, wealth, wisdom, rank or birth which decided whether citizenship could be acquired in that fashionable realm, for its governess, mode, fickle as she is, only too often allowed chance to rule.[4]

Corroborating this view, Blumenbach criticized the salons for their ambivalence toward political events:

The elements of animated discussion, of interesting conversation, seem wanting in Austria. Politics, public affairs, the sitting of parliament, news from abroad, literature, the periodicals, the courts of law, afford inexhaustible materials either for instructive or agreeable conversation in England and France. In Austria, politics and the affairs of the state never form the elements of conversation unless it be in a corner, or in the *embrasure* of windows, between two persons. Literature is as seldom introduced. Some remarks on the play or opera, the fashions, a drive on the Prater, a ball *masque* at the Ridotto, or at Eisenstadt, a reception at court, the cholera, an excursion to

Baden, Carlsbad, Teplitz or Marienbad, the chase, a favourite topic, and lately the steamboats on the Danube, or perhaps a little *terror* imported in the shape of *émeute* from Paris, or how very shocking the radicals are going on in England, comprise the most that escapes in the hearing of all, either at a dinner party or a soirée (I, 145–6).

Musical performances, either by isolated virtuosi or talented noble-women, also seem to have had less of an impact on the city's composers, for fewer works were now commissioned by aristocrats, and composers no longer depended solely upon them for advancing their careers.

SALONS OF JEWISH BANKERS

Generally excluded from the social circles of Austrian aristocrats, Vienna's Jewish financier families fostered their own salons, which in their own right became centers of learning and art (Mayer, Kaindl, Pirchegger, III, 100). Through familial and business ties, these families established contact with creative artists and scholars throughout Europe, but especially in Paris and Berlin. Writing in 1844, Tuvora testifies to the vitality of the activity: 'The salons of the financier families, especially a few of these...acquired a certain renown. Foreigners stream in and out...one can certainly find there distinguished, monied, well-placed and educated men...[5]

Outstanding was the salon of Nathan Adam Freiherr von Arnstein and his wife Fanny.[6] Fanny Arnstein's unusually broad education in foreign languages and science well equipped her for her duties in the salon. In fact, she and her sisters – Sara Lewy, Rebecca Ephram, and Cecilia Eskeles (members of the wealthy Itzig family in Berlin) – all directed lively musical and literary salons. Together with Cecilia, who also lived in Vienna, Fanny Arnstein virtually dominated Vienna's salon life between the years 1780 and 1818. Even the chronicler of the Vienna Congress, Cadet de Gassicourt, called the Arnsteins one of Austria's 'first families' (204).

In contrast to aristocratic salons, the Arnstein salon avoided undue formality and etiquette. A young Bavarian traveler in 1804 was impressed by the remarkable difference:

From midday, about 12 o'clock, until late after midnight, one meets the most sought-after society here, to which one has daily entrance without a special invitation. In order to make available the 'honors' of her house without interruption, she

[Fanny] never or seldom goes out, truly no small sacrifice, the gravity of which the foreigner can not gratefully enough acknowledge. One comes without great ceremony and goes without taking leave; every burdensome etiquette of the 'higher circles' is banned; the spirit, released from the restraints of propriety, breathes freer here.[7]

Eleven years later, the celebrated salon hostess of Berlin, Rahel Varnhagen also complimented the Arnstein salon on its relaxed and easy atmosphere.[8]

Every Tuesday evening, the Arnsteins presented musical soirées. Herself an amateur pianist and singer, Fanny probably had performed for her guests, but an index of amateur and professional musicians living in Vienna during the year 1797 indicates that by that date she no longer played. Despite the obvious flattering and poetic tone of the entry, the index gives an idea about the spirit in which amateur musicians probably performed:

Frau von Arnstein: the most learned and difficult compositions are her favorite. She reads very well, has a light hand and a masterful touch. In speed she excels. It is regrettable that she seems to have lost the taste for it a few years ago, for she very rarely touches the piano any more. People of her ability should not abandon the impoverished art which, in any case, more and more lacks active encouragement. She has a very pleasant voice and agile throat. Also her daughter promises likewise [to have] perhaps talents in music.[9]

Fanny usually invited young women amateurs as well as professional virtuosi to perform in her home. In 1809, J. F. Reichardt counted between three and four hundred guests at one salon concert. He noted that

Frau von Pereira [Fanny's daughter] together with Frl. von Kurzbeck played a very brilliant double sonata by Steibelt truly masterfully, and then, with unbelievable patience and kindness, many beautiful waltzes, to which the beautiful young world happily circled, in the ever growing throng... As soon as the outer room was opened for supper, I left: it was toward midnight.[10]

At another soirée in 1815, Carl Bertuch, a well-known publisher, recalled having heard the piano virtuoso, Ignaz Moscheles, play the overture to *Fidelio*, in addition to vocal duets and other chamber music (Spiel, 426). Another time he heard the opera composer, Giacomo Meyerbeer, play piano variations and choruses from the oratorio *Timotheus* or *Die Gewalt der Musik* (Spiel, 427).

The Arnsteins supported Viennese musicians in other ways. For example, they took in Mozart for eight months before his marriage and arranged for his subscription concerts in their home (Spiel, 103). The Arnstein banking firm also advanced loans to Beethoven and handled the financial affairs of the Friends of Music.[11]

The Arnstein salon reached its zenith of prestige during the Congress of Vienna when diplomats and artists from all parts of Europe attended. At one point in the city's celebrations, Nathan Arnstein rented and outfitted the entire Mehlgrube dance hall for a grand soirée, which began with a concert of Vienna's finest musicians, and ended with a great dinner and ball. Count August de la Garde wrote of the occasion, 'Excellent music, such as one could hear only in Vienna then, enchanted the air. The most distinguished society of Vienna crowded into the salon, all influential personages of the Congress, all foreigners of rank, all heads of lordly houses were present. Actually only the sovereigns were missing.'[12]

After Fanny's death in 1818, Henriette Arnstein-Pereira assumed her mother's social duties. Following her marriage to Ludwig Pereira, an adopted son of her father and the heir to the banking firm, Henriette moved to Baden, about sixteen miles southwest of Vienna, where she entertained another generation of artists including Beethoven, Caroline Pichler, Theodor Körner, Franz Grillparzer, Felix Mendelssohn (her cousin), Ottilie Goethe, Wolfgang Mozart Jr, Karl Holtei, Baron von Schörnstein, and Franz Liszt (Spiel, 484–5). But writers and friends confess that Henriette lacked her mother's intelligence and grace, and that her salon did not have its former brilliance. By 1830, after marital and personal problems, the Pereiras abandoned most of their social activities.

Closely connected to the Arnstein salon was that of Bernard Eskeles, for not only were Bernard and Nathan Arnstein business partners but their wives, Cecilia and Fanny, were sisters. It is likely that both salons carried on similar activities, but virtually no descriptions of the Eskeles home survive. However, some accounts condemn both Fanny and Cecilia for admitting some unsavory guests. The Austrian statesman, Friedrich Gentz, for example, complained to a friend in 1803: 'As much as I honor both sisters, the society in both these houses borders too closely on *mauvaise société*. I go there now with great reluctance; but it would be crass ingratitude if I were to neglect them.[13]

Taking the salons of the banking families together, Tuvora criticized them for patronizing what he saw as light, fashionable art and, with bitterness, reproached them for neglecting native intellectuals:

In these haughty salons, one often meets Viennese aesthetes and artists, seldom, on the other hand, the truly deserving, native professors and scholars, not that these have kept themselves withdrawn, but because no one takes the trouble to draw them in; and that can really not be different under the circumstances. The financier families do not consider the arts and sciences in their sovereign splendor; they appear to them solely as a means to decorate and glorify life.[14]

Precise information about the banking families in Vienna is still too limited to allow any pronouncements upon their full relationship to the city's patronage of the arts. But even the brief allusions by eyewitnesses suggest that their salons were at least as imposing as those of the aristocracy, and, most likely, were more cosmopolitan. The contribution of these families, therefore, seems to have been not so much any one brilliant soirée or concert but rather their expertise and leadership in planning large musical events by bringing together performers, concert organizers, and monied concert subscribers – a role which aristocrats no longer could perform and with which the middle-class bureaucrats still had little experience.

SALONS OF THE MIDDLE CLASS

The majority of salon descriptions written by travelers and city residents refer to the homes of middle-class bureaucrats and business-men. In contrast to the formality and opulence of aristocratic or financiers' salons, bourgeois salons were small, informal, congenial gatherings which met primarily for entertainment. Parlor games were numerous and varied. Hugo von Weckbecker recalled that in his home guests were expected to compose their own essays and poetry (123). Richard Bright observed other pastimes:

Not content of requesting young ladies to recite verses, they will sometimes invert the natural order of things and compel children to act plays, or grown people play cross questions and crooked answers, or standing in a circle, and holding a card in their hands, pass a ring from one to another, imposing it upon someone of the party, to discover in whose possession it is to be found. Acting riddles is a favourite game, and one which is well calculated to amuse those, who wisely resolve to be amused when they can. (123)

As the wealth and prestige of the middle classes increased after 1820, more families could afford the material benefits such as a piano, music lessons, and sheet music. By 1834, J. B. Weis declared, 'You must know, I continued, that now almost all of Vienna is musical; you will seldom find a house where a piano does not stand beside the other furniture, even if no one among the family is musical, but it is a part of *bon ton* to own such an instrument.'[15] Sealsfield noticed that middle-class families took pride in their children's ability to play the piano. Children began lessons at four or five years old and were 'pretty proficient' by six years old (203–4).

A genuine love of music along with the prominence accorded music by society accounts for the large number of musical amateurs and private concerts in Vienna. Some households were so active that the residents needed to reserve times for rehearsal. Hans Normann vividly describes the scene outside one apartment:

Furthermore the number of amateurs is immense. In almost every family of several members there is an amateur. Pianos are certainly never missing in prosperous houses, and in narrowly built houses often the comic situation arises that the parties must make appointments regarding the hours in which they want to practice. Very often one hears in a house violin playing on the ground floor, piano on the first floor, flute on the second, singing and guitar on the third, while, into the bargain, in the courtyard, a blind man exerts himself on a clarinet.[16]

Most amateur musicians probably regarded music as a social obligation or innocent entertainment rather than as a serious art, for writers mention music only incidentally or refer to it as a pleasant background for other salon pastimes (Russell, 306; Normann, 107). However, a correspondent for the *Allgemeine musikalische Zeitung*, writing about a Viennese salon in 1800, suggests that domestic music-making had a far more influential role in social advancement.

Every well-bred girl, whether she has talent or not, must learn to play the piano or to sing; first of all it's fashionable; secondly, it's the most convenient way for her to put herself forward in society and thereby, if she is lucky, make an advantageous matrimonial alliance, particularly a moneyed one. The sons likewise must learn music: first also, because it is the thing to do and is fashionable; secondly, because it serves them too as a recommendation in good society; and experience teaches that many a fellow (at least amongst us) has musicked himself to the side of a rich wife, or into a highly lucrative position. Students without means support

themselves by music…if someone wants to be a lawyer, he acquires a lot of
acquaintances and clients through music by playing everywhere; the same is true
of the aspiring physician. (Quoted in Locsser, 138)

Such valuation of music apparently was not universal, for, as Cyril
Ehrlich has pointed out, at least in Victorian England, making music
was considered effeminate for men and the source of 'chloroses and
neuroses' in young women.[17]

The music performed in Viennese salons was varied both in genre
and level of difficulty. The most common salon instruments were the
piano, violin, flute, and guitar. Sonatas, theme and variations, dances,
and programmatic pieces constituted the bulk of the repertory. In
addition, transcriptions of orchestral works for solo or four-hand piano,
Lieder of all kinds, and small chamber works (duets, trios, quartets)
for a variety of combinations were popular salon fare.

The level of difficulty in salon music seemed to increase throughout
the nineteenth century. The entreaties by Beethoven's and Schubert's
publishers to keep salon music simple testify to their concern that the
music be attractive and within the technical grasp of the Viennese
market. By 1840, however, with the reign of the piano virtuoso and
wider music-making public, a specialized genre of distinctive 'salon
music' emerged. Key figures in this development include Chopin,
Hiller, and Raff.[18]

After an impromptu concert, instrumentalists were often called
upon to perform dance music – the latest waltzes, quadrilles, marches,
and galops. According to an anonymous writer in 1834, a family's
music teacher or their servants frequently provided this service:

In the meantime, a musical choir performs favorite pieces and, if there are daughters
in the house, then too a little dance will be organized. Every respectable household
has not only its own music teacher, but also a few servants who are also good
musicians. The parlor is laid with parquet, swept and varnished, that is, ready for
dancing at any moment.[19]

Some of the best and most typical qualities of Vienna's middle-class
salons during the 1820s were to be found in those of Hofrat Josef
Witticzek (1781–1859), Karl Ritter von Enderes (1787–1861), and Josef
Freiherr von Spaun (1788–1865). The three men, all good friends,
shared similar backgrounds, education, and social rank. Not natives of

Vienna, they came to the city to receive a university education and to work in the Austrian bureaucracy, for which they all eventually received titles. Each man lived in a comfortable home or apartment, each enjoyed entertaining his friends with music, and, because of their friendship with Schubert and the performance of his music in their homes, descriptions of their salons have been preserved.

Having met Franz Schubert through Josef Spaun, both Enderes and Witticzek often organized 'Schubertiades' at which they performed Schubert's Lieder and piano music (Deutsch, *Biography*, 397, 399, 401, 403, 571). As with most informal social gatherings, few of the guests bothered to record the details of these meetings – either the kinds of music or the performers. But thanks to the diaries of Fritz and Franz Hartmann, two brothers and students of law from Linz, a few details of these parties in Spaun's home between 1825 and 1827 survive.[20]

To his Schubertiades, Spaun invited a large number of family friends, business associates, and friends of his son. Such gatherings later inspired the drawing by Moritz Schwind, 'A Schubert evening at the home of Josef Spaun', completed in 1870. The names of those present in the drawing are listed in Appendix D.[21] Upon examining the occupations of those present, one is struck immediately by the number of government employees, artists, and students, many of whom worked in the same offices or who were friends during their school days. Since Enderes and Spaun were bachelors during most of their Schubertiade days, young men outnumber women considerably. (The female guests were either relatives or wives of the guests.) The large proportion of young men, however, probably accounts for the salon's unique character and its vigorous activities besides music.

Schubertiades tended to follow a similar pattern. For instance, on the evening of 15 December 1826, Michael Vogel, a retired opera singer and close friend of Schubert, sang almost thirty of Schubert's songs. Then Josef Gahy and Schubert played a number of piano duets. A 'grand feast' and dancing followed (Deutsch, *Biography*, 271–2). At two subsequent parties, Schubert's songs and piano music again were performed, followed by big meals and games, which included gymnastic stunts at one meeting and a drinking bout at another – another testimony to the mostly male participation in the salon (Deutsch, *Biography*, 729). While music historians have tended to concentrate only on the musical aspects of these gatherings, the eyewitnesses report that the eating, dancing and games were equally important to them. In this respect, the Schubertiades are examples of typical middle-class socializing, for, apart from their attention to the music of Schubert, Schubertiades were neither formal concerts nor serious salon groups. In fact there is little evidence that Schubert performed his more serious chamber or symphonic works there or that Vienna's wealthy and influential music patrons ever attended them.

Accordingly, the music Schubert wrote and performed for these circles was, however fine, still generally bourgeois in character. Lieder with sentimental texts, jocular men's vocal quartets, piano duets, dances, and variations based on his songs perfectly suited the setting and demands of his amateur, yet discerning, audiences. His concert arias, string quartets, piano trios, overtures, and symphonies, written in a more serious and pretentious style, were intended for his father's quartet, certain aristocratic or professional patrons, theaters, or music societies. In contrast, Beethoven's nominal interest in this genre is understandable, since he rarely participated in such activities in middle-class homes. Instead, he played his own piano works or improvised for aristocratic salons and wrote songs (the majority of which were transcriptions of British folk songs for George Thomson), dances for the piano, and other trifles by commission only, or for quick cash profit from music publishers.

A few middle-class salons seriously pursued the arts and had some impact on the city's dramatists, writers, and composers. One of these was the literary salon of Caroline Pichler.[22] Like other bourgeois reading circles, her salon was patterned after the aristocratic circles of the eighteenth century, no doubt reflecting her youthful experiences. Caroline's mother, Charlotte Greiner, a lady-in-waiting to Maria Theresia, had entertained many artists and intellectuals connected with the court. Herself a writer of novels and plays and a regular contributor to literary journals and almanacs, Caroline Pichler encouraged close contact between Viennese writers and scholars by holding bi-weekly soirées during which writers read and discussed each other's works.

The salons of Professor Zizius, Josef Hochenadel, and Ignaz Sonnleithner specialized in the performance of art music. The travel notes of Louis Spohr from the year 1815 mention that Johann

Nepomuk Zizius (1772–1824), a professor of statistics and one of the founders of the Friends of Music, was an avid music lover. Visiting musicians were invited to his private home concerts to perform and to compete with Viennese artists who also attended regularly (Spohr, *Journeys*, 109).

Josef Hochenadel (1752–1842), an official in the Imperial Ministry of War, arranged home concerts for the benefit of his two musically gifted children, Katharina (piano, voice) and Thomas (cello). At their height around 1820, the home concerts were held every Sunday between November and Easter, and featured chamber music, vocal and instrumental solos, and large accompanied choral works from opera and oratorio by Austrian composers of the eighteenth and nineteenth centuries such as Haydn, Mozart, Beethoven, Mayseder, Schubert, and Hellmesberger (Sonnleithner, 739). Sonnleithner's memoirs also recall rare performances of Gluck's *Orfeo* and Naumann's *Cora*. He praised the concerts highly, claiming that they provided a 'rare artistic pleasure in an era which was unfavorable for serious music' (740). Even if such impressions were exaggerated, certainly the Hochenadel concerts brought together some of the city's leading professional and amateur musicians. Outstanding among the participants in the concerts are Caroline Unger, the Fröhlich sisters, Georg Hellmesberger, and Ludwig Tietze, performers connected with court theaters and the Conservatory who performed alongside such prominent men as Franz Gebauer, Raphael Kiesewetter, Josef Barth, and even a few noblemen such as Baron Nikolaus von Kruft and Prince Louis of Prussia (739). But after Hochenadel's second wife died in 1825, the concerts ceased.

Another active musical salon was that of Ignaz Sonnleithner (1770–1831), a barrister and professor of commercial law. On alternate Fridays throughout the winter, as many as one hundred and twenty guests came to hear and perform symphonic overtures, chamber music, vocal and piano solos, and large choral works (Deutsch, *Biography*, 112, Sonnleithner, 468–9). Sonnleithner's salon was responsible for arranging the first publication of Schubert's songs, as well as introducing him to many prominent Viennese music lovers. In addition, the salon may have brought Grillparzer and Schubert together, for Grillparzer was Sonnleithner's nephew.

Two other salons made considerable contributions toward the

revival of early music. Already in the eighteenth century, a handful of music collectors and antiquarians had begun systematically to assemble and transcribe music manuscripts from previous centuries. In Vienna this activity was initiated and fostered by Baron van Swieten, the emperor's physician. Swieten's private 'historical concerts' provided the model for succeeding performances given by Raphael Kiesewetter a generation later. Kiesewetter, however, went farther than Swieten by collecting and analyzing music from earlier centuries, and by opening concerts of such 'ancient' music to a wider audience.

As chairman of the Imperial War Council, vice president of the Friends of Music Society (from 1821 to 1826), administrative director of the Society's Conservatory (from 1817 to 1826), and as an active participant in the private musical circles throughout Vienna, Raphael Kiesewetter (1773–1850) had close connections with many of the city's finest musicians, music patrons, and music collections, including that of the court.[23] Through his ties with the government and the Friends of Music, he was able to locate, inventory, collect, and edit music from various European collections. His studies led to an essay, 'Die Verdienste der Niederländer um die Tonkunst', which won for him first prize from the Dutch Institute for Science, Literature, and Arts in 1828. Six years later, he published one of the first universal music histories (*Geschichte der europäischen-abendländischen Musik*, 1834) in addition to numerous other studies of the performance practice, notation, and biographies of early musicians.

Beginning in 1816, Kiesewetter organized about five historical concerts each year in his home. After only a brief pause in 1838, the concerts continued until 1843 – a total of about 270 performances of 178 works.[24] In a letter of 3 September 1828 to a fellow collector, Georg Pölchau of Berlin, who was just about to visit Vienna, Kiesewetter described his home concerts:

Please do not come with great expectations: it is only my small domestic- portable- and itinerant orchestra, which gathers, and the performances are impromptu. We meet at 6.30, make music until about 10; then we take some small refreshments, which may also perhaps not end without some singing.[25]

Six years later, he explained to Bottée de Toulmon, another collector, the difference between his concerts and those of his counterparts abroad.

In the musical season I have, for 18 years, had music of the old masters played. There are not concerts of the kind of Herr F[etis], who, in the course of two hours [surveys] the history of centuries, nor are they to be compared with the purely classical productions of Herr Choron. But the people who attend my concerts receive a correct impression of the course of history, since it is the object of my programs, and since I have whole pieces performed, or notable excerpts of all kinds.[26]

Most of the concerts featured choral works from the seventeenth and eighteenth centuries, which were performed by a mixture of professional and amateur musicians, many of whom were students at the Conservatory. Table 7 lists the participants in Kiesewetter's concerts. The list reveals the names of the Fröhlich sisters, Ludwig Tietze, Randhartinger, Kandler, Fuchs, Schoberlechner, Gebauer, and Pechaczek – all familiar in professional and middle-class musical circles of the period. Accompanied by the piano and possibly a few strings, the singers usually read the music at sight without any rehearsal. A typical program, given on 10 November 1822, included these works:

Motet (à 5) 'Exultata de Domini' – Palestrina (alla Capella)
Psalm (à 3) 'Notus in Judea' – A. Biffi (alla Capella)
Kyrie (à 5) 'Fugue and chorale' – J. S. Bach
Motet (à 2) 'Caro mea' – A. Caldara
Psalm (à 4) 'Beatus vir' – F. Durante
Magnificat (à 4) – N. Jomelli

Other concerts reveal some startling programs. For example, in 1829, the group performed Schütz's 'Das Gebeth des Herrn', *five* years before Winterfeld reputedly 'discovered' Heinrich Schütz.

In addition to his historical concerts, Kiesewetter also performed modern works. Through his children, Irene and Karl, Kiesewetter became acquainted with Schubert and his friends – with mutually beneficial results. Johann Jenger began to take an active role in the historical concerts, and Kiesewetter sponsored a number of Schubert-iades, which were attended by professional musicians and people associated with the Friends of Music. At one such concert, Michael Vogel, Ludwig Tietze, Benedickt Randhartinger, and Karl Schönstein sang songs by Schubert, and Irene Kiesewetter and Jenger played piano duets by Schubert and Beethoven. It is also possible that Schubert's acquaintance with Kiesewetter led to more performance possibilities and musical commissions through the Friends of Music.

Table 7. *Participants in Kiesewetter's Hauskonzerte*

Soprano	Alto
Therese Komper	Josephine Fröhlich
Sophie Linhardt	Barbara Fröhlich
Anna Fröhlich	Therese Miretti
Katharine Fröhlich	Marie v. Würth
Caroline v. Salken	Karoline Graziosi
Marie Weiss	Julie Goldberg
Wilhelmine Baumann	Leopoldine Direlt
Leopoldin Tuczek	Karoline Bodgorschek
Karoline Mayer	Therese Schwarz
Marie Ehres	Scherer
Fanny Goldberg	Betti Bury
Marie Sanger	Therese Janda
Josepha Albrecht	(12)
Vincentia Jeckal	
Amalie Tewilie	
Karoline Sack	
Therese Hefft	
Amalie Kierstein	
Magdalene Benda	
Mathilde Graumann	
Luisa Afell	
Fredericke Pinschoff	
Katherine Leib	
Rosalina Schodl	
Sidonie Turba	
(25)	

Tenor	Bass
Georg Kubner	Raphael Kiesewetter
Georg Hoffmann	Franz Sales Kandler
Peter Lugano	Karl Schoberlechner
Benedickt Randhartinger	Luigi Lablache
John, Comte Ferigotti	Gottfried Reggla
Michael Vogel	Arkadius Klein
Ludwig Tietze	Alois Fuchs
Kolumban Schnitzer	(7)
Mathias Lutz	
Joseph Barth	
Theobald Rizy	
(11)	

Conductors
Johann Hugo Worischek (died 1825)
Franz Gebauer
Franz Pechaczek
Johann Jenger (began in 1827)

Taken from Sonnleithner, 756–7.

Simon Molitor (1766–1848), a military commissary official, also held bi-monthly historical concerts after his retirement (from 1832 to 1848) (Kier, 89–90). But, unlike those of Kiesewetter, Molitor's concerts featured older instrumental music. He occasionally gave his concerts titles or themes. One program was called 'Instrumental Compositions of Netherlanders and German Masters from the Period 1500 to 1800'. The level of performance may have been higher than that of other comparable concerts because Molitor's performers were professional musicians. The group's string quartet, for instance, with the exception of Molitor, were all members of the Court Chapel: Josef Böhm and Leopold Jansa (violins), Molitor (viola), and Aloys Fuchs (cello) (Kier, 89). Unfortunately, almost no records of these concerts survive and thus their impact is uncertain.

In his monograph on concert life in Vienna during the years 1830 to 1848, William Weber asserts that the abundance of middle-class music salons delayed the modernization of the city's classical music concerts and the establishment of a professional orchestra (78–81). But he fails to credit sufficiently the bourgeois salon hosts with the preservation and promotion of art music during the previous decades, at a time when it was not fashionable to do so. After all, it was primarily these music-loving civil servants who sponsored the Friends of Music and the other concert series, and in whose salons a new generation of musicians learned the repertories of the past. Bourgeois salons also supported Vienna's music publishers and provided livelihoods for music teachers and instrument builders. A further tribute, however, was paid by the city's composers, who, throughout the nineteenth century, maintained close ties with these salons and for them continually wrote much excellent music.

6

MUSICAL INSTITUTIONS: RELIGIOUS AND MILITARY

Established much earlier, Austrian churches, synagogues, and military bands continued to play a role in Vienna's musical culture during the nineteenth century. These institutions are considered together here because they both required particular musical genres which had well-defined purposes, and they trained and employed performing musicians, thereby offering a composer both the opportunity to compose and perform new music. Further, the reputed abundance and public nature of sacred and military music suggest that works in these genres were heard by most Viennese residents and thus were an integral part of the city's musical environment.

MUSIC IN THE CHURCH AND SYNAGOGUE

Continuing traditions begun in the seventeenth century, Vienna was still a center for sacred music and the oratorio. At the same time, the city's synagogue was reputed to have been one of the most progressive in Europe. Both institutions were important patrons of music.

Throughout the nineteenth century, the great majority of Viennese citizens were Roman Catholic – the state religion of Austria. The next three largest religious sects were Protestants (Lutherans and Calvinists) among the German and Bohemian communities, Greek Uniate and Orthodox Catholics from Middle Eastern immigrants,[1] and Jews, most of whom had come from Eastern Europe (Poland and Russia). Table 8 presents nineteenth-century estimates of the size of the various groups in the years 1790, 1834 and 1836. The very slight percentage of change between 1810 and 1840 indicates that Vienna's Catholic community remained stable and the overwhelming majority during the first part of the century.

Habsburg rulers had long served as models of Catholic piety and

Table 8. *Religious groups in Austria and Vienna*

Austria

	1790[a]	1834[b]	1838[c]
Roman Catholics	unreported	22,000,000	26,790,000
Greek Uniate Catholics	2,916,000	130,000	3,040,000
Greek Orthodox		2,500,000	
Lutherans	304,000	1,500,000	1,190,000
Reformed (Calvinists)	926,000	2,000,000	1,660,000
Jews	290,000	430,000	500,000
Armenians	unreported	170,000	13,500
Unitarians	86,000*	50,000	50,000
Moslems	unreported	1,500	1,500
Mennonites, Hussites	unreported	3,500	unreported
Other	unreported	8,800	unreported

Vienna

	1790[a]	1824[d]	1834[e]	1836[f]
Greek Uniate Catholics	unreported	unreported	4,000	10,000 (together)
Greek Orthodox	unreported	unreported	600	
Lutherans	3,000	8,790	9,000	8,000 (together)
Reformed (Calvinists)	700	800	1,000	
Jews	unreported	unreported	1,600	1,600

Percentages of change in religious populations from 1810–40[g]

	Catholics	Protestants	Jews
1810–20	97·4–98	1–1·2	0·3–0·4
1820–30	97–97·4	1·2–1·5	0·4–0·6
1830–40	96·5–97	1·5–2·3	0·6–0·8
% of change:	−1·5	+1·3	+0·5

[a] Pezzl, *Skizze*, 390.
[b] Bäuerle, *Was Verdankt*, 427.
[c] Strombeck, *Darstellung*, 112.
[d] Pezzl, *Beschreibung* (1826), 41.
[e] Schmidl, 15.
[f] Pezzl, *Beschreibung* (1841), 28–9.
[g] Hickman, 29–30.
* *Note:* The Unitarians in Siebenbürgen were counted with Socinians.

devotion. Even the sweeping reforms of Josef II around 1780 did not last, for Franz I called for the return of strict observance of numerous religious holidays, he re-established the Jesuit order, and he reinstated a number of religious pilgrimages (Blumenbach, II, 161–74; 193–208). However, like his predecessors, Franz took pains to insure that the church would never usurp the power of the crown. Thus at the beginning of the nineteenth century, the church wielded power mainly in matters of religion, social service, and education.

As a center for a number of religious orders, Vienna was home for many clerics, monks, and nuns. In 1837, Schmidl tallied 170 priests, 450 monks, and 160 nuns (39). Three years later Pezzl tabulated: some 30 priests, 160 prelates, 231 ordained ministers, 138 foreign clerics, and 287 nuns living within Vienna's 10 monasteries, 5 convents, and 67 cloisters.[2] The colorful garb of each religious group added to Vienna's already motley street scenes. Blumenbach viewed the population as 'generally well-dressed and well-looking, a good sprinkling of soldiers in white uniforms and black gaiters; of priests, with black cassocks and white belts; of friars, with dust-brown habits, and head uncowled; of some hundreds of Jews' (1, 45).

During the period, a common perception expressed by visitors and residents was that the Viennese were not very religious. Diplomat Franz Andlaw charged that many Viennese attended church more out of habit than out of spiritual need, and that their indifference to religion paralleled their apathy toward politics (203). John Strang concurred in 1831:

...the great mass of the people are comparatively indifferent to all religion. The majority, no doubt, are nominally Catholics; but under this holy and intolerant title, I understand there lurks a vast quantity of unbelief and free-thinking. In short, it seems to be characteristic of the Viennese, that whatever be their nominal creed, they are never over-scrupulous about acting up to its requirements. Even the Jews of Vienna are less strict in their observance, than those of other towns in Germany (280–1).

The Viennese themselves admitted to a certain laxity in religious self-sacrifice. As early as 1790, Pezzl reported a relaxation of Lenten fasting observances. By 1844, an old fish wife complained that the trend had gone further: 'The great people don't trouble themselves about fasting and eating fish, and even the monks are grown more impious' (Kohl, 141).

Some churches apparently served functions other than for worship. In 1828 Sealsfield wrote that Mass at St Stephan's was more a social than religious occasion:

The priest who is able to do it [say Mass] in the shortest time, about 12 minutes, is surrounded by the greatest crowd. In the pews, which run up on both sides of the aisles, the fashionable world is seated; and, in the outer space of the nave, are the dandies of Vienna, walking to and fro, ogling, holding conversation, not only with their eyes, but even *viva voce* (200)..

Friedrich Nicolai reported that some churches harbored beggars and criminals. The midnight Mass acquired the nickname 'Hurenmesse' (whore's Mass), since prostitutes would solicit men in the churches to avoid the police patrolling the streets (90).

Hans Normann summarized what he believed to be the pervasive Viennese attitude toward the church in 1833 by quoting the advice of a woodcutter to his son: 'Remain an honorable fellow, follow your father, and believe what you want.'[3] To be sure, many writers criticized such religious negligence (Schlamperei), but to Glassbrenner such aversion to radical religious dogma, particularly the Pietism of northern Germany, was refreshing.

Also Pietism, that spiritual contagion which in the North carried off innumerable victims and which blocks the way toward Enlightenment, finds no adherents in Vienna...He [the Viennese] demands little ceremony and finds God everywhere where he finds pleasure and beauty. I still savor the world, he calls, why should I starve?[4]

One reason for the apparent indifference, even animosity, may have been the corruption of the church and the hyprocrisy of its clergy and monastic houses. Normann found that Austrians were cynical about their leaders' vow of poverty in view of their actual incomes. In 1822, these were reported to be 54,000 fl. for the archbishop and over 100,000 fl. a year for many Hungarian bishops (Pezzl, *Beschreibung* (1841), 26). Another point of contention was the large revenues extracted by big landowning monasteries: 'The country groans under a large number of oppressive cloister rulers, who drink a lot, amass treasures, and who divest the people of their best resources. For this reason the dissatisfaction among the general populace is also quite widespread.'[5] Like Normann, Blumenbach was skeptical about clerics' morals, and he insinuated that many of the religious foundling homes, often located near cloisters, cared for illegitimate children fathered by the churchmen (II, 177–8). Such accusations, however, he was unable to substantiate.

But if the Viennese seemed apathetic to theology and antagonistic toward the temporal affairs of the church, they reveled in religious ceremony and pageantry. On Sundays alone, hundreds of church bells rang from six in the morning until noon (Sealsfield, 202). Unaccustomed to such rich and theatrical religious spectacle, Protestant observers were deeply impressed. Nicolai was almost overcome by the experience.

The large mass of clerics of every kind, the large number of monks in every dress and form, the pictures of the saints and their veneration, fasting, crossing oneself, lowering of the eyes, beating one's breast, the mechanical saying of prayers, the scapular and girdle, vestments, the illumination, and music, the sprinkling of holy water, praying the rosary, the constant sound of the bells – all these things came into view everywhere in Vienna. If he saw the same things, a Protestant would believe himself to be in a totally new world.[6]

Blumenbach too observed the rich trappings of the churches, but he was repulsed by their veneration: 'Most of them exhibit gilding, and gaudy images of the Virgin, with the most barbarous representations of crucifixes and dead Christs, that bad taste and priestly terror could represent to dupe or terrify poor ignorant superstitious humanity' (I, 220).

The high feast days of Holy Week, Trinity, and Corpus Christi were celebrated with great ceremony. Frances Trollope describes with awe the formality and theatricality of Holy Week traditions – churches hung in black, silencing of the church bells, and the closing of the theaters. She was intrigued also by the annual foot-washing ceremony on Maundy Thursday. On that day, the twenty-four oldest citizens of Vienna were invited to the palace, where the emperor and empress, along with the members of the court, washed their feet and personally served them dinner as a demonstration of Christian humility and charity (II, 240–6).

Some religious observances incorporated pagan rituals or became general folk holidays. On Saturday in Holy Week, Holman witnessed the customary burning of Judas in effigy in the city's streets and at the doors of certain churches (275). Saints Brigitte, Leopold, and Anne were venerated with traditional folk celebrations. On Brigittenkirchtag (movable feastday in summer) the Viennese celebrated outdoors in the Prater or Augarten with picnics and dancing. On St Leopoldstag (15 November) in Klosterneuburg, it was customary to slide down a certain wine cask for good luck. And on St Anne's day (26 July) on 'Nannerl Tag', all Viennese women named after the saint were honored with serenades, gifts, or plays.[7]

Occasionally, exaggerated acts of piety created problems for state authorities, judging from an amusing order issued by the provincial government of Bohemia which, in November 1826, forbade the production and sale of any baked goods in the shape of the crucifix, the infant Jesus, Mary, or any other sacred symbol. The report explains that the items had become the subjects of extremely irreverent jokes when people bit off the figures' heads or other parts in public places, including the environs of the city churches.[8]

SACRED MUSIC

Music was always an essential part of the pageantry. In fact, Andlaw placed the church alongside the concert hall, theater, and salon for its cultivation of art music (204). Even the doubting Blumenbach confessed in 1836 that Vienna's liturgical music alone offered a 'splendid and imposing attraction' (I, 222).

At the beginning of the century, Vienna's church music differed little in style from its counterpart in the theater or concert hall. Contributors to musical journals repeatedly complained that sacred music had grown too secular and that the great concerted masses actually diverted attention from the liturgy's significance. Sealsfield infers as much from his description of Mass at St Stephan's in 1828: 'As soon as the concert, either vocal or instrumental is over, the whole crowd hastens to the doors, leaving priests, divine service, everything to do its business unmolested and alone' (201).

Periodically, the court made some attempt to reform particular abuses in the churches. In 1825 a court decree charged that music in its Court Chapel and St Peter's 'presently served more as amusement than as a means to promote religious devotion'. Henceforward, women, other than the wife, daughter, or sister of the choir director or the schoolmaster, were banned from performing with the church musicians, and no piece of music was to be performed that was 'better fit for the theater than the church'.[9]

Standard fare thus included polyphonic Mass and Vespers items, hymns, and music for sacred cantatas and oratorios. In Vienna, much of this music was newly composed by local composers: Beethoven, Schubert, Salieri, Albrechtsberger, and Weigl.

In general, liturgical practice and the role of church musicians in

Musical institutions: religious and military

Vienna attracted neither the attention of contemporary travelers nor of modern scholars.[10] Hence the few surviving practical guides on these matters have become valuable sources of information. One such handbook, entitled *Kirchenmusik-Ordnung-Erklärendes Handbuch des musikalischen Gottesdienstes für Kapellmeister, Regenschori, Sänger und Tonkünstler* (The Handbook that explains the Regulation of Church Music in the Musical Divine Service for Chapel Masters, Choir Directors, Singers, and Composers), was written in 1828 for the diocese of Vienna and Linz. The guide first divides sacred music into two genres: Choralmusik, loosely defined as vocal polyphony, three-part chorales or old mensural music; and Figuralmusik, described as 'solemn instrumental music'.

The handbook's anonymous author explains that sacred music expressed three sentiments: praise, trust or joy; supplication; or sorrow and mourning. To enhance these affections were the special characteristics associated with the various keys or tonalities. The author probably adopted the key characteristics from C. F. D. Schubart's *Ideen zur Aesthetik der Tonkunst* (Vienna, 1806) or Schubart's original sources, since the guide's key attributes and choice of words are essentially a paraphrase of the older work. The following example illustrates the similarities:

	Schubart 1806	Handbuch 1828
B Major	happy love, good conscience	happy love, good conscience, hope
Eb Major	love, devotion, talk with God	3 flats = holy; devotion, intimate talk with God
C Minor	penitential lament, intimate conversation with God, the friend and companion of life	penitential lament, intimate talk with God

The affirmation of Schubart's classifications provides further evidence that a composer's choice of key, for some sacred music, continued to have at least symbolic meaning well into the nineteenth century.

Next, the handbook outlines the responsibilities of the church musicians. The choir director was to select music to create the appropriate 'spirit' for the day. If he were not a composer, he was to judge the suitability of the music by examining the character of the vocal parts or by translating the text (usually in Latin) (7–8).

The organist's duty was to play preludes and interludes during the Mass and to provide correct tempi for the choir. Church instrumentalists were asked to tune their instruments *before* the service 'without great noise', to forgo 'fantasias and extraneous playing, and to strictly follow the directions of the conductor' (11). Singers were entreated to pay close attention to the liturgy so that they sang the correct response in 'pure accord', and to insure that their diction was understandable to the congregation (30). But the handbook's emphasis on practices to be avoided, by its very insistence, suggests that these probably were common occurrences in city churches.

Attempting to reform some of its sacred music in the eighteenth century, Viennese churches had instituted congregational singing of German sacred songs (Volksgesänge) (Pezzl, *Skizze*, 281). The songs must have been sung too quickly or too slowly, though, for the guide instructs the church musician to provide a moderate and even tempo for the congregation, observing the customary pauses after each phrase in order that the 'dignity of the song be not lost' (38). In addition for congregational singing, a leader or Tonführer was chosen for his 'insight, good judgment and self-respect' to select the most suitable pitch for the hymn and to alter the song's tempo if necessary without causing confusion in the congregation (39). From such statements, the guide implies that congregational songs were sung *a cappella*, since the leader, and not the organist, gave pitches.

Finally, the handbook discusses the kinds of music appropriate for Mass, funerals, and processions. As early as 1791, musical Masses had been restricted by the court to Sundays and special feast days. Instrumental music was allowed exclusively in city and market-town churches (20).

Music for funerals was prescribed by the funeral's class. The simplest and most inexpensive funeral provided only a choral litany, the 'Miserere'. A second-class funeral included a sung Requiem and a litany accompanied by brass instruments. Only the most expensive of funerals featured trombones and brass instruments in a sung Requiem and a special funeral motet (32). At funerals of young children, 'Laudate pueri' was sung; and for non-Catholics, a Trauerlied was performed (Schmidl, 289).

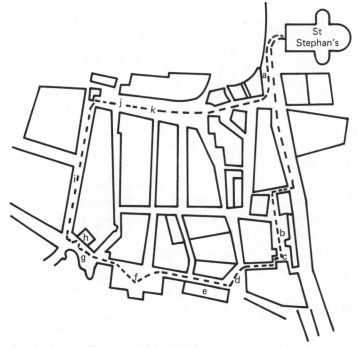

6 Order of procession for Corpus Christi, 30 May 1825

1. From the main door of St Stephan's to Stock am Eisen Platz[a] down the Kärntnerthorstrasse to Spital and Neuer Markt[b] to the palace of Prince Schwarzenberg[c]: first Gospel

2. Through the Kapuzinerkloster to Spitalplatz[d]: second Gospel

3. Pass the Augustinerkirche[e], Josefplatz[f] and Michaelerplatz[g] to the Michaelerkirche[h]: third Gospel

4. On Kohlmarkt[i] to the Graben[j] by the three pillars (?): fourth Gospel

5. On the Graben, a battalion of grenadiers from the Imperial Army will parade and after the procession will fire a threefold volley

(VA, P.H. 4247/1825 – Order for Procession 1825)

The handbook suggests that the procession for Corpus Christi was the most elaborate, with choirs and trumpet fanfares alternating with conventional prayers and recitations. If the Host was carried in the procession, however, only the 'Pange Lingua' (traditional Corpus Christi hymn) could be performed (30–2). Illus. 6 reproduces the stations of the procession along its route through Vienna. Restrictions were placed on the use of instruments in processions; trumpets and drums were reserved for feasts of first and second rank; all brass instruments were forbidden in Lent; and new music could be added if the emperor were to be honored at some point in the procession (30–2; see also VA, P.H., 4247/1825, 'Order for Processions at Corpus Christi').

INDIVIDUAL CENTERS OF SACRED MUSIC

Hofkapelle – Of all the churches in Vienna, none was more prestigious and boasted finer musicians than the small Hofkapelle or Court Chapel near the imperial palace. In 1825 the ensemble, consisting of 2 Kapellmeisters, a Chapel Composer, 10 singers (5 tenors, 5 basses), 2 female singers, 10 choir boys, an organist, and 24 instrumentalists (12 violins, 2 violas, 2 celli, 2 string basses, 6 oboes) performed sinfonias and fully orchestrated masses for the court and a limited number of guests every Sunday at 11 a.m.[11] Between the years 1824 and 1846, the Chapel ensemble included many notable musicians, such as Joseph Eybler, Anton Salieri, Joseph Weigl, Anna Kraus (née Wranitsky), Therese Grünbaum, Ludwig Tietze, Benedict Randhartinger, Ignaz Schuster, Aloys Fuchs, Hugo Woriczek, Leopold Jansa, Ignaz Schuppanzigh, Joseph Böhm, Joseph Mayseder, and Ignaz Umlauf. Furthermore, the Chapel usually performed the compositions by its own Kapellmeisters and native Austrian composers such as Josef and Michael Haydn, Mozart, Beethoven, Preindl, Salieri, Seyfried, and Eybler.

English travelers had high praise for the Chapel's music. In 1825 George Smart exclaimed about a performance of a Mass by Albrechtsberger: 'The boys were most excellent and the performance here was the best I have heard without wind instruments' (113). Four years later, Mary Novello praised the musicians for their 'correct and judicious' renditions of classical music. She commends, in particular, Josef Eybler: 'Eybler made no fuss or clatter but beat time steadily and calmly like a sterling and accomplished musician himself who knew that he was surrounded by others who knew their business without much interference from him' (180–1). That same year Edward Holmes was impressed by the performances, calling them 'the most delicate and finished service to be heard in Vienna' (161). In passing, he noticed that instrumental music was played where the English normally used a voluntary.

St Stephan's — Vienna's largest church, St Stephan's cathedral, impressed visitors with its Gothic design, its awesome atmosphere, and its grand, concerted Masses presented by an ensemble recruited from the two court theaters (Hecke, 46). On Sundays and feast days, Low Masses were recited by priests in chapels throughout the cathedral. Around 11 a.m., Vienna's wealthier citizens assembled for an elaborate High Mass.

Despite its grandeur, St Stephan's services received much pointed criticism. In 1781, for example, Nicolai judged the orchestra's performance to be below that of the court theaters in spite of its few gifted musicians. He also complained bitterly that the music resembled *opera buffa* more than sacred music (107). Forty years later, Mary Novello also complained about the level of performance, but now she found the church music too old-fashioned: 'The mass was in a poor commonplace old style like what might have been written by Hasse or Vinci; all the movements are short and unsatisfactory. The best voices were the trebles. The orchestral performers were of the mediocre kind.'[12] In 1839, on the feast of the Assumption of Mary, Friedrich Hurter judged the cathedral music to be excellent, but he found the incessant ringing of the bells to be 'ear-splitting'. Like Postl ten years before, he also was annoyed by the streams of people entering and leaving the sanctuary — their restless movement reminding him more of a trade fair than of devotional service (1, 283). According to Pezzl, the services occurring simultaneously throughout the cathedral caused confusion: 'The Holy Mass was likewise held in a kind of disorder. So many were read simultaneously that, instead of keeping the devout in an edified spiritual assembly, they scattered them instead.'[13]

Church of St Augustine — The Augustine church's reputation rested upon its performance of modern music, but only a few details of its repertory and performers have been preserved (Smart, 121). From archival documents, Biba found that in 1783 the church's orchestra consisted of 55 violins, 1 cello and 2 trombones, and the choir had 2 tenors, 2 basses and some choir boys from the nearby St Dorothea school ('Kirchenmusik', 26–7). Later (in 1837), Schmidl commented that music students from the Conservatory would perform there on special festivals at High Mass (11 a.m.) (233). The highest compliments were paid by Blumenbach in 1836, although he was vague about details: 'The instrumental execution in the German churches may not be so powerfully impressive as the vocal orchestra at St Peter's in Rome; but where else on earth can the public hear such exquisite music performed with such masterly excellence as at Vienna, and generally throughout Germany' (I, 222). He also makes a brief reference to 'military Masses' held by the church. Comparing them to those of Munich, he writes, 'In Vienna, military masses are less frequent, but they are executed in the highest style of grandeur' (I, 222). The sources do not explain what is meant by a 'military Mass', but a few oblique references suggest that in some way they featured brass choirs and that they were connected with important state celebrations. Perhaps they were associated with the memorial observances of All Saints' Day in honor of Austrian veterans, or with the funerals of knights from the Maria Theresian Order within the Augustine Church (Pezzl, *Beschreibung* (1826), 99).

Information about the musical practice of other Viennese churches is equally limited, although the churches of St Anne, St Peter, St Michael, and St Charles were cited specially for their instrumental music (Pezzl, *Beschreibung* (1826), 113; Novello, 179). Somewhat helpful are the notes taken by George Smart regarding the city's organs and church orchestras. For example, he praised the twenty-member orchestra of the Karlskirche for its performance of Beethoven's Mass in C, but he was disappointed with the organ, finding most Austrian instruments 'too squally' for his taste (127). He assessed the orchestra at St Peter's as 'weak' and expressed surprise to find trumpet and kettledrum flourishes performed between the verses of psalms at St Michael's – a practice at least as old as the eighteenth century.[14]

The suburban churches also supported small musical ensembles, for Franz Schubert wrote a number of concerted works expressly for them. For the Liechtenthaler church, Schubert wrote Masses in F and B♭. For the Alt Lerchenfelder church (April 1820) he set six antiphons for 'consecration of the palms on Palm Sunday', and two years later he wrote a Mass in E♭ for the St Trinitas Kirche in the Alsergrund (Deutsch, *Schubert Thematic Catalogue*, D. 223, 678, 696; and Deutsch, *Biography*, 44, 455, 804).

Seitenstettengasse synagogue – In April 1826, Vienna's older Latzenhof synagogue (on Katzensteig) was replaced with the consecration of a new building on the Kienmarkt, Seitenstettengasse (Normann, xxii; Pezzl, *Beschreibung* (1826), 22). The new synagogue quickly gained distinction for its excellent *a cappella* choir and gifted cantor Salomon Sulzer (1804–90).[15] Sulzer, a powerful baritone who often sang in Vienna's theaters and who later taught in the Conservatory, served as the synagogue's cantor for fifty-six years (from 1825 to 1881). His leadership was felt immediately in Vienna and abroad.

Sulzer encouraged the commissioning of new sacred music by local, contemporary composers. Beethoven was asked to compose a new cantata for the consecration of the new synagogue, for example. Although he could not comply, other respected and talented composers, among them Joseph Drechsler, Ignaz Seyfried, and Josef Fischof, contributed many excellent works. In July 1828, Franz Schubert set Psalm 92 (in Hebrew) for baritone solo (Sulzer) and mixed chorus (D. 953) for the synagogue. The Psalm's antiphonal style, alternating between a simple, declamatory full chorus and more ornate solo group and the interpolation of the rhapsodic baritone solo lines, provides some insight into the style of synagogue music that so impressed the eyewitnesses.

In accordance with the tenets of the Jewish Reform Movement led by Isaac Noah Mannheimer around 1825, Sulzer also revised the music of the service by harmonizing and giving rhythm to traditional Hebrew melodies. These were eventually published in two volumes entitled *Schir Zion* ('Harp of Zion', vol. I in 1838 and vol. II in 1865), and became standard liturgical collections in Europe and the United States.

As Alexander Ringer has pointed out, Josef Mainzer, then a priest and advocate of massed communal singing, heard the synagogue choir in 1827 and was among the first to publish its praise. In an article printed in the Parisian *Gazette Musicale* in 1834, he even suggested that Vienna's synagogue music serve as a model for the reform of Christian sacred music (Ringer, 'Salomon Sulzer', 360–4).

Unfortunately, few of the other travelers ventured into the synagogue or bothered to record their experiences. Glassbrenner, however, mentioned in 1834 that there were between ten to twelve boys in the choir. He praised Sulzer's 'wohl tönende' voice, but he thought that the music sounded too much like Rossini or Bellini – a criticism also lodged against the music of the city's churches (182). Two years later, both the American scholar, George Ticknor, and Frances Trollope extolled the novelty and beauty of the unaccompanied singing (Ticknor, 4; Trollope, 1, 286) Trollope wrote: 'There is, in truth, so wild and strange an harmony in the songs of the children of Israel as performed in the synagogue in this city, that it would be difficult to render full justice to the splendid excellence of the performances, without falling into the language of enthusiasm' (1, 286).

To a music historian, the accomplishment of the Viennese synagogue holds special significance, for its progressive *a cappella* music antedates the reforms of the Cecilian Movement by at least ten years. As a source of inspiration, at least to Mainzer, its choral music served as the model of the avant garde – a surprising feat in view of Vienna's restrictive and generally conservative artistic environment.

PATRONAGE OF SACRED MUSIC

Among its duties as a patron of music, the church fostered music education. Some of the city churches supported private musical societies and music schools in addition to providing their own liturgical music. One such society, Verein zur Verbesserung der Kirchenmusik auf dem Lande, was founded by Prince Ferdinand Lobkowitz in 1827. The organization's six hundred members formed a music school, located in St Anne's church, which offered classes (eighteen hours a week) in sacred music, choral music, choral and psalm singing, Latin, music theory, figured bass, violin, and organ. According to Schmidl, the school had 78 pupils in 1840 (231; Pezzl, *Beschreibung* (1841), 254). The title of the society implies that the school sought to improve the level of performance in Austria's rural churches, although subsequent writers do not offer further explanation.

A similar school was established by Father Honorius Kraus with the help of the Kirchenmusik Verein of Schottenfeld in 1823. Again, no information is available about the school's curriculum or enrollment (Bäuerle, *Was Verdankt*, 174).

Another avenue of musical patronage came from the municipal government, which, through the church, subsidized certain music and

Masses throughout the year. According to the city's account books, an important occasion was the annual November Mass for 'Our Savior' (possibly the dedication of the cathedral). The accounts show that from 1812 through at least 1830, the city paid a fixed sum of 11.11 fl. (CM) for additional brass instruments used in the Mass, and 11.36 fl. to the Kapellmeister of St Stephan's (WStA, Oberkämmeramt, Ausgabe, 1816–30). In addition, the city paid for daily votive Masses between the years 1816 and 1830, but the word 'Lesung' and the low sums cited in the ledger probably indicate that musicians were not used in these services (WStA, Oberkämmeramt, 11/8 Erforderniss fixirte Ausgabe 1823–6, 157, 159, 163, 165).

The city endowed other votive Masses during the year because lump sums of money were allotted to certain churchmen for 'singing and other religious services'. Between 1822 and 1830, for example, the city gave 19.12 fl. (CM) to two chaplains for such duties. The accounts also show that the position of Kapellmeister at St Stephan's was endowed by the municipal government 360 fl. (CM) a year (*Ibid.*, 160, 167). In addition, the city contributed money to special celebrations by individual churches, for, in October 1824, the city paid 160 fl. (CM) to a parish church in Leopoldstadt in honor of its one-hundredth anniversary (WStA, Ausgabe, 1823–6, 4/11 no. 16836, 21 October 1824).

In summary, the church served three important functions for Vienna's musicians. The first was to educate young musicians in the fundamentals of singing and music theory in its schools. Joseph and Michael Haydn, Franz Schubert, and Johann Hellmesberger all began their careers in this way at the k.k. Konvikt as choirboys for the Court Chapel. Its second function was to serve as a platform for the performance of new musical works. Franz Schubert, for example, wrote his first and some of his last compositions for the church, probably not so much out of religious zeal, but because in the church he had the opportunity for a public performance. Finally, for some composers, singers, and instrumentalists, the church offered employment or additional income. By mid-century, however, church reforms and an increasing interest in restoring polyphonic music of the sixteenth century caused the genre of church music in Vienna to lose much of its attraction for contemporary composers.

MILITARY MUSIC

Like the church and synagogue, the Austrian army indirectly served as a musical patron. Compulsory marches and parades created a demand for appropriate new music and able performers. In turn, the frequent performances of military bands helped to disseminate new music and raise much art music to a popular genre.

Austrian military life – After the Napoleonic Wars, Austria's army, numbering about 270,000 (down from 650,000 men during the war), was considered to be one of the strongest military forces in Europe, employing one of the best cavalry and artillery (Sealsfield, 235, n. 163). About 12,000 of these men were stationed in garrisons outside Vienna (Schmidl, 236; Pezzl *Beschreibung* (1820), 242). By 1837 two permanent infantry regiments, consisting of grenadiers and three divisions of cavalry, and an artillery unit of 1,000 men, were stationed around Vienna, the largest camp being located in the Alservorstadt.

The army had long been the traditional career of the second or third son of Austrian aristocrats, and it was considered a passable living for members of the lowest classes despite the hard life and slow rate of promotion. The gulf between the ranks of aristocratic officers and infantry soldiers, however, remained insurmountable throughout most of the century.[16]

Evidence that military service was something to be avoided is provided by the government which punished certain criminals and unruly students with military duty. From personal experience, Hans Normann relates the brutality of military life and the bitterness of Austrian students over new draft regulations of 1826 which abolished their student military-service exemptions, while nobles and civil servants were still free from duty. He warned that, even more than censorship, forced military service would stifle Austria's 'spiritual life' by denying youth the opportunity to develop their talents (99–100).

In the provinces, military recruiters, who filled their quotas by impressing men into service by force or through cunning, were dreaded visitors. Some fathers averted them with large bribes, while the poor resorted to self-imposed injury to make themselves unfit for duty. Normann writes:

How different it has become since the year 1826. With terror a father hears that a son is born to him, and when he is grown, he [the father] has no other worry than to take him out of school as quickly as possible and to make him military-free. The poor mutilate themselves and the rich pay and bribe, crimes are committed, and a scurrilous business carried on by the recruiting officials, who hold in their hands the power over life and freedom of the people. Tragicomic is the sight of the youth in school, among whom the number of cripples and destitute increases at the same rate, [while] the number of healthy declines.[17]

No wonder the recruiters were feared; according to Langenschwarz in 1836, the normal term of service for an Austrian was fourteen years and, for a Hungarian, a lifetime (15)!

Military life had many disadvantages. The pay was low even though the government provided billeted lodgings, a 50% discount on meat, and a 30% reduction on certain theater and ballroom tickets. Indeed, the wages for lower-ranking officers just about matched those of a factory worker (See Table 2). Furthermore, soldiers often were treated as social outcasts. The traditional Austrian policy of stationing troops of one ethnic background in areas of another exacerbated old national antagonisms and isolated the soldiers from civilian life. In Vienna, citizens distrusted the soldiers, whom they suspected, sometimes rightly, of theft, brawling, and rape.

Within their own ranks, there was enmity. Tuvora charged in 1844 that arrogant officers hardly bothered about their duties. Instead, they indulged in banquets, hunts and pleasure trips (37). Soldiers and petty officers, however, were closely watched and often beaten for minor infractions. Normann deplored the disrespect for the common soldier: 'A great defect of the Austrian army is the poor treatment of its soldiers. The rank and file and petty officers...are addressed with Er [third person pronoun used with servants] and are [subject to] degrading corporal punishment, flogging, and running the gauntlet.'[18]

But its indignities and hard life aside, the Austrian army also was distinguished by its splendid appearances in public – the stylish uniforms and precision maneuvers of its infantry, cavalry, and artillery, and the well trained military band attached to each regiment. In 1828 Sealsfield gave them uncharacteristic praise: 'But the musical bands of all these regiments and troops are the best of their kind. Their playing is plainly electrifying – "If I want to hear music", Professor

W. from Berlin told me at the performance of Spontini's *Olympia*, "then I go to Austria. Their military marches are more pleasing to me than this entire opera" (14). Baroness Blaze de Bury also attested to their excellence: 'Any real lover of music ought to go to Vienna, if for no other earthly reason than to hear the march of the fourth act of the *Prophete*, played by the military band' (108).

Military bands – According to the research of H. G. Farmer, Austrian military bands, organized around 1741, were small ensembles restricted to infantry and a few artillery units. The musicians were civilians, hired by officers, to accompany the marching and to provide them with evening entertainment (serenades, dinner music, etc.) (72). The instrumentation of these groups (understood as Harmoniemusik), called for eight parts consisting of varying pairs of trumpets, horns, bassoons, oboes or clarinets. Joseph Haydn's *Feldpartiten* or 'Field Suites' are good examples of the genre.

During the last quarter of the eighteenth century, a craze for Turkish Janissary band music swept Europe. The Janissary imitators imparted to most military bands shrill oboes or fifes played in unison and a noisy percussion section of a bass drum, cymbals, triangle, 'jingling Johnnie' (bells on a staff) (Farmer, 76–7). In his Singspiel, *Die Entführung aus dem Serail*, Mozart capitalized on this band craze as well as the then popular 'Turkish harem' plot.

The French Revolution boosted the position of wind band, now employed for public singing and other republican entertainment. Napoleon later drew upon the excellent French wind players in his military bands and directed the creation of new cavalry bands which relied mostly on brass instruments (Farmer, 81). English, Austrian and German bands were influenced profoundly by the French musicians who, like them, often played in the front lines to inspire the soldiers to fight (Farmer, 88).

Drawing upon their own traditions and French reforms, Austrian military bands reached a peak of excellence and influence from *c.*1820 to 1845 (Rameis, 30). Relying on communications between the emperor and the Imperial War Council, Emil Rameis has pointed out that, before 1820, most Austrian military bands were unruly, undisciplined ensembles of 50 to 60 musicians, who wore garish, unmatched outfits and who performed poorly. But after 1820, thanks to such able band masters as Joseph Dobyhall, military bands were reorganized, given uniforms, and trained to play challenging contemporary music (mostly operatic overtures, marches, and dances) (32). Farmer adds that other typical genres included the military concerto (works featuring solo clarinet, horn, or flute), the serenade, and divertimento (dance suite) (100–1).

The new bands reduced their number to about 26 musicians and relied heavily on woodwinds: 2 flutes, 2 oboes, 1 clarinet (in F), 2 clarinets (in C), 2 basset horns (in B♭), 1 serpent (in C), 2 horns, 2 trumpets, 1 tenor trombone, 1 bass trombone, 2 bassoons, 1 contrabassoon, small drum, a great drum, cymbals and triangle (Rameis, 36–7). Soon many of the improvements in brass instruments (keys and valves) changed the bands' makeup. The Austrian Infantry Band in 1827 reflects the changes: 1 piccolo, 2 clarinets (in A♭), 1 clarinet (in E♭), 9 clarinets (in B♭), 1 bassoon, 1 serpent, 2 keyed trumpets (in E♭), 2 trumpets (in A♭), 3 trumpets (in E♭) trumpet (in F), 1 trumpet (in C), 2 horns (in E♭), 2 horns (in A♭), 2 trombones, 1 bass trombone, 1 side drum (Farmer, 99). Farmer points out that, compared to their English counterparts, Austrian bands lacked strength in the bass range, but the technical expertise of each bandsman must have compensated for the instrumentation because, along with Italians, Austro-German band members were actively recruited for British bands (Farmer 95, 99).

Military bands in Vienna were used primarily for parades and military reviews, but their duties often included civic and religious functions as well. Coronations, royal weddings or funerals required ceremonial masses and processions complete with fanfares and military band music. Such religious observances as the Corpus Christi procession were given official sanction with the appearance of regimental bands and the attendance of the emperor. Troops lined the processional route through the city; an artillery unit headed the parade, and a battalion of grenadiers officially ended the procession with a threefold volley (Pezzl, *Beschreibung*, (1820), 131–2).

Newspapers and court records describe other functions in which military bands participated. The emperor's birthday (12 February), for example, was celebrated with great pomp. In Troppau (1820) on that day, the city's theater produced the play *Rudolph von Habsburg* in the emperor's honor, after which the audience sang the national anthem. Then the city's church bells rang, while Franz reviewed the troops en route to the cathedral for a special Te Deum sung in his honor (*Wiener Zeitung*, 3 March 1820, 317). Seven years later in Trieste, the day began with a cannon salute and special Mass. In the evening the theaters produced a new cantata, *Igea*, whose finale culminated with shouts of 'vivat' for the emperor. Then followed the opera, *Mose in Egitto*, with ballet selections during the intermission.[19]

For special events, regiments or noblemen commissioned new music. In 1809, Beethoven wrote a March in F (also known as the 'York March') for Archduke Anton's Bohemian militia band to play at the palace in Laxenburg for the archduke's equestrian exhibition (Kinsky, *Beethoven Verzeichniss*, WoO 18, 457). The next year Beethoven wrote another march for the archduke in honor of Maria Ludovica's nameday (WoO 19). Again in 1816, the 'bürgerliche Artillerie Corps der k.k. Haupt- und Residenzstadt Wien' asked Beethoven to write a piece of band music with Janissary percussion instruments. Agreeing, he wrote a March in D (WoO 24).

In Vienna, military bands played every evening around 11 p.m. at the changing of the guard near the Burgthor. In the summer, once or twice a week, the bands also gave outdoor concerts in a circular pavillion in the Volksgarten. For only 24 kr. entrance fee, one could hear the bands play dance music, marches, and popular operatic works (Blumenbach, I, 156). In 1836, Frances Trollope witnessed a special Volksgarten concert given by two military bands and one civic band in honor of Emperor Ferdinand I's return from Prague, where he had been crowned King of Bohemia. A cannonade commenced the concert of mostly waltzes. Around 9 p.m., the three bands merged under the direction of Joseph Lanner to play marches, a 'Jubilate', and coronation anthems. The presentation ended with a display of fireworks (I, 296–7).

Austrian military bands inspired new music throughout the period. Marches, for parading and dancing, consequently became a large part of the Strausses' output. Among the most popular were the Radetzky March by Johann Strauss Sr and the Kaiser Franz Joseph March by his son. Table 9 lists marches and military music composed by Beethoven, Schubert, and the two Johann Strausses. Many of the titles

Table 9. *A listing of military marches by Beethoven, Schubert and Johann Strauss (I, II)*

Beethoven:

WoO 18 March in F 1809
WoO 19 March in F 1810
WoO 20 March in C 1810 'Zapfenstreiche'
WoO 21 Polonaise in D for Military Band 1810
WoO 22 Ecossaise in D for Military Band 1810
WoO 23 Ecossaise in G for Military Band 1810
WoO 24 March in D 1816
WoO 29 March in B♭ 1820

Schubert (Schubert's military music was originally written for piano duets, but they were subsequently transcribed for band by his contemporaries)

3 Marches héroïques Op. 27	*c.* 1818
3 Marches militaires Op. 51	*c.* 1822
6 Grandes Marches Op. 40	1824
'Nicholas March' – 'Grande March héroïque composée à l'occasion du Sacre de sa Mag. Nicolaus I' in A minor Op. 66	1826
'Alexander March' – 'Grande funèbre à l'occasion de la morte de SM Alexandre I' in C minor Op. 55	1826
2 Marches caractéristiques Op. post. 121	1826
1 Kindermarsch in G (for the nameday of Karl Pachler)	1827

Johann Strauss Sr:

Op. 102 Original-Parade marsch
   144 Parademarsch
   188 Oesterreichischer Festmarsch
   209 Oesterreichischer Defilir-Marsch
   221 National-Garden Marsch
   223 Marsch der Studentenlegion
Op. 226 Freiheits-Marsch
   227 Marsch des einigen Deutschlands. Militär Marsch
   228 Radetzky-Marsch
   231 Brünner-National Garde Marsch
   240 2 Märsche für die spanische Nobelgarde
   244 Jellacic Marsch
   245 Wiener Jubelmarsch
   246 Wiener Stadt-Gardemarsch

Johann Strauss Jr:

Op. 49 Fest-Marsch
   54 Revolutions-Marsch
   56 Studenten-Marsch
   58 Brünner National-Garde Marsch
   67 Kaiser Franz Joseph Marsch
   69 Triumph-Marsch

Table 9 (*cont.*)

77	Wiener Garnisons Marsch
83	Ottinger Reitermarsch
93	Kaiser-Jägermarsch
107	Grossfürsten-Marsch
113	Sachsen Kürassier-Marsch
126	Jubelmarsch
133	Karoussel-Marsch
149	Erzherzog Wilhelm Genesung-Marsch
156	Napoleons-Marsch
158	Alliance-Marsch
212	Fürst Bariatinsky-Marsch
284	Deutscher Krieger-Marsch
289	Persischer Marsch
353	Russische Marsch-Fantasie

Taken from the following indices: Deutsch, *Schubert Catalogue*, 267, 335, 395, 416, 427–8, 482; Kinsky, *Beethoven Verzeichniss*, 456–63; Rudolf Prohaska, *Johann Strauss* (Berlin: n.p., 1900), II, 113–21.

of Strauss marches suggest that they were commissioned by or dedicated to specific regiments – Brünner National-Garde Marsch, Wiener Garnisons Marsch, Sachsen-Kürassier Marsch.

Little is known about the lives and careers of Austrian band musicians except that they continued to hold civilian status beyond 1850, unlike similar musicians in England. Also, unlike either France or England, Austria formed no schools to train its military musicians. An advertisement in the *Wiener Zeitung* (2 March 1820) gives an indication of qualifications required of band masters. Candidates were invited to apply for the vacant position of Kapellmeister of a band attached to an infantry regiment stationed in Galicia (now a part of Poland). The applicants had to be fluent in Czech or Polish, proficient on a brass instrument, and knowledgeable about conducting military music (363). Unfortunately, no other information about the position or band ever followed.

After 1840, Continental military bands declined in comparison with new English bands. Farmer points out that, in 1856, the French closed their military-music academy and that by 1860 all Austrian bands attached to cavalry, chasseur, and artillery units had been disestablished

(137–8). Of course, the remaining Austrian military bands continued to accompany the parades and reviews as well as to give informal concerts in Vienna. But, like the city's sacred institutions, they seemed to lose the will and confidence to improve their ensembles or to foster new, dynamic music.

7

POPULAR MUSIC

From Vienna's ballhouses, inns, and parks poured forth another kind of music whose distinctive style and message had great social significance and came to represent an era and Viennese lifestyle.

BALLROOM DANCING

Dancing was so popular in Vienna that at the time of the Vienna Congress Prince Charles de Ligne is reputed to have said that the Congress danced! (Nicolai, 109–110). Throughout the period writers commented on this Viennese passion and its effect on their character. In 1830 one writer called dancing a 'Viennese obsession' and likened it to an hypnotic transformation: 'In the dance hall, the Viennese is an entirely different person. His spirit, which before was already lethargic, goes into the most formal *sleep* and *trance*, while his body newly revives, and his every nerve trembles in 6/8 time.'[1] In 1844 Joseph Tuvora placed dancing next to eating as Vienna's favorite pastime and claimed that the sensual waltz mirrored the innermost essence of the Viennese character (115). Blaze de Bury even drew an analogy between the love of dancing and the temptation of Eve:

One thing is proved to me, namely that if mother Eve had been a Wienerin, the evil one might not have offered her all the apples in Normandy without success, whereas if he had tempted her with a 'Tanzerl', we her heirs, and the perpetrators of her misdoings, would have gone on twirling like dervishes, and have probably seen 'inordinate love of dancing' take the place of gluttony on the list of the seven capital sins (II, 62).

Balls were evening entertainments, beginning around 8 or 9 p.m. and lasting late into the night. In his guide, Sealsfield explains that men were usually expected to dress formally in black frocks, silk breeches, black stockings, and maroquin shoes (179). For women of the upper and middle classes, ball gowns were an indispensable part of any wardrobe. Wealthy women often owned a number of gowns, with which they wore their finest jewelry or fresh flowers (Trollope, ii, 94–5; 189–91).

Balls were great social occasions for all ages. Usually only the young danced, while the elderly looked on, played cards, or conversed with friends in adjoining rooms. Refreshments consisted of punches, fruit, ices or candy, and were available throughout the evening until about midnight when a supper was served. Dancing resumed until 3 or 4 a.m.

Like the salon, a ball provided a socially acceptable means to make new acquaintances and possibly to meet one's future mate. The diaries of Fritz and Franz Hartmann provide an inkling of what two young men deemed important and interesting at such balls. Both men attended a dance on 10 February 1827, and came away with different impressions. Franz wrote down the names and evaluations of new acquaintances, and described the pleasant task of escorting home one of the young women (Deutsch, *Biography*, 603). Fritz recalled the looks and manners of his dancing partners, and complained about having to dance with the ugliest girl at the party (Deutsch, *Biography*, 604–5). Martha Wilmot summed up the ball's social importance in a letter to her sister, writing, 'no girl will speak to a man who does not dance...' (304).

Dance regulations – As with other public entertainments, balls were subject to Austrian laws. On the following religious and commemorative days, dancing was forbidden: Advent to Epiphany, Ash Wednesday through the first Sunday after Easter, Pentecost, Corpus Christi, Marian feasts, beyond midnight on the eve of a religious holiday, birthdays or namedays of the royal family, and official days of mourning (*Sammlung der Gesetze*, 1828, 450). On Sundays, dancing was not allowed to begin until one hour after the afternoon Mass (and some writers say not until after evening prayers). Hence, dancing on Sundays usually began after 6 p.m. (VA, P.H., 1972/1822; Witzmann, 6).

These requirements also applied to the Austrian provinces and non-Christian residents. A letter to the police marked 'Urgent' and dated 10 March 1822 (during Lent that year) reported that a soirée, given by Hr Bittermann, a Jewish wholesaler formerly of Pressburg, included a performance of an amateur theatrical work and dancing. Such violations were probably common, since a year later the court issued an explicit order forbidding Jews to hold balls during the Lenten season (*Sammlung der Gesetze*, 1822, 472).

In 1822 even the respected actor Heinrich Anschütz was reprimanded by the police for a similar offense. His memoirs tell of a party to which Franz Schubert and other friends had been invited. As part of the festivities, Schubert played a number of his piano works, among which were some dances. (His memoirs are vague about whether the guests actually danced.) Suddenly, the music was interrupted by a passing police commissioner who reminded the actor that, since it was Lent, dancing was not allowed even in the home. He pressed no charges, but warned about the consequences should the music continue. When Anschütz returned to his guests to relate the message, Schubert allegedly remarked that such orders were difficult for him since he loved to play dance music (Anschütz, 266).

All public balls required the prior permission of the police. In this way the ballrooms could be inspected for safety and the police could arrange for uniformed guards or spies if they deemed it necessary to keep order. The regulations also facilitated the collection of a mandatory tax on the music, called Musik Impost. An ordinance of 23 August 1821 declared that every owner of a restaurant in Vienna that offered dancing during the Carnival season would be charged a tax of 4 fl. 30 kr. (for public dances) and 6 fl. (for private balls) (*Sammlung der Gesetze*, 1821, 371–2). A year later, Jäck and Heller mention an additional 15 kr. charged for each musician participating in balls in private homes (284). Hence, even at private Hausbälle, guests were usually asked to help defray the cost of the music. In addition, Hans Pemmer has pointed out that if a ball continued beyond midnight, an additional 45 kr. was added to the tax.[2] Even dance masters giving lessons were charged impost tax, a fee they usually passed on to their students (Witzmann, 17).

Table 10 presents the official record of impost taxes collected in Vienna between the years 1819 and 1830. The figures reflect both the predictably active months during Carnival (January through March), the sudden drop during Lent (March and April), and the slackened

Table 10. *Music impost taxes 1819–30*

	Nov.*	Dec.	Jan.	Feb.	Mar.	Apr.	May	Jun.	Jul.	Aug.	Sep.	Oct.
1819	211·48	200·54	60·48	638·24	419·54	16·36	94·18	84·18	75·00	188·12	168·42	80·36
1820	266·36	80·30	549·24	1,254·54	38·12	none reported	103·30	67·12	98·36	159·30	156·30	43·40
1821	226·48	128·36	136·06	399·00	496·42	none reported	40·36	54·48	67·42	144·06	none reported	271·24
1822	106·12	186·00	259·25	1,169·15	—	288·05	128·35	105·05	146·55	none reported	491·55	177·00
1823	164·10	187·35	510·20	1,012·10	163·45	37·00	161·35	112·50	147·10	250·30	317·05	161·55
1824	208·10	161·30	238·13	714·45	941·35	none reported	74·40	110·40	104·05	189·05	272·50	106·00
1825	255·05	151·23	160·05	116·45	91·55	16·50	81·30	109·30	88·10	230·05	323·05	109·55
1826	192·55	188·00	272·55	1,005·00	9·43	27·15	88·30	88·05	90·00	238·45	302·50	124·10
1827	139·10	186·25	89·35	650·25	780·45	10·00	39·40	101·15	74·40	308·10	223·10	156·15
1828	140·30	204·50	87·40	895·55	284·25	21·05	67·20	80·40	99·05	205·30	310·05	146·40
1829	189·40	191·55	55·55	458·25	966·30	none reported	40·20	98·45	95·10	272·05	200·00	160·20
1830	118·20	170·10	85·40	537·10	572·50	23·20	21·10	106·45	113·20	212·25	201·50	109·10

Total tax:

1819 – 2,239.30 fl.	1823 – 3,226.05 fl.	1827 – 2,759.50 fl.
1820 – 2,818.34	1824 – 3,121.33	1828 – 2,543.45
1821 – 1,965.48	1825 – 2,704.20	1829 – 2,729.05
1822 – 3,058.27	1826 – 2,627.43	1830 – 2,272.10

Taken from: WStA, Oberkämmeramt, 'Empfänge' for the years 1819–30.

* The arrangement of the months is by 'Military Year'. All figures have been converted into CM (the change to CM began in January 1822 in the municipal accounts).

activity in the summer. But the totals for each year also show a peak between the years 1822 to 1824 and an erratic decline toward 1830. No city records, current events, or eyewitness accounts, however, offer an explanation for the fluctuation.

Often stricter rules were imposed on dances in rural Austrian provinces. During the previous century (1751) a young girl could be sent to prison if she were caught three times staying too late at a ball; a young man could be handed over to the military recruiters for two of the same offenses (Witzmann, 7). The mass of old dance regulations for the provinces of Bohemia, Silesia, and Moravia were combined and updated in 1827. The new rules emphasize the need to inform the police of any costume balls and social dances even if given in private homes. On holidays, dancing was forbidden until after the day's Mass, and it was permitted until midnight in provincial towns and only until 10 p.m. in small villages. Organizers of public dances were responsible for maintaining order at all times. If the dancers refused to leave, or if musicians played beyond the closing hours, both the dancers and players were liable to fines or arrest.[3] In addition, a music impost tax of 1 fl. (for towns and market places) and 40 kr. (for smaller villages) was charged (*Sammlung der Gesetze*, 1830, 4).

The Viennese municipal government regulated the times and location of certain dances through the granting of official dance-hall status, Tanzsaalprivilegium. Such privileged halls differed from regular inns that offered dance music in that they were larger, had 'better music', and required 'respectable' attire of their guests. They could also advertise their balls in journals and handbills and could charge an admission fee (Witzmann, 8–9). These advantages were great because the halls could offer dancing year round, stay open later each night, and would have to renew their licenses much less frequently.

Police records of an investigation of one dance hall in 1821 illustrate the kinds of concern in granting the privilege. Aloys Persa, Hofrat of Police, reported that the inn, Zum Stadtgut, had received the status of Tanzsaal. But, when district police inspected the premises, they judged the place to be 'more like a tavern than a public dance hall', despite the efforts of the owner to enlarge and better decorate the rooms. In addition, they reported that the clientele consisted of mostly lower-class tradespeople, apprentices, and servants, with 'seldom a single respectable middle-class family'. Furthermore, a dance hall next door was reputed to have been a regular haunt of soldiers and prostitutes, where many 'excesses' had been committed in the past, which neither the inn's owner nor the local civil police could contain. Thus Persa requests that the inn's privileges be revoked, since the rooms were too small to qualify as a dance hall, the district did not employ sufficient policemen to protect the patrons and the neighbors, and the neighborhood could contribute to the 'ruin of the morals of the lower classes' (VA, P.H., 8038–1821).

Carnival balls – Vienna's most elaborate festive balls were reserved for Carnival or Fasching season, which began after Epiphany (6 January) and lasted until midnight on the eve of Ash Wednesday. Since Lent is not a fixed feast, Carnival could last several months, although the church attempted to limit very long seasons.[4] To the Englishwoman, Martha Wilmot, it was a 'most absurd thing' that the year's balls were crammed into one season (219–20), but, for the Viennese, carnival was a welcome time of concentrated revelry and dancing. In 1809 Reichardt called the dancing a 'mania' (I, 322). Anecdotes about fashionable balls dominated conversation; socialites vied for invitations to the most prestigious fêtes; and one was inevitably obliged to attend balls arranged by one's relatives and business associates.

The Carnival also brought lucrative business opportunities, for the countless balls created a demand for ball apparel, party delicacies, banquets, entertainments, party favors, and gifts. Viennese music publishers offered new collections of dance music for the home, and musical souvenirs of each Carnival or of a particular dance hall. Composers also took advantage of the demand by composing dance music or novelties to be performed during festive balls. Accordingly, Franz Schubert contributed new waltzes, galops, and quadrilles to special Carnival anthologies every year from 1822 through 1828 (see Illus. 7):

11 Feb. 1822	Neueste Tanzmusik zum Carneval 1822, Cappi-Diabelli.
10 Jan. 1823	Neue Tanzmusik/Carneval 1823, Sauer-Leidesdorf.
31 Jan. 1824	Halt's enk z'samm, Sauer-Leidesdorf.
21 Feb. 1824	Der beliebte neue Tanz. Galoppes und Eccosaien, Sauer-Leidesdorf.

7   Titlepage of *Halt's enk z'samm* ('Hold on tight') – *A Collection of Original Austrian Ländler for the Pianoforte*, by Moritz von Schwind 1824
    (Historisches Museum der Stadt Wien; Inv. Nr. 66.085)

8 Jan. 1825	Tanz-Musikalien für Karneval 1825, Cappi & Co.
20 Jan. 1826	Fünfzig Neue Walzer, Sauer-Leidesdorf.
11 Jan. 1827	Neue Krähwinkler Tänze, Sauer-Leidesdorf.
22 Jan. 1827	Valses nobles, Haslinger.
10 Jan. 1828	Grätzer Walzer, Haslinger.[5]

Entrepreneurs were able to reap big profits from public Carnival balls only if they managed to attract large crowds and were careful about controlling costs. Ball expenses could be staggering judging from financial records of the public balls given in the Redoutensaal, the Apollosaal, and a private ball given by Prince Johann Adolf II von Schwarzenberg (presented in Table II). The itemized list from the Schwarzenberg ball reveals that lighting costs (which included the candles, fixtures, and labor) alone equalled the annual salary of a Kapellmeister! Lighting for a ball in the Apollosaal likewise was expensive – about 42% of the total expense. The total costs for each of the balls in the Redoutensaal averaged about 1,500 fl. The Schwarzenberg ball cost more than ten times as much.

But, if the expenses were high, so too were the profits. The earnings from the balls in the Redoutensaal, also shown in the table, easily outweighed the expense. An average of about 7,500 fl. was raised each year.

The Carnival season reached its peak on its last day, called *Fastnacht* or Faschingdienstag. Revelry began early in the morning. Luncheon was served between 2 and 4 p.m. followed by more dancing. At 6 the guests retired to change into more formal evening attire. Dancing resumed shortly thereafter. At midnight, the music ceased and the crowds dispersed to attend church in observance of the beginning of Lent. In the Redouten halls, the 'elegant world' made a traditional silent procession once through the ballroom at midnight to close the Carnival officially (Trollope, II, 104–39, 170, 182; Hebenstreit, 143; Pietznigg, 32).

The Carnival season of 1823 was so brilliant that it warranted a number of chronicles. Despite the specter of cholera, which plagued the city the previous year, F. A. Kürlander estimated that Vienna held no fewer than 772 balls, which were attended by over 200,000 persons (Pictznigg, 152). The official count of balls that season reveals that many of the balls were held in the suburbs, especially in large restaurants like the Casino, Sperl, and Zum Römischen Kaiser (Schmidl, 24). The number of tickets sold to the two balls in the Redoutensaal that year also indicates that about four thousand people attended.

In 1832 the season's most successful events were two children's balls sponsored respectively by the Russian embassy and by Lord Cowley. At these, children of aristocrats and wealthy families dressed and danced with all the regalia and pomp of their adult counterparts (Pietznigg, 26–7). Kürlander relates that other balls offered diverse entertainment as well. One ambassador presented a French comedy; the banker Geymüller arranged special party games. In addition to the balls given by foreign dignitaries and royalty, balls were held by the Musikverein, and by charitable organizations (Pietznigg, 26–39 *passim*).

One of the most popular types of Carnival ball was the masquerade. Once banned by the police because they were considered too

Table 11. *Financial records of balls*
Accounts of masked balls in the Redoutensaal 1831–4

1831 Masked balls on 6, 10, 15 February		
Masked Flora–Devisen ball	3,222 tickets @ 2.00 fl.	6,444·00 fl. CM
Masked Fest ball	235 tickets @ 2.00	470·00
Masked ball	2,968 tickets @ 2·00	5,936·00
	Total	12,850·00
Expenses		−2,395·09
	Total Profit	10,454·51
1832 Masked balls in March		
Masked ball	633 tickets @ 1.36 fl.	1,012·48
Masked ball	3,313 tickets @ 2.00	6,626·00
	Total	7,638·48
Expenses		−1,381·31
	Total Profit	6,257·17
1833 Masked balls on 14, 19 February		
Masked ball	462 tickets @ 1.36 fl.	739·12
Masked ball	3,682 tickets @ 2.00	7,364·00
	Total	8,103·12
Expenses		−1,375·46
	Total Profit	6,727·26
1834 Masked balls on 6, 11 February		
Masked ball	1,338 tickets @ 1.36 fl.	2,140·48
Masked ball	4,036 tickets @ 2.00	8,072·00
	Total	10,212·48
Expenses		−1,994·46
	Total Profit	8,218·02

Taken from HHStA, R-42 Redouten Säle 1835.

dangerous, by 1826 masked balls were permitted in Vienna and certain provincial capitals, but only during Carnival and with special restrictions. Apparently their appeal declined from the eighteenth century, for by 1815 many persons attended masked balls without costumes or masks – a situation that occurs in Strauss' operetta *Die*

Table 11 (cont.)
Apollosaal – expenses for 1 evening ball in 1824

Hr Lanner for music	300.00 fl. WW	120.00 fl. CM
Lighting of office	11.00	4.24
Wax candles (140 @ 2.30)	350.00	140.00
Gardener	25.00	10.00
Oil for misc. lighting	37.46	15.00
1½ cords of wood (transport, labor)	57.12	22.48
Military guard	33.00	13.12
Police guard	20.00	8.00
Coach porters	67.30	27.00
Hanging of signs	3.00	1.12
Cleaning of ballroom (½ price)	35.00	14.00
Lighting, cleaning, removal of candles	12.00	4.48
3 dance inspectors, 1 dance master		
@ 2.30 @ 12.30	20.00	8.00
Heater @ 3.00; porter @ 10.00	13.00	5.12
English *Retiratmacher* (?)	5.00	2.00
Chimney sweep	7.00	2.48
Lighting of fires	2.30	1.00
Washing of terrace	4.48	1.54
Lighting of candles	12.30	5.00
2 coaches	4.00	1.36
Total	1,020.16 fl. WW	*c.* 408.00 fl. CM

Taken from Stöger, 'Apollo Saal', 62.
Note: Conversions to CM have been rounded off to the nearest kr.

Table 11 (cont.)
Expenses of a ball given by Prince Johann Adolf II Schwarzenberg in 1840

18 February 1840	
Food	1,912.20½ fl. CM
Lighting	1,598.45
Heating	222.24
Music	182.46½
Labor	13,346.40½
Miscel.	1,254.21½
Total	18,517.18 fl. CM

Taken from Stekl, 149.

Fledermaus. Instead, 'theme' balls as the Fratschl or Washmaidl balls – with everyone dressed in similar costumes usually depicting members of the lower classes – gained popularity during the nineteenth century (Witzmann, 4–5).

The masked ball was a favorite, largely because of the air of mystery and intrigue engendered by the costumes and masks which hid one's identity and age. Schönholz wrote that masked balls were the arena for every kind of affair: diplomatic plots, court intrigues, amorous flirtations, and marriage proposals (74). Hence they gained the reputation of being a 'playground for the city's adventurers and a favorite haunt of married women and widows', according to Tuvora (62).

Most of Vienna's masquerades were held in the Redouten halls located next to the Winter Riding School in the palace (see Illus. 8). The larger of the two halls had an area of 674 meters and a height of 15 meters (Stöger, 24). A travel guide from 1829 reports that there three major masked balls were held during the Carnival: the third Sunday in Carnival, the last Thursday in Carnival (known as 'fat Thursday') and on the last day of Carnival (Hebenstreit, 143). These balls drew huge mobs of up to six thousand persons and observers often complained that the ventilation was very poor and that the ballrooms were unbearably hot and stuffy (Reichardt, 1, 324).

An anonymous Bavarian attended a Viennese masquerade in the Redoutensaal in 1804. He was impressed by the large number of police and cavalrymen stationed outside the halls to direct traffic and keep order. Inside he described adjoining rooms which provided masks, refreshments and uninterrupted dance music performed by a large orchestra. He noticed that, in spite of the costumes, certain class distinctions were still observed, since members of the court did not dance, and aristocrats danced only sedate quadrilles, if they danced at all. But in general, the man was surprised by the lack of troublemakers and rowdiness – features, he said that were common at similar balls in Berlin (*Bemerkungen*, 119–20).

To combat the risqué image of the masked ball, some dance-hall managers devised 'subscription' balls for respectable people. For such balls, guests were required to sign up and buy tickets in advance. The

8   Formal masquerade ball at the k.k. Redoutensaal *c.* 1815 (Historisches Museum der Stadt Wien, Inv. Nr. 19.877)

resulting guest lists aided those seeking to avoid any disreputable persons, they alerted the police to potential civil unrest, and they provided the ball organizers with a means of collecting any unpaid bills incurred by the guests during the ball (Pietznigg, 34).

Ballroom music — At festive balls, orchestras usually provided the music. Karl Postl counted around fifteen to twenty instrumentalists in 1828 who performed in galleries above or behind the ballroom. The ensembles varied widely, but stringed instruments usually provided the foundation for the melody and harmony.

  Most balls began with a formal promenade accompanied by march music, allemandes, or polonaises. The opening Grand March of a gala costume ball in Vienna given in 1826 by the English ambassador, Sir Henry Wellsley, was impressive by all accounts:

...the company assembled, and the procession, arranged according to quadrille, began. The glistening of jewels and embroideries eclipsed the thousands of tapers, and the dazzled eye could scarcely endure the splendor arising from the union of the utmost magnificence and the highest elegance. A page, as a herald, preceded each quadrille and the name of the novel, to which characters belonged was displayed on a banner.[6]

Another formal ball held in 1834 opened with a polonaise and a cotillion. The orchestra of between fifteen and twenty musicians played three chords to announce a special 'chain dance', which was accompanied by castanets and hand clapping. The remainder of the evening was filled with acceleration waltzes and a final allemande (*Seufzer*, 111).

Throughout the 1820s, the quadrille, a contredance consisting of at least five different sections and performed by four couples standing in square formations, was popular in Vienna. By 1831, when the English had begun to favor the galop or gallopade, the older quadrille retained its Viennese following (Strang, 312–13). As late as 1844, Tuvora even claimed that the quadrille had usurped the waltz (115)!

But no dance is more closely associated with Vienna than the waltz. In 1829 waltz music permeated every corner of the city, much to the disapproval of Mary and Vincent Novello. About a group of musicians playing in the Caroline gardens, Mary wrote: 'The performers here were of a better class than those I heard before at the Volksgarten, but the pieces they played were not a wit better, nothing but waltzes, eternal commonplace waltzes. Germany really appears to me at present the land of galops, waltzes, and Quadrilles' (161). Nine years later, Frances Trollope also was disappointed by the honor accorded popular music: 'Vienna is in truth just now suffering severely from an access [*sic*] of waltzes, and rococo Haydn, Mozart and the like are banished from 'ears polite' while Strauss and Lanner rule the hour' (1, 372).

At first the waltz was controversial because of the close position of the dancers, its 'suggestive' turns, and the unhealthful exertion (Carner, 20–1; Witzmann, 47–51). Glassbrenner best expresses the image of the Viennese waltz as a sensual madness or Totentanz:

In Vienna, however, this frenzy has become degenerated. One no longer sees dancers there, but only Bacchantes. The women feverishly thrill as soon as they are touched by the arm of the man, then they press their breast close to his, their head on his shoulder, and now they let themselves be swept about, imbibing in this voluptuous posture with every movement of the man and that lascivious music; imploringly innocence flees, terrified from the hall, femininity drags itself beseechingly at their feet, and death stands in the corner and laughs up his sleeve.[7]

Martha Wilmot also worried about the health of the young dancers: 'While it [Carnival] lasts the young people almost dance themselves to death, and then the last thing is a Ridout [= Redoute or 'masked ball'] where the *cram* and *mob* is suffocating, the dancing and music maddening' (219–20). Despite the apparent absurdity, such worries were not without foundation. The strenuous whirling dancing by tight-corseted women often caused them to faint. The clouds of dust whipped into the air by their skirts aggravated respiratory ailments, a common Viennese malady. Even when some ballrooms washed down their floors with water during intermissions, the rooms filled with dust (*Das constitutionelle Dresden*, 71; Witzmann, 12). Others suffered heart attacks and strokes while dancing.

Other writers condemned the secondary effects of dancing. Tuvora, for example, believed that the waltz magnified the worst weaknesses of the Viennese character – their apathy toward spiritual and intellectual pursuits and their overdeveloped sensual appetites (118). Those interested in political reform blamed the waltz for pacifying the will of the populace. Eduard Boas suggested in 1834 that the only way the Viennese would turn out to revolt would be if Strauss played waltzes long enough to collapse the 'old legs' of the aristocracy (141). And in 1836 Langenschwarz asserted that the dance 'inflamed the head, clouded the brain, aroused sexual appetites, and quashed any thought of revolution'. Just as the press ordinances of Charles X had caused a riot, he continues, only prohibitive measures against dancing would turn the Viennese against the emperor (22–3).

Suburban dance halls – Most of Vienna's twenty or thirty dance halls were located in the suburbs and catered to middle- and lower-class families. On Sundays, the only free day for most workers, the inns and dance halls were crowded with couples, children, and families. A few of these were notable and were praised by travel guides or memoirs.

The Mondschein auf der Wieden in Matzleinsdorf was described in 1785 by Friedrich Nicolai as a place where one could find many merchants, well-to-do citizens and families of civil servants. 'Everything was respectable' (127). A ball announcement in 1820 which describes the hall's interior mentions that the first and second floors provided candlelit dining tables where the manager promised his guests 'true' drinks and prompt service. The dance floor accommodated about twenty couples, who could dance to the music of Josef Wilde, Josef and Johann Faistenberger, and Valentin Czeyka, the inn's music director. On that same occasion, the ball was to begin at 8 p.m. with a polonaise from the ballet *Das Waldmädchen*, and it lasted until 5 a.m. Admission was a modest 2 fl. WW (48 kr. CM) (*Wiener Zeitung*, 5 February 1820, 189).

The Mondschein gained infamy for its Langaus dance, a strenuous, fast, forward-turning dance, which Adolf Bäuerle wrote caused the physical collapse of many dancers.

The Mondschein-Saal made an immortal name for itself by the mortality among the young people who visited it, and there danced nothing but the Langaus. At that time it was the fashion to be a dashing dancer, and the man had to waltz his partner from one end of the hall to the other with the greatest possible speed. If one round of the immense hall had been considered sufficient, one might perhaps have allowed this bacchantic dance to pass. But the circle had to be made six to eight times at a breathless speed and without pause. Each couple tried to outdo the other and it was no rare thing for an apoplexy of the lungs to put an end to the madness. Such frightful intermezzi finally made the police forbid the Langaus. (Schenk, 301–2; Carner, 25)

The ban on the dance proclaimed in 1791 had to be reaffirmed in 1794, 1803, and 1804. A fine of 20 fl. was threatened if owners allowed the dance in their halls. But the repeated bans and warnings testify to the continued practice of the dance and probably increased its popularity (Witzmann, 51–2).

The Sperl, in Leopoldstadt, was a beloved meeting place for middle-class families on Sundays and holidays. In importance, Heinrich Laube compared Metternich to the Sperl: 'The former is the minister of the exterior and the latter the minister of the interior!'[8] He also characterized the hall's clientele as typically Viennese: 'To be sure no *haute volée* gather there, it is a very mixed society. But the ingredients

Die hüpfen, als ob sie kalte Füße hätten. —   Das nennt man begeistert Krauteintreten

9   Examples of dances probably done in suburban dance halls
(Schliemann, *Schattenbilder*, 145)

are not to be taken lightly, and the mixture is classic Viennese.'[9] Later
studies concur that the Sperl represented middle-class, Viennese social
solidarity and affluence (Aspöck, 35–6) (see Illus. 9).

The Sperl was known for such Viennese delicacies as Backhuhn and
Krapfen, as well as for its music and dance floor, which held about
two hundred people (Jäck and Heller, 288). Also famous were its
orchestra and conductors, many of whom were talented composers:
Michael Pamer (1820), Reichmann (1826–8), Josef Lanner (1829), and
Johann Strauss Jr (1829–36) (Pemmer, 155).

On special occasions the Sperl presented concerts by brass bands in
combination with its orchestra. A ball announcement from 25 August
1830, advertised a 'Great Ball Festival', promising an evening of
entertainment and music, directed by and for the benefit of Johann
Strauss. Strauss was to direct the forty-five piece orchestra while
Nowak directed the trumpet corps from the regiment of Count Giulay.
Strauss promised to perform the waltzes, 'Gute Meinung für die
Tanzlust', 'Wälzer a la Hietzing', and the 'Einzugs-Galop', and to
première 'Souvenir de Baden'. The whole evening cost only 30 kr.
CM and lasted from 7 p.m. to 5 a.m. (GdMf, Concert Program,
'Grosses Ballfest im Saal zum Sperl').

Once a flour depot in the Neuer Markt, the Mehlgrube, a hotel and dance hall, first catered only to aristocrats. By 1716, however, members of the middle class were admitted, thus making the Mehlgrube the oldest bourgeois dance hall in Vienna. In 1798 it was refurbished in 'Italian style' and reopened as a public dance hall (Pemmer, 194). The Jäck-and-Heller guide from 1829 reports that for only 1 fl. WW (24 kr. CM), one gained admission and that dance music was performed from 8 p.m. to 3 a.m. (284). During the Carnival of 1832, Kürlander wrote that 4 fl. CM covered the cost of admission, supper, and refreshments for the Mehlgrube's subscription ball, which, he adds, even some noblemen attended (Pietznigg, 36). The hall's facilities were put to other uses as well. In 1819, for instance, Franz Gebauer presented the first of his Concerts Spirituels, concerts of sacred and instrumental music (Deutsch, *Biography*, 212). No writers mention anything about the hall's accoustics, however.

The largest and most extravagant of the suburban dance halls was the Apollosaal, in Mariahilf, built by Sigmund Wohlffsohn, an English inventor and entrepreneur.[10] The Apollosaal had a narrow, long dance floor (in proportion of length to width, 4:1), with adjoining coves and 'modern' smooth, polished floor to facilitate the newer fast dances (Witzmann, 9). At the height of its splendor (roughly 1808 to 1820), the Apollosaal attracted heads of state and aristocrats, who marveled at its exotic decor, fountains, and lighting effects. In 1809 Reichardt called it 'an entirely strange, fantastic monster of splendor and variety, which, when illuminated, however, had a totally dazzling, magical effect' (160).

From 1 to 5.30 in the afternoon, the Apollosaal served meals in its gardens while music was performed in the background. After 5 p.m., for an additional 1 fl. WW (24 kr. CM), one could dance in the ballroom (Jäck and Heller, 285, n. 21).

The music in the Apollosaal was admired throughout Vienna. The orchestra, located overhead, was relatively large (57 pieces). Josef Hummel, the father of the pianist and composer Johann, was the first conductor, and after 1819 he was followed by many talented men, including Sigmund Sperber, Thomas Storch, Mathias Schwarz, and Josef Lanner. Some composers wrote music specially for the hall. For its gala opening in 1808, Johann Nepomuk Hummel composed twelve

Der „Walzerkönig" trägt seine Krone
Mit Würde und kühlem Blut;
Doch auch sein Bruder ist nicht ohne —
Ihm steht halt das Tanzen so gut.

10   The two younger Strauss brothers – 'Waltz kings'
(Schliemann, *Schattenbilder* 9)

Minuets and Trios (Op. 27); and later Johann Strauss Sr wrote
'Apollo-Walzer' (Op. 128), possibly in memory of the hall.

But in 1821, Jäck and Heller admit that the hall's elegance and prestige had declined. The admission price for men sank from 10 fl. WW
(4 fl. CM) to a mere 30 kr. Women entered free (284). By the 1830s,
the hall had further deteriorated so much that respectable families no
longer attended. The hall went bankrupt soon thereafter. Converted
into a candle factory in 1839, the Apollosaal was destroyed by fire
in 1876.

The suburban dance halls would probably be ignored by modern
historians were it not for their orchestras and compositions by Josef
Lanner, Franz Morelli, and Johann Strauss, who launched and advanced
their musical careers there and who dedicated many of their finest
dances to the halls (Illus. 10).

The meteoric rise to fame of Vienna's waltz kings began late in the

1820s and continued throughout the century.[11] In 1833 Hans Normann called Johann Strauss Sr the 'darling of the Viennese', and claimed that his music issued from every piano in the city. Josef Lanner he classified as 'good, but too sluggish and slow'; Morelli he called 'more a musician than an artist' (Normann, 39). The following year, Strauss, Lanner and Morelli were again named as the best dance composers in Vienna. For example, the satirical *Hans Jörgel* journalist wrote that Strauss' compositions were as valuable as ostrich feathers; Lanner had the variety of a nightingale; and Morelli gave the impression of a blackbird that sang sweetly when the weather was fair.[12] To this list a German visitor added the name of Czermak. The writer was impressed not only by the music, but also by the sensitivity and execution of his orchestra: 'The musical corps is reliable and every instrument so fervent that everything is one bow, one note, one crescendo, one fortissimo or piano. Seldom have I heard wind instruments so delicately handled as at the Zwei Tauben [a dance hall] where Lanner's group, under his direction, performed from 6–11 p.m.'[13] He claimed that Morelli and Czermak were fashionable, but he correctly predicted that their fame would not outlast that of Strauss (*Meine grosse Reise*, 79).

Thus Vienna's suburban dance halls provided not only entertainment for the city's working classes, but also a good livelihood for talented musicians from the lower classes. The great demand for new dance music for these halls promoted competition and experimentation that contributed to the high quality and unique character of the classical Viennese waltz. Around 1830, at a time when the music in the city's public concerts and private salons was not very distinguished, the suburban dance halls and restaurants fostered the only new and lasting music – a music which clearly reflected the city's predominantly bourgeois taste. That the Viennese waltz earned respectability by gaining admittance to concert halls, opera houses, and foreign courts throughout Europe testifies not only to the excellence and wide appeal of the music itself, but also to the growing influence and power of the working classes in artistic matters.

Popular music

To Vienna's lower classes, the neighborhood family restaurants (Gasthäuser), coffee houses, taverns, and public parks served as both salon and concert hall. For, wherever food and drink were served, folk and popular music was performed by folk singers or small bands of instrumentalists. In 1836 Blumenbach praised these establishments and ranked them above any in Paris or London:

I don't know of any town, not even Paris, where the citizens have so many pleasurable resorts as those of Vienna. The many public coffee-houses, ball-rooms, Lusthausen [sic] (pleasure houses), with numerous concerts, are all open to them at trifling expense. For from twelve to forty-eight Kreutzer, a much less sum than each of many thousands of all ages and sexes in London pay on Sunday for *blue ruin* [gin?], the tradespeople, high and low, at Vienna, amuse themselves once a week, or oftener, at a ball or concert, and the military bands play to them every evening for nothing. (I, 156).

Most restaurants offered light Tafelmusik consisting of marches, quodlibets, dance music, and popular songs. But in some of the larger establishments, like Zum roten Igl, Zum römischen Kaiser or Gasthaus alla Biedermeier, the musicians often played operatic overtures, or sections from symphonies by Gluck, Haydn, Mozart, or Beethoven.[14]

Vienna's wine and beer halls featured zither music and folk singers. Zither players usually played solo dance music and folk tunes, but sometimes they encouraged the audience to provide accompaniment. Hans Normann explains, 'Songs without text are performed in beerhalls usually by a zither player, while those who are present whistle and clap along. A few even achieve virtuosity on this instrument, such as the world famous Viennese Bierwirth Heiligschein, who even plays concerti on the zither.'[15] Normann also provides two musical examples that may have been performed by such musicians (Illus. 11). The first, 'Hernålser Dånz' (dance of Hernals, a Viennese suburb), contains the characteristic triple dance meter, simple melody, and grace notes often heard in zither music. But the phrase structure of the second period (measures 9–19) is irregular. The second example, 'Volkslied', illustrates a simple, triadic melody in Bar form, with typical grace notes by thirds – a feature of many yodeling songs – and short, balanced phrases.

11 Two zither tavern songs

Translation: Swaying in the meadow stands a pear tree with leaves, and what grows on the pear tree, a lovely nest. Nest on the tree in the meadow, swaying in the meadow stands a pear with leaves.

(Normann, 37)

Folksingers, called Bänkelsänger, sang ballads and other popular songs, accompanying themselves on harps or guitars. Franz Rebiczek's research found that the folksingers improvised recitative-like strophes which they accompanied with simple chords. Typically the songs were about historical events, catastrophes, sensational crimes, or about contemporary public figures (46–7). The best of the songs often were

— „frische Würstel g'fällig — vom letzten Distanzritt!"   Ein „Blumenmädchen" vom Graben, genannt „die g'schoppte Flora".

12   Other Viennese street hawkers
(Schliemann, *Schattenbilder*, 147)

printed as broadsides and sold on the streets. Normann was fascinated by the colorful saleswomen hawking music:

> In Vienna a real business is also done in songs, and even in the city one finds on the open street an impressive assortment of 'entirely new worldly songs, which we have just received'. Such saleswomen of songs either walk along the streets or have their own selling place where sacred and secular songs hang on a line, with the stories of the four Heumann children, of Genovesa, the illustrated presentation of all the ages of man, the wicked world, the man who is beaten by his wife, and vice-versa, a microscopic enlargement of a flea, and such.[16]

Usually the songs sold for a groschen near the Jägerhorn am Neubau or on the upper Jesuitenplatz. Professional music publishers later collected some of the songs and made large profits by printing them in anthologies (Werner, 7)

Sometimes the musicians joined forces to present costumed, theatrical scenes or to perform 'folk cantatas' (Weis, lvi). In 1796 and 1797, for instance, Ludwig Bleibtreun, a folksinger and worker in a publishing company, published the texts of his cantatas for singer and harp. *Bund der Treue*, a 'small cantata by Ludwig Bleibtreun, sung by the harpists

Leopold Bürger and Sebastian Frohnhofter (1796)', commemorated Austria's entrance into the war with France.[17] *Unser Dank* (1797), another cantata with music by Bürger, celebrated the surrender of Mantua. Both works contained recitatives, arias, and choruses accompanied by folksingers' harps or guitars. Other groups were families such as the Familie Linnbrunner, Scharinger, Kwapili, Herzog, and Früholz (Schlögl, 158).

Although most of Vienna's folk singers were known only to small local audiences, a few gained wide popularity and are known by name today. Johann Schmutzer was a guitar, zither and violin virtuoso; Stelzmüller was known for his dances; and Petzmayer was reputed to have been the city's best zither player (Ludwig, 7). Prominent around 1830 was Johann Baptist Moser (pseudonym for J. B. Müller, died 1863), son of a pedlar, who turned from teaching school to become a folk singer in 1829. First playing the harp, he later turned to the piano for accompaniment in the inns Zur Bretze and Zum Grünen Tor in Lerchenfeld. Eventually he organized a society for folksingers and gained for them a greater respectability. Amalie Zeidler was also a popular folk singer in the Griechen Beisl. Both she and Moser gained national recognition for their music and story-telling skills (Werner, 19).

Also performing in Vienna's taverns, but more often in the city's parks or from door to door, were itinerant harpists (Boas, 98–9). The harpists were notorious for their quick, biting wit and their ability to satirize even the most serious subjects in improvised, rhyming verses, sung to the accompaniment of harps (Schmidl, 23). Viennese audiences apparently enjoyed the harpists and repeatedly saw them as stock characters in their folk comedies. However, foreigners were usually offended by their vulgarity and cruel insults (Werner, 19). Building upon this reputation, in his play, *Die gefesselte Phantasie*, Raimund features a harpist, called Nachtigall (nightingale), who uses his wit and insults to wring a few Kreutzer from a foreigner in a local beerhall (Act I, xx). Even Glassbrenner, a satirist himself, was wholly unsympathetic to the humor of the harpists:

In the Wurstelprater and in Lerchenfeld sit Father, Mother, son and daughter, and all laugh heartily over the most poisonous, smutty jokes which, sugared over with clever melodies, come out of the mouths of so-called harpists and are accompanied by graphic expressions and gestures to heighten their effect...[18]

Although most of the harpists' songs are now lost, Eduard Boas recorded one of the song texts in his travel notes. Devised by an unnamed harpist, the poem would surely have been banned had it been printed in Austria:

In Schönbrunn, sagt er	In Schönbrunn, says he
Is an Aff, sagt er	Is an ape, says he
Hat a G'sicht, sagt er	Has a face, says he
Wie a Pfaff, sagt er	Like a priest, says he
Frisst an Zucker, sagt er	Feeds on sugar, says he
Sauft an Wein, sagt er	Swills on wine, says he
So an Aff	Such an ape
Möcht' i sein.	I'd like to be.

(98–9)

The obvious point of the song is that not only was Schönbrunn the site of the municipal zoo, but it also was the summer palace of the emperor.

The police received many complaints about the harpists from their informers. A lengthy report by Sedlnitzky to the first chancellor, Sauer, dated 1821, lodges an official protest against harpists, yodelers, and other 'music makers' who performed in the city's beerhouses and taverns, and whose 'immoral and irreligious songs' offended the audiences (VA, P.H., IV-M-7, Ministerium von Inneren, Carton 1370, 1821) (Illus. 13). But the lack of subsequent information, and reports that harpists continued to perform their songs throughout the 1820s and 1830s, suggest that the police actually took few measures to silence them. Rather, the police tended to ignore the musicians until they posed a real threat. In 1831, a letter by a man named Adalbert Zaleisky (his position is unknown) reveals that the police had been warned recently of some satirical songs circulating among tavern musicians. Claiming that the musicians stirred up the lower classes by alluding to contemporary events, Zaleisky calls for renewed watchfulness by the police to isolate and punish any offender.[19] Whether the police heeded the advice is unknown.

The seeming tolerance of harpists by the police in spite of the former's poor reputation and the government's stringent regulations of speech again illustrates the paradoxical and arbitrary nature of law enforcement in Vienna. As long as the harpists, social outcasts, entertained the working classes who remained deeply loyal to the

— „Tauch an Schackerl, was thät'n denn d'Leut
sag'n, wann um Zwölfe no' ka Werkel da wär!"

13   Street musicians with a barrel organ
(Schliemann, *Schattenbilder*, 131)

emperor, the government could afford to tolerate a modicum of free speech.

In a class even below the harpists were other itinerant street musicians, who were little more than beggars or vagabonds, and many of whom were blind, crippled, or maimed. Although begging was officially forbidden in Vienna, scores of unfortunates lined the city walls and hid in dark passages. In 1830, Meynert observed how some were experts in displaying their deformities to play upon the sympathies of passers-by, but that when money was thrown, they became veritable gymnasts to retrieve it (79). Four years later, J. B. Weis commented on their music:

Yet, in order to hear music, one need not even visit a tavern, for in the city there is not a single so-called Durchhaus (that is, where one can arrive, through two facing gates, from one street into another) where, because no peddling is allowed, there does not stand a boy or girl with a harp or guitar. These are mostly blind, or half-idiotic, pitiful creatures, who seek their sustenance through their playing.[20]

Such poor street musicians seemed to be accepted and pitied by Viennese residents. Certainly they left lasting impressions on Vienna's visitors. Boas described a certain blind woman who always moved her audiences to tears with her flute (192). In 1830 Meynert was struck by the playing of a lame organ grinder. He remembered the man's whimpering voice and watery eyes 'that always looked so dejected', and 'with his worn out songs he always strangely knew how to accompany the true melody of my heart...they [the songs] sound so simple, so sweetly attuned to our hearts, like an ancient folk tale which everyone can know and recite, and which stands unnoticed high above the everyday.'[21] Both Wilhelm Müller and Franz Schubert must have had similar reactions, for their poem and song 'Der Leiermann' projects just such a pathetic person. With 'numb fingers' and 'barefoot on the icy ground', the musician plays incessantly to an unfeeling, uncaring world. The music's unchanging open-fifth drone and repetitive, almost recitativo, melody perhaps imitates the style of the contemporary street musicians. Resignation seems his message, for 'he lets everything go as it will; he grinds and his hurdy-gurdy is never silent'.[22]

The Austrian government was anxious to regulate the number and activities of the itinerant musicians to prevent them from threatening its citizens and from committing crimes. In 1819, the police gave notice that strict licensing and restrictions were to be placed on travelling theater troupes, rope walkers, musicians, folk singers, traveling animal shows, menageries, marionette theaters, traveling side shows, medicine men, and wax museums (*Sammlung der Gesetze*, 1820, no. 28080, 441–2). Two years later, Sedlnitsky expressed concern about the increase of able-bodied men among the ranks of musicians, idlers, and beggars in the city, who he believed posed a threat to Vienna's security. Hence, his report concludes, only musicians who were blind, maimed, or crippled would be allowed to perform on the street for money, since 'daily experience teaches that those invalids attracting [crowds] with their barrel-organs and side shows, are often dangerous vagabonds, and that, even if they are not criminals, they could only too easily become so, with the disorderly, idle life they lead'.[23] Sedlnitsky adds that it would be better if the state found a way to help the poor instead of simply issuing more music licenses.

The itinerant musicians thus added another dimension to Vienna's unique musical culture. With their guitars, harps and hurdy-gurdies, these musicians and their songs were as much a part of the city's visual and aural color as the opera houses, salons, and dance halls. Moreover, the harpists, like modern-day political cartoonists, exercised one of the few means open to Austrians to speak out about the foibles and ironies of their times and about their government and society, even if their statements were disguised as humor. Had more of Vienna's popular music survived, we might have a broader understanding of what Viennese life was like and to what extent itinerant musicians influenced the daily experiences and artworks of writers and composers.

SUMMARY
Music in its cultural context

Viennese culture following the Napoleonic Wars was a complicated fabric of contradictory tendencies, attitudes, and policies – a confluence of old and new.

The city's physical appearance clung to the past. The ancient walls and guarded gates still divided the cramped, overgrown inner city from the suburbs. The architects of even new court buildings, palaces and formal gardens retained their Baroque designs; and, as late as 1829, the city lacked gas lights and steam engines. The policies of the court, bureaucracy, and church also worked to restore the old order, resisting new ideas and more efficient methods of attaining their goals. In social intercourse, class barriers and regional mores stubbornly persisted, as did the custom of addressing each other with archaic and exaggerated titles. The popular expression, 'Küss' die Hand' (I kiss your hand), of course derived from the older courtesy, and was still practiced as a phrase and deed in a variety of social situations (Glassbrenner, 60). And, as Blumenbach noted, tradespeople addressed their customers with such reverent titles as 'gracious Lady' and 'my Lord', regardless of their class (1, 147). Thus, despite its size, political importance, and cultural achievements, Vienna clung to old ways.

Unlike either London or Paris, Vienna began the nineteenth century as a provincial Eastern city, owing to its distance from industrial centers, its close ties with the Middle East, and its own sizable population of Eastern European peoples. Moreover, in many ways, the city resembled a rural town, since vineyards, vegetable gardens, woods, and game preserves were close to even the most populated areas. The suburbs' rivers, woods, rolling hills and plains invited many country rambles, outdoor parties, and a rustic lifestyle. Even the most worldly Viennese aristocrats spent a good part of every year at their country estates or hunting lodges outside the city, to devote themselves to their horses, hunts, and other outdoor sports.

As a result, allusions to the city's picturesque and still rustic countryside permeate not only the local literature and art, but also the music, from the imitation of folk music in works by Beethoven and Schubert to the incorporation of hunting horns, bird calls and zither music in the dance music of Johann Strauss and the tavern songs of itinerant musicians.

Vienna's proximity to farms and wilderness, the sources of dairy products, grains, meat and fish, helped to keep the price of food low compared to that in other large European cities despite its poor communications. In view of the plentiful supplies of food and an abundance of excellent local wine and beers, it is no accident that eating was an important social occasion and that many artistic activities, including musical performances, took place in restaurants and taverns.

Such pleasures may have been the only physical comforts of many citizens, who, like other urban dwellers in the nineteenth century, suffered from a lack of pure drinking water, improper sewage disposal, and ignorance about the causes and control of disease. Urban life was uncertain, with illness and sudden death almost commonplace occurrences. In addition, there was a shortage of housing, leading to severe overcrowding; heating fuels were prohibitively expensive; and unemployment was widespread.

In some ways, the hardships of city life may have contributed to the extreme manner in which the Viennese sought escape through amusements and the arts. Intensely popular, the theater offered an imaginary world of illusion and a parody of real life; elaborate religious and state holidays provided the excuse for public displays of piety and expiation; and the Carnival, with its frenzy of parties and balls, offered a kind of communal catharsis. Intrigued by this paradox, Henry Schnitzler argues that the gaiety of Vienna was the gaiety of escape 'frequently born of anguish, even of despair; it is invariably a gaiety with, deep down, a bad conscience or at least an awareness of its dubious character...'[1] He points to the cholera epidemic of 1831–2 when during the Carnival people danced to 'Cholera Gallopades', and later to the devastating stock market crash of 1873 when 'Crash polkas' seemingly make light of the situation. He concludes that Karl Kraus' maxim that the situation in Vienna was 'hopeless, but not serious' has always been a leitmotif of Viennese life (100).

Some citizens sought escape from political matters also. In 1815, Vienna was physically and spiritually scarred, having twice experienced the assault and humiliation of foreign occupation. The long years of war took their toll in human life, property and financial resources of the government. The country entered a period of depression, from which it did not fully recover until around 1830.[2] Many expressed cynicism about idealistic revolutions and devoted themselves, instead, to leading quiet family lives. Foreign nationals within the city felt bitter disappointment about the failure of the French Revolution to free their lands from Austrian domination, while devoted anti-monarchists were disillusioned by Napoleon's failure to help their republican cause. Thus few people in Vienna were willing or able to organize new political movements.

Immediately after the war, the emperor affirmed the political tenets of Joseph II — to maintain a strong, centralized government ruled by an enlightened, but absolute, monarch. Accordingly, the Austrian government was reordered, political power was redistributed, and the bureaucracy grew rapidly. In turn, its offices and officials enacted new decrees and regulations to bring more order and control over foreign and domestic affairs.

The political upheavals in France instilled grave fears about similar events occurring at home. Such fears were not totally unwarranted, since, even before the wars, subjects in Austrian provinces voiced discontent and worked for independence. Thus, along with centralizing the government's offices, Austrian leaders took strong measures to thwart the adoption of liberal ideas. Official censors now took special care to revise or ban revolutionary and controversial writings, whether they were of a political, theological, scientific, or artistic nature; the secret police uncovered and crushed plots intended to overthrow the monarchy.

Between 1815 and 1829 Austria's conservative policies were successful. Metternich dominated the negotiations and settlements at the Congress of Vienna. In 1819 at the Carlsbad Conference, Austrian statesmen persuaded German leaders to divest German universities and student associations of many academic freedoms and any political power. With sheer military might, Austria crushed two uprisings in Italy, thereby frustrating that area's aspirations for unification and independence for another four decades. Austria also helped to prolong the war between the Greeks and the Turks by unofficially supporting the Turks, the recognized, albeit unpopular, 'legitimate' monarchs.

For Vienna's musicians and music lovers, the country's political policies also had impact. The centralization of political power and the accompanying flurry of regulations led to revised and new rules about public decorum in the theaters; restrictions on the time and place of concerts and balls; limitations on travel; impost taxes; and even attempts to curb the number of itinerant musicians allowed to play on the streets and in taverns. Censorship was applied to melodies, texts set to music, concert programs and handbills, and musical dedications. Secret police and spies were present at most concerts, balls, and public places where artists and musicians congregated, in order to gather information not only about their political activities but also about their moral character. In these ways, the government acquired a voice in deciding which musicians would be hired by state institutions or be granted court privileges, and whether their compositions would be allowed to be published or performed.

Such a reactionary political system proved both a hindrance and a boon to Vienna's artistic community. As long as the court controlled and directed the majority of the city's musical institutions, musicians were forced to deal with the government's inherent inefficiency, political intrigues, and corruption if they wished to find a secure, salaried position or to gain a promotion. The censors not only denied easy access to foreign literature and musical publications, but could also delay, forbid, or seriously mutilate a composer's works. The secret police contributed to an atmosphere of insecurity and distrust because their information could be detrimental to persons applying for court positions, for permission to travel, or for other privileges. In addition, the police could arrest or fine musicians for performing at inappropriate times, such as on Normatagen or after the curfew. Furthermore, the welter of bureaucratic paperwork hampered not only native musicians from traveling abroad, but also impeded foreign artists, deemed politically or morally undesirable to Austrian society, from entering the country or finding work. Thus, beside creating irritations for musicians, the government most likely also encouraged political and social conformity.

Yet Austria's conservative policies may also have had their advantages, for its stability and peace offered musicians an environment free from the disruptions of political tumult or the privations of war. The process of censorship and review hindered blatant plagiarism and protected performers from undeserved harassment by the press. From a liberal viewpoint, the official discouragement of political activity may actually have benefited works that made satirical social comments, since they attracted a wide and probably more attentive audience. Certainly the folk comedies of Raimund and Nestroy satirized contemporary issues and foibles of Viennese society, and the stinging wit of the harpists' songs enjoyed popularity throughout the years of severest censorship.

In addition, at a time when Austria could boast few national heroes, the Viennese lionized their musicians and actors. A person who excelled in music or the theater could therefore gain the fame and wealth that normally would be accorded elsewhere to statesmen, military leaders, or scientists. The Viennese thus seemed to compensate for their ignorance of and impotence in political affairs by turning to esthetic and artistic issues. They fought battles over the supremacy of German opera and led rowdy factions for or against celebrated virtuosi.

Finally, even if the government appeared to be rigid and severe, eyewitnesses and documentary evidence suggest that persons with wealth, position, or influence could circumvent the law for their own purposes. The 'Metternich system' could be tempered by bribing officials, applying for special court dispensations, convincing a nobleman to use his influence to take the case to a higher court. Even in the cases of less fortunate members of the working classes, the police and government appear benevolently to have tolerated a certain amount of illegal trade or misbehavior so long as it did not appear revolutionary or pose a real threat.

Another outcome of the Napoleonic Wars was the financial ruin of many aristocrats who had speculated in war commodities or had been forced to contribute money for troops and supplies. By 1811, the government had gone bankrupt and its currency been devalued by two-fifths. As the economy collapsed, inflation and poverty grew. More and more, Austrian leaders were forced to rely upon Viennese bankers and merchants to finance the empire's reconstruction, invest in new industry, and to support the military. Thus pragmatic businessmen, rather than aristocrats, gained new influence and social prestige after the wars.

Having lost a dominant role in political and financial matters, the aristocrats increasingly retired from positions of authority in artistic and musical affairs. Many of their salons became refuges, aloof from the society and musical tastes of the middle class. Much of the responsibility for music patronage fell on Vienna's Jewish banking families, who had cultivated salons since the eighteenth century, but who were ostracized by aristocratic society because of their religion and race. Their salons became a focus of musical and artistic activity and a haven for visiting foreign performers. In addition, the bankers' experience in raising and investing money and their ability to organize profitable business ventures made possible the establishment and support of the city's first public Music Society as well as many other charitable institutions.

Civil servants also took greater responsibility for the city's musical life. In keeping with their middle-class education and values and their experiences in the highly centralized bureaucracy, these music-loving bureaucrats worked hard to organize and democratize amateur musical circles and to educate the new audiences' musical tastes. As a result, respected civil servants filled most of the administrative posts in the Society's conservatory. They also founded and contributed to Vienna's musical journals, whose purpose was to inform and educate. Their domestic musical activity brought together amateur and professional performers and provided a platform on which young and unknown artists could launch their careers. In the cases of Kiesewetter and Molitor, their home concerts of early music sparked greater interest in the systematic study of early music, leading eventually to a new branch of historical inquiry.

As the middle classes became more musically active, commerce related to music boomed. Music publishers turned out both serious art music as well as popular salon pieces, dances, and illustrated musical almanacs. Piano makers created handsome salon instruments and supplied a widening bourgeois market. Theater and restaurant owners set up small stages for concerts and dancing. Concert programs became more varied and performers sought to please wide audiences by displaying virtuosity. Music quickly became a fashionable commodity.

With the growth of audiences, musical tastes began to polarize. The educated middle-class families tended to support art music by native German composers, while less discriminating businessmen and newly titled aristocrats tended to support fashionable foreign artists. Although the two factions were still loosely defined at the beginning of the nineteenth century, by around 1840 both groups had coalesced. Some of the bureaucrats became inflexible pedants in regard to music, unduly harsh critics and self-appointed guardians of orthodox classical tastes. And not unlike the government, for which many of them worked, they too resisted change and musical influences from abroad. Musical Liebhaber, on the other hand, became little more than musical philistines whose tastes and regard for composers changed as quickly as fashion. In the year 1828 alone, for instance, Vienna was rocked by two musical crazes. The arrival of the first giraffe to the city's zoo inspired giraffe fashions, theatrical parodies, and giraffe waltzes.[3] Likewise Paganini's concerts led to the creation of new foods, new figures of speech, more theatrical parodies, and many transcriptions of his works.

In such a culture both Beethoven and Schubert could be considered to be failures, according to the standards of their contemporaries. Neither man received a secure salaried position in any of the city's musical institutions; neither had influential patrons among the new class of monied aristocrats; neither was very successful at writing for the theater beyond a few overtures and incidental music; and neither man made much profit from personal benefit concerts. Their lack of success after the wars was surely due, in part, to the currents of social and economic change as well as to Vienna's political conservatism.

From the time he settled in Vienna (1797) until the Vienna Congress, Beethoven took full advantage of the city's musical life. Like other performers of his day, he established his musical reputation first as a virtuoso in public benefit concerts and, then, in the salons of rich and powerful aristocrats who, in turn, became his protectors, benefactors, and students. As a composer, Beethoven turned for commissions primarily to Vienna's nobility, but he also tapped the lucrative local market for popular music by writing dances, military marches, chamber music, and folk-song arrangements.

In his leisure hours, Beethoven behaved like most other citizens of Vienna, taking delight in long walks in the city parks and environs.

Like other professional musicians, he spent many hours in the salons of piano manufacturers and in coffee houses to hear the latest news and gossip about visiting performers, recent concerts, new theatrical pieces, and publications of music.

But during the years 1820 through 1827 – a period of intense family problems, illness, loss of face in the courts, and full absorption in a new musical style – Beethoven generally withdrew from society. By 1820 many of his generous patrons such as Kinsky and Lobkowitz had died or had gone bankrupt, and many of his middle-class benefactors had lost patience with his erratic behavior and his failure to honor his growing debts (Thayer, 558; Marek, 436–7). Even some professional musicians resented his arrogance. Of course, he was still a local celebrity and his music was performed in many Viennese salons, concert halls and churches, but his new works were deemed to be incomprehensible, crude, and undisciplined by many, even knowledgeable, contemporaries (Solomon, 310, 319–20). Even worse, anecdotes dating from this period suggest that the police were condescending toward him, treating him as a local eccentric.[4] Although Beethoven was honored after his death with a grand and regal funeral attended by thousands of Viennese, his last works received little acclaim outside isolated circles of connoisseurs.

Beethoven was well aware of his fall from current fashion when he told Rochlitz, the editor of Leipzig's musical journal, during his visit in the summer of 1822:

'You will hear nothing of me here.' 'It is summer now', I wrote. 'No, nor in winter either', he cried. 'What should you hear? Fidelio? They cannot give it, nor do they want to listen to it. The symphonies? They have no time for them. My concertos? Everyone grinds out only the stuff he himself has made. The solo pieces? They went out of fashion here long ago, and here fashion is everything.' (Thayer, 801)

Two years later while in Baden, Beethoven told Karl Freudenberg that Rossini's music, then very popular in Vienna, was better suited to the 'frivolous and sensuous spirit of the times' (Thayer, 804).

Perhaps no one incident better demonstrates how far Beethoven had fallen in the estimation of the city than his last public concert in 1824. The concert arrangements, from the selection of the hall to the pricing of the tickets, were fraught with disagreements, protests, and even appeals to the police. Beethoven won only a few of these battles, and these through the intervention of a few aristocrats on his behalf, but the delays in preparing the concert cost him the advantage of presenting his works during the regular concert season. The program itself was not attuned to the Viennese spirit of 1824 either. Both the French revolutionary idealism echoed in the Ninth Symphony, and the profound religious sentiments expressed by the Missa Solemnis, fell on the unattentive or disillusioned ears of the Viennese, who had lost faith in the spirit of revolution and religion. After their second performance, these pieces quickly fell out of the Viennese concert repertory. The Friends of Music Society, which made a point of performing Beethoven's symphonies during the years 1820 to 1830, only had the means (or desire) to perform the first and second movements of the Ninth Symphony once in 1827. Even then, a critic found the music worthless because it was too difficult to understand: 'But of what value is a composition which one can neither understand nor comprehend? Est sonus inanis proeteraque nihil – (*Allgemeine musikalische Zeitung* (2 June 1827), 449). As Vienna's musical tastes and patronage became more bourgeois, the city no longer held the promise of critical acclaim or financial security for Beethoven. He turned to aristocrats and musical societies in Prussia, Russia, and England, but with only moderate success. When the lucrative prospect of travel to London arose in 1825, Beethoven hesitated (Thayer, 929–31). Soon thereafter, the opportunity was gone.

Franz Schubert was unsuccessful in gaining acceptance as a composer of serious art music, since he failed to produce successful, popular works in the exalted genres of opera, concerto, or symphony. Partly to blame were his age and untimely death, for Schubert was too young to be a real contender for most court positions, and too inexperienced for the opera conductor's post at the Kärntnerthor Theater to which he applied in 1821. Furthermore, as Deutsch has pointed out, the prospective Italian management at that theater made his hiring rather unlikely (*Biography*, 159–62).

Schubert's circle of friends – talented aritists and writers, many of whom were still university students or just beginning their careers – could offer him no assistance beyond introducing him to their friends and certain bourgeois salons. But their youth and relatively large amounts of free time allowed them the luxury of a bohemian life, frequenting coffee houses, parties, and taverns to smoke, drink, talk long into the night. Unfortunately this period was short lived, since one by one each man finished his education, found employment, married, or moved away.

Another impediment to Schubert's career may have been his temperament. Schubert's friends and acquaintances repeatedly observed that he was unassuming, shy, and self-conscious in society – traits which certainly would have put him at a disadvantage when negotiating with shrewd music publishers, arranging public concerts, or seeking the opportunity to perform in the private salons of influential patrons. At the time, Schubert was stubborn, even defiant of authority. His association with Johann Senn led to a near-arrest by the police in 1820; he was reprimanded by the police for playing dance music in Lent; he purposely omitted from the Credo of his Masses certain portions of the text; and he set to music an unsanctioned German translation of the Mass and a number of opera libretti even before they had been passed by the city's censors. Such actions were not politic for so young a musician and one who had not yet established his reputation in these genres, nor had attained a secure living from his compositions.

Other factors may have obstructed his career. Unlike most other well-known composers, including the young Beethoven, Schubert was not a performing virtuoso. Although he occasionally appeared in public to accompany his songs and played the piano in the salons of his friends, he rarely gave piano lessons, and did not regularly perform with any theater orchestras or church ensembles. Consequently, he probably had little contact with the city's professional instrumentalists or vocalists except for Michael Vogel, a retired opera singer, and Ludwig Tietze, a singer in the Court Chapel. In fact, though they lived in the city at the same time, Beethoven and Schubert seem to have had few friends in common. After 1816, Beethoven, an internationally acclaimed composer, associated with professional musicians of the court and theaters, music publishers and journalists, as well as the foreign virtuosi and tourists who came to pay homage. Schubert, on the other hand, surrounded himself with young artists, poets, and amateur musicians, whose affiliations usually extended only to the Friends of Music, its conservatory, similar societies in Graz and Linz, and to other middle-class salons in Vienna. And accordingly, much of Schubert's music was written for an audience whose musical abilities, expectations, and interests were different from those of Beethoven's followers after 1820. Certainly Schubert received high praise and offers of publication for his Lieder and dances, but his designation as 'Lieder composer' carried little artistic distinction. Indeed, in June 1827, one music critic for the *Allgemeine musikalische Zeitung* hints that Schubert should turn to other genres:

The tireless Lieder composer Schubert in the weekly meeting of the Abendunter-haltung club again had two new songs performed: 'Der zürnenden Diana' (Mayerhofer), 'Fräulein vom See' (Walter Scott). Also, he works in this genre almost too much, and the resulting wares hardly have the ability to surpass the splendid ones presented earlier. (449)

Schubert's friends also pressed him to write operas and symphonies. Even his epitaph, written by Franz Grillparzer, expresses the unrealized expectations of his supporters: 'The Art of Music here entombed a rich possession but even far fairer hopes' (Deutsch, *Biography* 899–90). But whenever he wrote large or serious works, Schubert's friends and publishers found the music technically too difficult, unmarketable, or unsatisfactory.[5] Thus it appears that Schubert failed to live up to the expectations of his friends and even his own ambitions because his middle-class audiences were reluctant to accept his salon music as serious art music, and they were not proficient enough to perform his other works. Given the changes in the musical climate discussed in this study, it seems no accident that Schubert's collected works were unknown until ten years after his death, when his Lieder had gained a higher artistic estimation and when more accomplished, professional orchestras, like that in Leipzig, could perform his symphonies. The piano sonatas had to wait another century before their general acceptance as masterpieces (Deutsch, *Biography*, 910–11).

But if Beethoven and Schubert were seeming failures in the 1820s, who were the successes? One group in this category were the Kapellmeisters, composers and performers in the Court Chamber ensemble, state theaters, and large churches, who were employed by the state, often as a result of many years of service and of political influence. In view of the government's scrutiny of their loyalty and good behavior, these musicians tended to be men and women who were conservative in their personal affairs as well as their music. Men like Antonio Salieri, Josef Eybler, Franz Krommer, Adalbert Gyrowetz, Ignaz Mosel, Josef Weigl, Phillip Riotte, and Franz Gläser, who enjoyed relatively secure incomes, faithfully executed their musical duties, and wrote and performed many works; but their music lacks distinction and is forgotten today.

Another group of successful musicians were those who won the admiration of audiences by displays of technique and musical showmanship. During the first part of the nineteenth century, two great virtuosi conquered Vienna. In the summer of 1822, Rossini arrived in the city to produce his latest operas with his new Neapolitan company. They created a sensation. Not only did he reap huge profits from his guest appearances at concerts and salons, but he also left an indelible mark on contemporary opera composers who immediately imitated his brilliant melodic style and stirring overtures.

Six years later, the violin wizardry of Paganini created another furore. Like Rossini, Paganini dazzled his audiences with incredible feats of technique, musical effects, and highly ornamented versions of popular and national tunes. He heightened the effect by playing the role of a diabolical, supernatural, and inspired performer. For his efforts, his receipts were tremendous. Still financially comfortable, if to a lesser degree, were Vienna's own piano virtuosi, such as Johann Hummel, Carl Czerny, Ignaz Moscheles, and Sigmund Thalberg, whose music dominated Vienna's concert programs, private musicales, and musical publications.

A third group of musicians who achieved unreserved success, continuing to this day, were Vienna's dance composers, the most notable of whom were Joseph Lanner and the Johann Strauss family. Like Johann Strauss Sr, the son of an innkeeper, most of these composer-conductors were born into the working class and began their careers in neighborhood taverns and dance halls. By artfully composing dance music with haunting melodies and elements of local color, and then performing it with highly disciplined dance orchestras, these men gained for the waltz a respectability and acceptance as art music. The waltz eventually was received by courts throughout Europe, performed in public concerts, and incorporated into opera and operetta. Today the waltz 'On the Beautiful Blue Danube' has come to symbolize not only an era, but the essence of the Viennese spirit and thus is played at important events such as the stroke of midnight on New Year's Eve or the opening of the annual musical festival in June. That dance music should have so quickly and completely conquered European audiences surely confirms the powerful impact of the new patrons of music. Strauss and Lanner never held positions in court institutions, working instead as conductors in various dance halls. But, unlike Beethoven and Schubert in the same predicament, they struck a balance between sentimentality and musical craft in their dances that perfectly suited the desires of their immediate, and now monied, audiences.

EPILOGUE

Following the deaths of Beethoven and Schubert, political and economic events brought sweeping changes to the tone and character of Viennese life. Around 1830 Austria began to suffer major setbacks in foreign policy. The Peace of Adrianople, in March 1829, ended the brutal conflict between the Greeks and Turks. Greece emerged as an independent state, but Russia, now under the rule of Czar Nicholas, also emerged as a world power with lands on the strategic Black Sea. Friedrich Gentz saw Austria's future to be 'darker than any grave' (Mayer, Kindl, Pirchegger, 57).

A year later in Paris (July 1830) the Bourbon King, Charles X, was deposed in favor of Louis Philipe, Duke of Orleans. Sometimes called a 'bourgeois revolution' because its supporters were mostly middle-class tradespeople and artisans, the revolution did not entirely usurp the power of the French landed aristocracy, but it forced the government to represent middle-class interests.[6] The revolution sent shockwaves throughout Europe.

Only a few months afterward, the Belgians declared their independence from the Dutch. When Russian troops were called upon to suppress these insurgents, they were surprised and momentarily thwarted by Polish nationalists in Warsaw, their own territory! Meanwhile in Italy, rebels began to agitate against the Dukes of Modena and Parma.

In Austria, the uprisings raised fears about revolution in the provinces of Lombardy and Venice. Hans Normann reported that Poles in Vienna and in the Austrian province of Galicia hurried to join the fray, some sacrificing all their property and wealth for the Polish cause (49). Aristocrats like Lulu von Thürheim worried about their future, calling the recent political events a volcano whose flames ignited fires of revolt throughout Europe (III, 322). Even Franz Ritter von Heintl, who previously saw no threat of revolution in Austria, admitted that the atmosphere had changed:

A mood predominated, which was like that when one sees on the horizon a terrible storm gathering, which threatens to devastate everything around it. One sees it, trembles before it, and must await its success. The Parliament had been promised; the nation, with a sense of its power united through public opinion, confidently looked forward to the fulfillment of this promise.[7]

For Viennese intellectuals and artists, the July revolution created much excitement (Normann, 47). Eduard Bauernfeld's diary chronicles the change among the members of the old Schubert circle:

To the rest of us who now as then remained clinging to the ground, the July revolution, like a flaming meteor, cast a light into the troubled darkness of the imbecilic Austrian night. From then on we began to read newspapers diligently and fortified our courage with Börne and Heine's outpourings. Not to mention the 'Spaziergang eines Wiener Poeten' [a collection of controversial poems by Anastasius Grün, the pseudonym for Count Anton Auersperg].[8]

Throughout the next two decades, such writers as Bauernfeld, Lenau, Holtei, Frankl, and Grillparzer eulogized revolutionary causes and contributed to anthologies by liberal German writers known as *Das junge Deutschland*.[9]

Not only political events, but also the belated arrival of the Industrial Revolution brought changes to Viennese life. In 1829 the first steamboat sailed on the Danube River, and a year later steamship lines were established between Vienna and Pest. Transportation was further improved by the arrival of the steam locomotive, making its first run in Austria in 1837 between the Viennese suburb of Floridsdorf and Wagram. Soon thereafter, Vienna was linked to other European cities by railroad. Other technological advances followed. Gas lights, already widely used in London, Paris, and even Madrid as early as 1828, were finally introduced into Vienna in 1845.[10]

By 1830 Austria had also recovered from the economic depression that had begun around 1816, thanks to technological improvements imported from abroad and an expansion of investment capital (Slokar, 397–8). By the mid 1830s, Vienna produced most of Europe's silk and was a formidable competitor in cotton and linen textiles. Viennese leather products rivaled those of Turkey; and the city's older workshops of luxury goods such as porcelain, silver, fine soap, furniture, and musical instruments expanded.

As in other industrial cities, the initial success and expansion of industry brought to Vienna the fruits of prosperity. New jobs were created and many goods were cheaper and more plentiful than before. Prosperity also brought a sense of well-being, optimism, and self-satisfaction – characteristics today associated with the term 'Biedermeier'.

The fortunes made by enterprising financiers, speculators, and industrialists brought them increasing influence in government, economics, and even artistic matters. Affluent bourgeois families, who could now afford the leisure and culture previously enjoyed only by the upper classes, bought the trappings of that culture. Prosperity apparently touched the lives of some members of the working classes, for in 1844 Kohl recorded the lament of a fishwife, who claimed that the new wealth hurt her fish sales:

Now the domestics have become more independent, they have more wages and feed themselves, and like better to eat flesh than fish. Formerly a counsellor's lady would go herself to the market to buy fish; now she leaves all that to the cook, who is become a greater lady than the *court counsellor*'s, and people choose rather to buy from the game-market than from us. (141).

Despite the expansion of industry and wider distribution of wealth, Austria's finances were still unsound. Inflation, speculation in currency, and unscrupulous banking procedures led to money panics and the financial ruin of many investors. The government's irresponsible expenditures for the army and their inability to collect equitable taxes weakened the economy.[11] The tax burden eventually fell on Austrian farmers and on members of the lower classes through land and consumption taxes. By 1840 discontent was widespread. Gutzkow commented on the ensuing changes in Viennese life in 1845: 'If one searches for the reasons for this change, they are openly evident. The art of living has become more difficult. Money has a lesser value than before. One needs more for expenses and the incomes have remained the same.'[12] To exacerbate the problem, the bureaucracy continued to grow, thus seriously draining the national treasury. Complaints grew louder about the government's inefficiency and waste (Boehn, 485).

Vienna's literary culture also reflected many of the social changes around 1830. The literary salons, with their staid feminine leadership and formal, yet domestic, atmosphere were replaced by literary coffee houses, like the Silbernes Kaffeehaus, and such literary societies as Concordia, Aurora, and Hesperus, where male writers met informally to converse. Caroline Pichler, Vienna's foremost salon hostess at the turn of the century, blames changes in social habits for the salon's decline. The new, later dinner hour interfered with social obligations and there was now less time to gather and to read, she contends. Further, she complains that the growing habit of smoking tobacco isolates intelligent men and women:

Beyond this there is the ever more rapid growth of tobacco smoking, without which the greater part of men can now no longer live, and yet cannot practice in the presence of women or in the unhappy salon; the innumerable coffee houses and restaurants, supplied with all refinements of luxury and comfort, offer these smokers the most agreeable opportunities to indulge in their pleasure and, at the same time, to be free from all regard for politeness and courtesy.[13]

But, if men turned their backs on the domestic salon to spend more time in coffee houses, they apparently also abandoned the previous kind of salon conversation. While studying the history of the Ludlamshöhle, Otto Zausmer found that the groups that gathered in the Grüne Insel, Wirt Adelgast, Stern and Silbernes Kaffeehaus at first imitated the jovial and witty pastimes of the Ludlamshöhle, but, when political events grew serious, the men gave up such activities to read newspapers by themselves (111). Again, Bauernfeld best summarizes the change of atmosphere among artists and writers: 'The 'Concordia', the 'Hesperus' and other more or less literary societies hang together only loosely without the cheerful and friendly elements which united us so faithfully at that time. In short, the harmless days are over.'[14]

The 1830s were also troubled times for Vienna's theaters. The ownership and directorship of the theaters frequently changed hands, the Josefstadt Theater went bankrupt, favorite actors and actresses from the previous decade retired, and dramatic tastes changed. A temporary bright respite for the Burgtheater came with the appointment of Johann Deinhardstein to the position of deputy director in 1832. Deinhardstein improved the quality of the theater's repertory by hiring many outstanding actors and by producing new plays. Although the majority of these new serious works were translations of French or English plays, a few important plays by native Austrians, such as Grillparzer, Bauernfeld, Zedlitz, and Castelli, were presented.

The indigenous folk comedies also began to lose their appeal. The loss of such comedians as Therese Krones, Ignaz Schuster, and Ferdinand Raimund, upon whose improvisations and humor the charm of the works often rested, changed the character of the plays (Laube, 268). The fairy tales and allegorical comedies of the 1820s were replaced by the sarcastic and cynical humor of Nestroy. In addition, Glassbrenner reports, new folk comedies now featured live dogs, apes, bears, rope dancers, and magicians, of which the public soon tired (126–7). As the folk theaters declined, the lavish spectacles and sentimental melodramas of the Theater an der Wien gained popularity.

Like the theater, Vienna's music was affected by contemporary events. Opera, for example, clearly reflected the political turmoil and passionate national feelings. Indeed, in 1830 it is well known that the last act of Auber's *La muette di Portici* incited the audience in Brussels to begin their revolt. Andlaw stated that the opera's last act was so powerful that the theater directors often brought it to an end with Masaniello's stirring words, 'On, on once for freedom! Masaniello, the deliverer, leads you on!', thus omitting the denouement (232). In other French and Italian operas, such as Rossini's *Guillaume Tell* (1829), Bellini's *Norma* (1831) and *I Puritani* (1835), Donizetti's *Lucrezia Borgia* (1833), Halévy's *La juive* (1835) and Meyerbeer's *Les Hugenots* (1836), large, noisy crowd scenes, the brandishing of swords, the waving of flags, and the marching of troops no doubt mirrored both contemporary passions and, in some cases, current events, only thinly disguised by the operas' historical or exotic setting.

The founding of men's choral groups, reading circles, and gymnastic societies also had political overtones, for, beyond their immediate function, these clubs became organized, nationalistic lobbies encompassing middle- and lower-class workers. Austrian officials were acutely aware of the dangers of such patriotic groups. The censors continued to ban or neutralize inflammatory speeches against the state, and the organization of a Viennese Männergesangverein (men's choral society) was forbidden until 1843.[15]

National pride and revolutionary aspirations sometimes were associated with dance music. Polonaises and mazurkas, for example, were popular long before the political unrest in 1830, but, after the Polish revolt in Warsaw, the dances became a focal point of national pride and resistance. Realizing their potential danger, Austrian censors banned a number of these dances along with works dedicated to revolutionary heroes.

In the 1830s, Vienna lost many of her great artists and patrons. Between 1825 and 1830 Antonio Salieri, Hugo Worischek, Peter Winter, Ernst Fesca, Antonie Oster, Franz Danzi, and Ignaz Schuppanzigh, in addition to both Beethoven and Schubert, died; and the salons of Hochenadel and Pereira-Arnstein closed. Few of the remaining musicians were of the same stature and originality. Meanwhile, vigorous new musical developments took place elsewhere in Europe. For example in Leipzig, 1829, Mendelssohn advanced the revival of J. S. Bach by conducting his *St Matthew Passion*. In the same year Rossini introduced *Guillaume Tell*, one of the first French grand operas. And in 1830 Berlioz premiered his *Symphonie fantastique*, a pioneering, radical work in concept, structure, and orchestration. Of course Vienna remained an active musical center, offering innumerable public concerts, operas, private salon performances, but its music was no longer in the vanguard of German art music.

In view of the changes taking place in Vienna's culture, writers have often wondered what would have happened to Schubert had he lived longer. It is clear from the biographies of his friends that the group was already disbanding in 1827. Moritz Schwind, for example, first visited Munich's art academy in August of 1827 and then enrolled for the next year. Joseph Spaun, a key personality in the arranging of Schubertiades, gave his last party before marrying in April 1828. His brother Max (Spax) and the two Hartmann brothers returned to Linz in 1827. Franz Schobert's lithographic business faltered and then failed in 1829. Eduard Bauernfeld, having passed his university examinations, began his first civil-service job in 1828. His diary reveals that he was aware of the group's dissolution: 'What will become of all of us? Will we stay together?'[16] The answer was already apparent, for by the late 1820s their bachelor, university days in Vienna were over. For them and their Viennese contemporaries, 1830 marked the conclusion of a distinctive and colorful era.

LAMENT OF THE VIENNESE OVER THE DEPARTURE OF THE ITALIAN OPERA COMPANY

(Ignaz Castelli ?)

Die Wälschen[a] ziehn zum Thor hinaus Ade!
  Mit allen Rouletten u. Trillern is aus, Au weh
Verlängerte d'Ohren auch noch so sehr,
  A so a schönig Gsangel höhrts nimmermehr Au weh, au weh, au weh.

Verlassen und arm, ist da grosse Wien Au weh
  Wo tragen wir jetzt unsere 3 Gulden[b] hin O je
Wir haben uns Geld von Maul abstrahirt
  Und alles auf unsere Ohren spendirt Au weh, au weh, au weh.

Wer wird denn jetzt in de Opern gehn Au weh
  Und gar vielleicht hören an Gluck'sches Gstöhn O je
Man hat uns beraubt unsers schönsten Glücks
  Wir Deutsche können allzusammen nix Hehe, hehe, hehe.

Wan deutschen Opern aufgeführt wern O je
  Da soll me sogar was reden hörn Au weh
Wir aber gehn in Theater nicht
  Um zu hören was drinnet gschicht Ne ne ne.

Leb wohl Rossini du grosser Man Ade!
  Du hast uns so viels Gute getan O je
Wärst du nicht du himmlischer Compositeur
  Wo nematen wir den was zu sumsen her O je, o je, o je.

Es san de Tön, de du ans geben O je
  No süsser als Feigen u. Zibeben O je
Das Süsse, da ist zwar für den Magen
  Allein, d'Wiener können gar viele vertragen, hehe, hehe, hehe.

Du hast uns nix, was z'hoch g'schrieben O je
  Bis allwei nit unschön beym Boden blieben O je
G'merkt ham wir uns de Liedeln glei
  Man braucht gar nit viel verstand dabey, Au weh, au weh, au weh.

Lament over departure of the Italian Opera company

Du hast uns Deutsche geliebt und geehrt Per se
  Das ham wir in all deinen Opern ghört O je
A Kompliment hast du uns überall gemacht
  In aner jeden a paar deutsche Tanzerl mitgebracht, O je, o je, o je.

Und was du no alles für uns hast gethan O je
  Du nahmst unser Geld, bey deiner Einnahme an Per se
Anstatte dass wir dir ham a Nachtmusik gebracht
  Hast du uns selber an schöni g'macht Au weh, au weh, au weh.

Leb wohl, wir vergessen di nimmermehr Ade
  Und kommt an anderer g'scheiderer daher Per se
Und wo du bist auch in fernsten Ort
  Du lebst bey uns in den Werkeln fort Ade, ade, ade.

Wo nemen zu weinen wir Wasser gnug her Au weh
  Der David[c] geht fort u. kommt nimmer mer Au weh
Wem rugen wir den jetzt im Komödiehaus
  Fürs Schreien elfmal nach anander heraus O je, o je, o je.

Du bist zwar nit so weise u. nit so gscheid Ne ne
  Als wie der Herr David in alter Zeit Heu je
Singst a kani anfachen Psalmen wie er
  De san die z'fad u. viel z'weni schwer Au weh, au weh, au weh.

Auch machst du niemal, wie er a Gedicht, Ach nie
  Und bist auch kein König der Juden nicht Per se
Und dennoch verehren viele Juden allhier[d]
  Stets ihren König und Abgott in dir Au weh, au weh, au weh.

Leb wohl u. streng di nit gar Z'stark Ade
  Das man de türk'sche Tromel nit hören kan O je
Holt ein hübsch, wan's dir nit aussi g'lengt
  An Lungelflügel ist bald zersprengt Au weh, au weh, au weh.

Es andern es Salaminischen Leut Ade
  Dass wir eng g'sehn het, hat uns g'freut O je
In der Colbran[e] u. in der Ekerlin
  Du wat sicher gar viel Erhabnes drinn O je, o je, o je.

Nozari,[f] Ambroggi,[g] lebt alli wohl Ade
  De Augen san uns von Thränen vol Au weh!
Wer wird den in künftigen Winter no leben
  Wan's gar kani wälschen Opern wird geben. Ade, ade, ade.

Appendix A

O! grosser Babajo wir flehen zu dir O je
   Wir wollen kan Brod; wir wollen kan Bier Ne ne
Wennst unst nur a wälsche Opera schenkt
   Mit Rossinischen Zuckerwasser uns trankst Ade! ade! ade!

Taken from VA, P.H., 673/1822, Report from Baden, 24 July 1822.

a. Wälschen = Italians
b. 3 Gulden = ticket price
c. Giovanni David = tenor
d. Reference to Jewish banking families
e. Maria Colbran = soprano
f. Andrea Nozzari = tenor
g. Antonio Ambrogi = bass

EXAMPLES OF SONGS FROM FOLK COMEDIES

from *Aline oder Wien in einem anderen Weltteile* (1822) by Adolf Bäuerle

Act I, xix: Duet between Zilli and Bims — last strophe (Music by Wenzel Müller)

Z.   Nur noch ein Wört'l, was g'fällt denn in Wien?

B.   Ehrliche Leut' und ein fröhlicher Sinn.

Z.   Ist's denn wahr, reissen s' den Stephansthurm ein?

B.   Er muss ihnen grad' wieder z' fest g'wesen seyn.

Z.   Ist denn das Feuerwerk immer noch da?

B.   Brennen d'Raketeln, schreyen wir: Ah!

Z.   Was jetzt im Leopoldstädter Theater vorgeht?

B.   Da singt just die Zilli mit dem Bims ein Duett.

Z + B   Das muss ja prächtig seyn, dort möcht' ich hin!

Ja nur ein Kaiserstadt, ja nur ein Wien!

Appendix B

from *Der Verschwender* (1834) Raimund

'Hobellied' (Music by Konrad Kreutzer)

Da strei-ten sich die Leut' he-rum oft um den Wert des

Glücks der ei-ne heisst den an-dern dumm, am End' weiss keiner

nix! Das ist der al-ler ärm-ster Mann, der

an-d're viel zu reich; das Schick-sal setzt den

Ho-bel an, und ho-belt al-le gleich. Da gleich.

Taken from Richard Smekal's collection of *Altwiener Theaterlieder* (Vienna: Wiener Literarische Anstalt, 1920), 73, 79, 81, 113. The music for Raimund plays can be found in *Die Lieder Ferdinand Raimunds*, Herbert Waniek and Alexander Steinbrecher, eds. (Vienna: Universal Edition, 1940). See also: Rommel, *Das Parodistische Zauberspiel* (Leipzig: Verlag von Philipp Reclam, 1937), 115; and Prohaska, 123, 129, 175–9.

APPENDIX C

SELECTED EXAMPLES OF MUSICAL DRAMA
PERFORMED IN VIENNA IN 1825 AND 1826

Date	Title	Composer	Dramatist	Theater
1825				
Jan. 20	Der Berggeist	Riotte	Horschelt	Jo
Feb. 1	Nurredin, Prinz von Persien	Riotte	Gewey	TaW
Feb. 5	Philibert, Graf von Flandern	Gläser	Fasch	Jo
Feb. 11	Heliodor, Berherrscher der Elemente	Gläser	Gozzi	Ka, Jo
Feb. 11	Die Zauberbirn (opera)	Volkert	Rainoldi	Jo
Feb. 11	Der oesterreichische Grenadier	Müller	Meisl	Jo
Feb. 12	Bianca e Faliero (opera)	Rossini	Manzoni	Ka
Feb. 17	Agnese di Fitz-Henry	Paer	Buonovoglia	Ka
Feb. 22	Menagerie und optische Zimmerreise in Krähwinkel	Gläser	Gleich/Hopp	Jo
Feb. 24	Die Reise durch die Luft	Roser	Gleich	Jo
Feb. 25	Die Wunderbrille im Zauberwalde	Müller, Drechsler	Gleich	Leo
Mar. 1	Il turco in Italia (opera)	Rossini	Romani	Ka
Mar. 10	Rübezahl (opera)	Würfel	Marsano	TaW
Mar. 17	Fortuna vor Gericht	Gläser	Meisl	Jo
Mar. 21	I Pretendenti delusi (opera)	Mosca	Prividali	Ka
Mar. 22	Amossa (Bald Zauberer, Bald Schuster)	Müller	Korntheur	Leo
Apr. 29	Die Fee aus Frankreich	Müller	Meisl	Ka
May 4	Der verwunschene Prinz	Müller	Bäuerle	Ka
May 6	Das Zauberhorn (opera)	Lubin	Vogel	Ka
May 10	Der Erlenkönig	Gläser	Told	Ka
May 16	Die Müller	Starklop	Ravel	TaW
May 19	Das ländliche Fest	Berton	Ravel	TaW
May 21	Die Schweizerfamilie (opera)	Weigl	Castelli	TaW
May 23	Die geraubten Haarzöpfe	Volkert	Meisl	Jo
May 28	Armida, die Zauberin im Orient	Gläser	Meisl	Jo
Jun. 18	Die musikalische Schneiderfamilie	Müller	Bäuerle	Leo
Jul. 1	Sieben Mädchen in Uniform	Gläser	Angely	Ka
Jul. 7	Der Brief an sich selbst	Gläser	Meisl	Ka
Jul. 9	Der Weibertausch	Hérold	Artois Castelli	Ka

Date	Title	Composer	Dramatist	Theater
1825				
Jul. 9	*Meister Martin, der Küfner und seine Gesellen*	Seyfried	Holbein	Jo
Jul. 13	*Die Hubertusnacht*	Roser	?	Jo
Jul. 15	*Eine Prise Tobak*	Riotte	?	Ka
Jul. 25	*Jakob in der Heimat*	Müller	Gleich	Leo
Jul. 25	*Die sonderbare Laune* (opera)	Gläser	?	Ka
Aug. 1	*Kornblümchen*	Lubin	Perrault	Jo
Aug. 3	*Die sonderbare Laune* (opera)	Gläser	?	Jo
Aug. 4	*Eine Prise Tobak*	Riotte	?	Jo
Aug. 9	*Sieben Mädchen in Uniform*	Gläser	Angely	Jo
Aug. 18	*Die Unterhaltung in der Herrschaftsküche*	Volkert	Occioni	Leo, Jo
Aug. 20	*Der Freischütz*	Weber	Kind	Jo
Aug. 30	*Faustus Mantel*	Müller	Bäuerle	TaW
Aug. 30	*Der Weibertausch*	Hérold	Castelli	Jo
Sep. 3	*Joko, der brasilianische Affe*	Platzer	Meisl	Jo
Sep. 10	*Der Kampf mit dem Drachen*	Röth	Heigel	TaW
Sep. 10	*Bettina*	Gläser, Seyfried	Vogel	Jo
Sep. 12	*Die Glocke*	Lubin	?	Jo
Sep. 17	*Die Krähwinkler in der Residenz*	Gläser	Gleich	Jo
Sep. 23	*Das Abenteur im Guadarama Gebirge*	Röth	Heigel	TaW
Sep. 30	*Gisperl und Fisperl*	Drechsler	Bäuerle	Leo
Oct. 8	*Raoul der Blaubart* (opera)	Gretry	Sedaine Fischer	Jo
Oct. 18	*Alles in Uniform für unsern König*	Müller	Hensler	Jo
Oct. 29	*Die Drillingsschwestern und der Waldgeist*	Riotte	?	Jo
Nov. 4	*Der Schiffscaptain*	Blum	?	TaW
Nov. 4	*Gisela von Bayern, erste Königen der Magyaren*	Leidesdorf	Meisl	Jo
Nov. 5	*Der Barbier von Sevilla*	Rossini	Sterbini Kollman	Jo
Nov. 17	*Lisko und Saladino*	Drechsler	Lhotsky	Leo
Nov. 19	*Die Sonnenjungfrau*	Seyfried	Kotzebue	Ka
Nov. 24	*Aline, Wien in einem andern Weltteile*	Müller	Bäuerle	TaW
Dec. 11	*Henslers Gedächtnisfeier*	Gläser	Meisl/Hopp	Jo
Dec. 17	*Die Zauberrose*	Faistenberger	Occioni	Jo
?	*I due Forzati* (opera)	Lannoy		?
?	*Der Zaubersee* (opera)	Remde		?
?	*Der kleine Schadenfroh*	Fe. Schubert		?
?	*Der Wolfsbrunnen*	Roser	Gleich	?

Date	Title	Composer	Dramatist	Theater
1826				
Jan. 10	*Die diebischer Elster* (opera)	Rossini	Gherdini Seyfried	Jo
Jan. 18	*Thespis, Serapions und Jocus Wanderung in die Leopoldstadt*	Müller	Meisl	Leo
Jan. 24	*Staberl als Freischütz*	Röthe	Carl	TaW
Jan. 27	*Oskar und Tina*	Drechsler	Meisl	Leo
Feb. 3	*Der Tanzmeister Pauxel*	var. comp.	Carl	TaW
Feb. 28	*Die Zauberlampe*	Müller	Wilmann	Leo
Mar. 4	*Hans und Raphael, die wilden Brüder auf Bodmanin*	Anon.	?	TaW
Apr. 14	*Das grüne Männchen*	Drechsler	Meisl	Leo
Apr. 20	*Pansalvyn*	Riotte	?	TaW
Apr. 20	*Bozena*	Seyfried	Neil	Jo
Apr. 26	*Die Reise ins Bad*	Müller	Gleich	Jo
Apr. 26	*Die Begebenheiten zur Mahlzeit*	Müller	Gleich	Leo
Apr. 29	*Der Untergang des Feenreiches*	Kauer	Meisl	Jo
May 19	*Intermezzo*	Boieldieu	?	Jo
May 26	*Die Zauberrose*	Faistenberger	Occioni	TaW
Jun. 6	*Menagerie und optische Zimmerreise*	Gläser	Gleich	TaW
Jun. 7	*Sieben Mädchen in Uniform*	Gläser	Angely	TaW
Jun. 17	*Heliodor, Beherrscher der Elemente*	Gläser	Gozzi	TaW
Jun. 27	*Die lustige Werbung*	Kreutzer	R.B.	TaW
Jul. 1	*Der Hund von Gotthardsberg*	var. comp.	?	TaW
Jul. 6	*Die weisse Frau*	Boieldieu	Scribe Castelli	Ka
Jul. 13	*Tante Aurora*	Boieldieu	Lonchamp Lambrecht	Ka
Jul. 16	*Der Hund vom Gotthardsberg*	var. comp.	?	TaW
Jul. 18	*Lully et Quinault*	Isouard	Gaugiran Nanteuil	Ka
Jul. 21	*Die Braut aus dem Zauberbrunnen*	Müller	?	Jo
Jul. 22	*Le nouveau Seigneur de Village*	Boieldieu	de Lesset	Ka
Jul. 27	*La Lettre de Change*	Bochsa	Planard	Ka
Aug. 2	*Der Mauer und der Schlosser*	Auber	Delavigne	Ka
Aug. 4	*Les deus jaloux*	Bonnay	Gall	Ka
Aug. 9	*Le bouffe et la tailleur*	Gaveaux	Villiers Gouffé	Ka
Aug. 18	*Les rendezvous bourgeois*	Isouard	Hoffman	Ka
Aug. 26	*Ambroise*	D'alayrac	Monvel	Ka
Sep. 4	*Adolphe et Clara*	D'alayrac	Marsollier	Ka
Sep. 6	*Die umgeworfenen Kutscher*	Boieldieu	Dupaty Kupelweiser	Ka
Sep. 14	*Le delire*	Berton	Revéróni	Ka

Appendix C

Date	Title	Composer	Dramatist	Theater
1826				
Sep. 15	Glück in Wien	Müller	Bäuerle	Leo
Sep. 16	Felix und Gertrud	Volkert	?	Jo
Sep. 22	Jadis et aujourd'hui	Kreutzer	Severin	Ka
Sep. 27	Die steinerne Jungfrau	Gläser	Gleich	Jo
Sep. 28	Die Abenteuernacht	Drechsler	Lang	Leo
Sep. ?	Die Mahm aus dem Pustertale	Kauer	Gleich	Jo
Oct. 14	Mirana, Königen der Amazonen	Gyrowetz	Holbein	Jo
Oct. 27	Die Fee in Krähwinkel	Müller	Bäuerle	Leo
Oct. 30	Leicester (opera)	Auber	Scribe Castelli	Ka
Nov. 3	Der Rache Fluch	Seyfried	Lembert	TaW
Nov. 4	Die Weiber in Uniform	Gläser	Gleich	Jo
Nov. 4	Die Bürger Wiens im zwölften Jahrhundert	Lubin	?	Jo
Nov. 10	Le maitre de chapelle	Drechsler	Raimund	Jo
Nov. 22	Der goldene Fisch	Lubin	Roller	Jo
Nov. 28	Der Klausner auf dem wüsten Berg	Carafa	d'Arlincourt Planard	Ka
Nov. 29	Guido von Waldau	Riotte	Vogel	TaW
Dec. 1	Die schwarze Frau	Müller	Meisl	Jo
Dec. 12	Die schwarze Frau	Müller	Meisl	TaW
Dec. 14	Der Untergang des Feenreiches	Kanne	Meisl	TaW
Dec. 18	Marie (Verborgene Liebe)	Hérold	Planard Castelli	Red
?	Granada	Schlösser	Marlani	?
?	Laurina	Kessler	Walther	?

Compiled from Anton Bauer, Oper und Operetten (Graz, Herman Böhlaus, 1955); Anton Bauer, Das Theater in der Josephstadt zu Wien (Vienna, Manutiuspresse, 1957); Anton Bauer, 150 Jahre Theater an der Wien (Vienna, Amalthea Verlag, 1952); and from Alfred Lowenberg, Annals of Opera 1597–1940 (Geneva: Societas Bibliographica, 1955); Umberto Manferrari, Dizionario universale delle opere melodrammatiche (Florence: Sansoni Antiquariato, 1954), and Franz Steiger, Opernlexikon (Tutzing: Hans Schneider, 1978).

Abbreviations of the theaters: Jo = Josefstadt Theater; Ka = Kärntnerthor Theater; Leo = Leopoldstadt Theater; TaW = Theater an der Wien; Red = Redoutensaal.

SCHUBERTIADE GUESTS AT THE HOME OF JOSEF SPAUN

Government officials
1   Bauernfeld, Eduard – official in the Lottery Administration; writer
2   Castelli, Ignaz – librarian and secretary to the Lower Austrian County Council; writer/dramatist
3   Doblhoff, Anton – statesman; Austrian minister
4   Enderes, Karl – conveyancer for Ministry of Finance
5   Gahy, Josef – secretary of Court Chamber; pianist
6   Grillparzer, Franz – director of Court Chamber archives; dramatist/poet
7   Gross, Josef – secretary to Court Exchequer
8   Kenner, Josef – magistery official in Linz; draftsman/poet
9   Ottenwalt, Anton – assistant to Chamber procurator
10 Mayerhofer, Johann – Austrian censor; poet
11 Perfetta, Martin – official in Court War Accountancy
12 Schönstein, Karl – counsellor in Ministry of Finance
13 Rueskäfer, Michael – examiner of excise affairs (customs official)
14 Spaun, Josef – official in Lottery Administration
15 Witticzek, Josef (and wife) – conveyancer to Privy State Chancellory

Army
1   Mayerhofer, Ferdinand – lieutenant fieldmarshal; military surveyor
2   Senn, Johann – teacher in military academy (not present in 1824)

Professional/self-employed
1   Enk, Karl – private tutor
2   Feuchtersleben, Ernst – physician; poet/philosopher
3   Pinterics, Karl – private secretary to Prince Josef Palffy
4   Schober, Franz – actor; poet, later, secretary to Franz Liszt
5   Seligmann, Romeo F. – physician; professor of medical history
6   Steiger von Amstein, Johann – mining expert in Gmunden
7   Walcher, Ferdinand – timber dealer

Appendix D

Musicians

1 Lachner, Franz – conductor at Kärntnerthor Theater (beginning 1829)
2 Lachner, Ignaz – organist; theater conductor
3 Randhartinger, Benedict – Kapellmeister at Court Chapel
4 Schubert, Franz – composer; school teacher's assistant
5 Vogel, Michael (and wife, Kunigunde) – retired opera singer

NOTES

INTRODUCTION

1. Carl Dahlhaus, 'Romantik und Biedermeier. Zur musikgeschichtlichen Charakteristik der Restaurationszcit', *Archiv für Musikwissenschaft*, 31 (1974), 22–41.
2. Alice M. Hanson, 'Incomes and Outgoings in the Vienna of Beethoven and Schubert', *Music and Letters*, 64 (July 1983), 174.

I THE CIVIC ENVIRONMENT FOR MUSIC

1. Russell, 317. Nicht leicht wird man eine Stadt finden, wo das liederliche Leben so herrschend ist, wo die weibliche Tugend weniger geschätzt, und folglich auch sparsamer angetroffen wird.
2. *Vertraute Briefe* (1793), 83. Da der Boden aus einem feinen Kreis bestrebt, der durch die vielen Jahren sehr fein zermalmet wird, so hebt der Staub sich desto leichter; die Stosswinde führen ihn in dicken Wolken einher, die Luft wird davon verfinstert, und die Menschen wandeln gleich den Göttern des Olimps, aber nicht in einem Aether, sondern in dicken Staube, der sich auf Lunge und Brust setzt, und den Augen wehe thut...
3. Horn, 190–6. Lung infections presumably included all lung ailments except tuberculosis. Catarrh usually referred to bronchitis (see Cooper, 442). Nerve fever is considered by Otto Deutsch to have meant typhus or typhoid fever (*Biography*, 823n.). 'Wechsel' fever or intermittent fever is now the term used for malaria, but its former meaning is uncertain.
4. Cooper, Appendix A, 'Beethoven's Medical History', 434–6; Marek, 311–14; Solomon, 262.
5. Hickmann, 5. A Heller was an Austrian coin used from 1897 to 1925 and was worth $\frac{1}{100}$ Krone.
6. Pichler, I, 243. Schon damals zeigte sich, was die neuere Zeit viel öfters und auffallender ans Licht stellt, dass es trotz Jammer der niedrigen Klassen und trotz der menschenfreundlichen Klagen so vieler wohltätigen Seelen, welche jenen alles aufs Wort glauben und vom Mitgefühl für ihre Not durchdrungen sind, dass dieser beklagenswerte Zustand in den allermeisten Fällen nur ein relativer war. Wäre wirklich Not im allgemeinen vorhanden gewesen, wie in der Schweiz und in Hamburg, so hätte die Suppe Abnehmer und Liebhaber gefunden.
7. Stöger, no. 4, 62.
8. Pezzl, *Skizze*, 121.
9. HHStA, Oberstkämmeramt, von O.MeA. Rückgest. Akten (1792–1842), R-10, 594/1826.
10. *Ibid.*, R-22, 25 July 1841.

11. Among the most recent studies is the series by Alexander Weinmann entitled, *Beiträge zur Geschichte des alt-Wiener Musik Verlags* (Vienna, Universal Edition, 1967), Series 2, part 6, 11.
12. Marek, 481. There is speculation that the ring intended for Beethoven was stolen, and the inexpensive one was sent instead.
13. See Adolf Bäuerle, ed., *Das sechzigste Geburtsfest Sr. Majestät des Kaisers von Oesterreich Franz I* (Vienna, Anton v. Haykul, 1828).
14. Carl Czerny, 'Recollections from my Life', *Musical Quarterly*, XLII (July 1956), 313.

2 MUSIC AND THE AUSTRIAN POLICE

1. Beethoven (Anderson), III. No. 1186, 1042.
2. Novello, 142; Holmes, 114–15.
3. Glassbrenner, 97. See below note 34.
4. HHStA, Staat. Wissenschaft, no. 77, 13 July 1822.
5. HHStA, Staat. Wissenschaft, no. 11, 3 August 1823; 11 September 1827.
6. HHStA, Staat. Wissenschaft, no. 11, 11 August 1823.
7. Marx, *Zensur*, 4; Normann, 110; Oberhummer, *Wiener*, I, 194–5.
8. See Blumenbach. 259; Anschütz, 227–8.
9. VA, P.H. 941/1813, 'Theater Censur'.
10. Their fears materialized after the first performance when angry Bohemians sent Grillparzer threatening letters. Grillparzer, *Selbstbiographie*, 106–7.
11. Anschütz quoted by Frankl, *Erinnerungen*, 147. ... dergleichen Eseleien, im Hinblick auf meine Zukunft, übersehen könnte! So muss ich mir meiner Familie wegen, alle diese Dummheiten gefallen gelassen!
12. Meynert does not identify the Polacca, but possibly the music was connected with the rebellion that took place in Warsaw the previous year (1830).
13. HHStA, Kabinets Protokoll: 23 July 1799, CXXIV, no. 1089; 19 November 1797, CXXXIV, no. 2770.
14. HHStA, Notenwechsel von der Polizeihofstelle (old fascicle 11) new 10, 1822–3; Notenwechsel an der Polizeihofstelle (fascicles 352–3) 29 September 1825.
15. HHStA, Notenwechsel von der Polizeihofstelle (old 47–8) 1824–5, fascicles 559–60.
16. For a list of censored literature and music between the years 1798 and 1802 see WStB, 'Verzeichnis'. For a similar listing for 1835–48 see HHStA, 'Verzeichnis der vom der k.k. Central Censur verbotene Werken 1835–1848' (old fascicle 80) new 60, fos. 1–547.
17. Beethoven (Anderson), III no. 1278, 1120; Thayer, 906–7.
18. Deutsch believes that Goethe never gave his permission. Nonetheless the songs were finally published in 1825 and bear the Deutsch numbers 161, 369, 544 (*Biography*, 419).
19. The work's name also reflects the censor's wishes: 'Gesänge zur Feier des heiligen Opfers der Messe'. Deutsch, *Biography*, 682–3n.
20. VA, P.H. 887/1829.
21. See Normann, 112; Zenker, *Journalismus*.
22. VA, P.H. 3578/1829. The decision may have been made easier since the work had already been accepted in Germany.
23. HHStA, Noten von der Polizeihofstelle (old 50, 51) new 41, 10 Dec. 1830.
24. GdMf Archiv. Index der Gesellschaft der Musikfreunde des oest. Kaiserstaates von 1812–30; VA, P.H. 1968/1825.

25. HHStA, Noten von der Polizeihofstelle, carton 39 (old 47–8), fascicles 539–40. 19 August 1826.
26. Wilhelm Chezy, *Erinnerungen aus meinem Leben* (Schaffhausern: F. Hurter'schen Buchhandlung, 1863), II, 35.
27. For a list of Viennese periodicals during this period see Zenker, *Journalismus*; Maria Lanckoranska and Arthur Rümann, *Geschichte der deutschen Taschenbücher und Almanachen aus der klassisch-romantischen Zeit* (Munich, Ernst Heimeran Verlag, 1954).
28. Carl Junker, *Korporation der Wiener Buch, Kunst und Musikalienhändler 1807–1907* (Vienna, Franz Deuticke, 1907), 18.
29. *Seufzer aus Oesterreich*, 115. This work is probably a revision of Sealsfield's *Austria as it is*.
30. Forstmann, 34–5; Rudolf Till, 'Die Bibliothek des Hauptschuldirektors Johann Hoheisel – Ein Blick in die Geisteswelt des Wiener Bürgertum im Vormärz', *Wiener Geschichtsblätter*, III (1957) 49–54.
31. See Boas, 168; Schaden, 46; Sherer, 308.
32. Normann, 106. Man stellt diese Anstalt der spanischen Inquisition an die Seite, erzählt sich die schauderhaftesten Mährchen davon, schreit über Geistesinfibulation, und hält alle jene Männer, welche an der Spitze dieser Anstalt stehen, gleich wie jene, welche in ihrem Solde (so sagte die böse Welt) leben und wirken, für blutdürstige Tyrannen, Menschenfresser und Obscuranten.
33. Forstmann, 36. Davon wird jedoch von Seiten der Polizei wie billig keine Notiz genommen, denn man weiss bestimmt, man habe von dem Pöbel nichts zu befürchten, und glaubt nur einzelne Sprudelköpfe im Auge haben zu müssen. Der Teutscher bleibt ja so lange ruhig, als ihn nicht die drückendste Noth aus seiner Lethargie rüttelt.
34. Glassbrenner, 148–9. Und nun kommt man nach Wien, wird auf die freundlichste und artigste Weise von allen höheren Beamten behandelt, findet selbst unter den niederen nur wenigen Klötze; hört überall freimüthig politisiren, alle Tage neue bon mots, die Krone und Purpur berühren; findet in allen Familien verbotene Bücher, abonnirt sich für den Zirkel verbotener Journale: sieht alle Leute verbotenen Tabak rauchen, wo das Tabakrauchen verboten ist; kauft überall Waaren, die viel theurer sein müssten, wären sie nicht auf verbotenem Wege nach Wien gekommen, trinkt überall verbotenen Wein, und findet überall verbotene Mädchen! Wo ist die geheime Polizei; was thut sie? Selten hört man, dass Jemand eine Geldstrafe erduldet hat; die Wiener selbst zeigen dir hier und dort einen Naderer, aber frägt man, ob seit Jahren ein Wiener durch diese Naderer incommodirt ist, so erhält man ein entschiedenes Nein zur Antwort. Wahrhaftig!
35. For a discussion of the conference and its impact on students and foreign policy see Eberhard Büssem, *Die Karlsbäder Beschlüsse von 1819* (Hildesheim, HA Gerstenberg Verlag, 1974); Kissinger, 232–46; Doblinger, 'Gedanke'.
36. Except for Protestant theology students (mostly from Siebenburg and Hungary), Austrians were not allowed to study abroad. Letter exchanges between foreign students and professors were banned likewise. If convicted of an offense, a student received a sentence of fourteen or more years in the army.
37. Arthur Kopp, *Deutsches Volks und Studenten-Lied in vorklassischer Zeit* (Berlin, Wilhelm Hertz Verlag, 1899) 203–4.
38. Friedrich Harzmann, *Burschenschaftliche Dichtung von der Frühzeit bis auf unsere Tage* (Heidelberg, Carl Winters Universitäts-buchhandlung, 1930), 135.

39. HHStA, Verzeichnis der von der k.k. Central Censur verbotene Werken 1835–1848.
40. Doblinger, 55. Deutsch disagrees with Doblinger's implication of other members of Senn's circle of friends; however, he provides no further evidence. Deutsch, *Biography*, 130n.
41. Schubert had moved to Wipplingerstrasse No. 380 by around January of 1821. *Ibid.*, 163.
42. *Gesetzbuch über Verbrechen und schwere Polizey-Uebertretungen*, Part 2, 40. See also Thomas Frost, *The Secret Societies of the European Revolution 1776–1876* (London; Tinsley Bros., 1876) and Lennhoff, *Politische Geheimbünde*.
43. *Ibid.* (Frost), 264. The Spielberg prison was described briefly by Caroline Pichler when she visited the city of Brünn in 1817. While no one was allowed to enter the prison, she saw its exterior and some of the subterranean passages leading into the cells. Pichler, II, 104.
44. Castelli (1969), 99; Zausmer, 'Ludlamshöhle', 86–7; Sauer, 24.
45. The play was first performed in Vienna on 15 December 1817.
46. Castelli (1969), 98–9; Anschütz, 311; Rosenbaum, 21 November 1826, 31r; Weber, 314; Grillparzer, *Tagebuch* (4 March 1826).
47. Rosenbaum states that the largest gathering took place on Saturdays, but that some of the men also met on other days of the week. See also Zausmer. 'Ludlamshöhle', 91, 95; Anschütz, 316.
48. There is a controversy about the exact date. Castelli states that it was the 26th and Rosenbaum's diary shows that it was the night of 18 April.
49. See Meynert, 237–8; Boas, 170–1.
50. The Carbonari or 'charcoal burners' were a secret society originally organized in France (*c.* 1802–10) by members of the French army opposed to Napoleon. After the war, they championed the cause of Italian unity and universal suffrage. Lennhoff, 94.
51. Anschütz, 320. Seit Enthüllung der Carbonariverschwörung in Italien bedurfte es in Wien für die damalige Polizei nur weniger Anhaltspuncte, um gewaltthätig in das Leben der Gesellschaft einzureisen.
52. The explanation of the phrase was supplied by Karl Schwarz during his questioning. He states that his name was Schwarz (black) and his nose and face were bright red (rot). Hence, Schwarz was red, and red, black.

3 MUSIC IN THE THEATER

1. The most authoritative and comprehensive works dealing with one Viennese dramatic genre include: Otto Rommel, *Die Alt-Wiener Volkskomödie* (Vienna, Anton Schroll & Co., 1952); Emil Blümml and Gustav Gugitz, *Alt-Wiener Thespiskarren* (Vienna, Anton Schroll & Co., 1925); and Anton Bauer, *Oper und Operetten in Wien* (Graz, Hermann Böhlau, 1955). The best histories of individual theaters include: Heinz Kindermann, *Das Burgtheater* (Vienna, Adolf Luser Verlag, 1939); Gustav Zechmeister, *Die Wiener Theater nächst der Burg und nächst der Kärntnerthor von 1747 bis 1776* (Vienna, Hermann Böhlau, 1971); Robert Maas, *Die Wiener Oper* (Vienna, Brüder Rosenbaum Verlag, 1963); Anton Bauer, *150 Jahre Theater an der Wien* (Vienna, Amalthea Verlag, 1952) and *Das Theater in der Josefstadt zu Wien* (Vienna, Manutiuspresse, 1957); and Franz Hadamowsky, *Das Theater in der Leopoldstadt von 1781 bis 1860* (Vienna, In Kommission bei O. Höfels, ww., 1934).

2. The actors between the years 1816 and 1829, according to Eduard Bauernfeld, later were known as the 'Viennese School'. See Bauernfeld, *Erinnerungen*, 182.

3. Glassbrenner, 105. Das Burgtheater is heiliger als Gott. Wer nicht lobt und preist, ist verflucht!

4. See Ivor Guest, *Fanny Elssler* (Middleton, Wesleyan University Press, 1970), and Emil Pirchan, *Fanny Elssler – Eine Wienerin tanzt um die Welt* (Vienna, Wilhelm Frick, 1940).

5. References to other opera parodies are made in Rommel's *Volkskomödie*. See also Otto Rommel, *Ein Jahrhundert alt-Wiener Parodie* (Vienna, Oesterreichischer Bundesverlag, 1930) and *Das parodistische Zauberspiel* (Leipzig, Philipp Reclam, Jr, 1937); and Erich Joachim May, *Wiener Volkskomödie und Vormärz* (Berlin, Henschelverlag Kunst und Gesellschaft, 1975).

6. *Dizionario di Musica* (Turin, Paraviso & Co., 1959).

7. See Franz Mirow, *Zwischenaktmusik und Bühnenmusik des deutschen Theaters in der klassischen Zeit* (Berlin, Selbstverlag der Gesellschaft für Theater, 1927).

8. Joseph Mantuani, ed., *Tabulae Codicum Manuscriptorum Praeter Graecos et Orientales in Biblioteca Palatina Vindobensi* (Vienna, C. Gerold, 1864–99) IX–X, 316554 ANA 48E73, p. 174.

9. See Lanckoranska, *Taschenbücher*, and Zenker, *Journalismus*.

10. Glassbrenner, 179. In keiner Stadt der Welt spielt das Theater Publikum so viel Kabalen und Intriguen, als in Wien; es ist kein Schauspiel auf den Brettern, das sich in dieser Hinsicht mit ihm messen könnte. Hat sich eine Schauspielerin den heissen Wünschen eines Cavaliers geopfert, so wird sie so lange mit Beifall überschüttet, bis sie sich auch andern heissen Wünschen opferte.

11. Castelli (1969), 88–90. Adolf Bäuerle wrote a semi-fictional novel entitled *Therese Krones* in 1854 that dramatizes these events.

12. Hurter, II, 73–4. Was sonst als Mittel zur Erholung, als anständiges Ergötzen betrachtet wurde, wird nun von Manchen, wenn es nicht als ein Geschäfte, doch als Theil der Lebensaufgabe angesehen, und vor und nachher mit einer Einlässigkeit und Wichtigkeit behandelt, als wäre das Theater des Gegenstand, welcher neben den unentbehrlichen Bedürfnissen den Menschen vor Allem in Anspruch zu nehmen hätte.

13. Glassbrenner, 215.... Mütter lehnten sich gegen Väter und liessen ihre Gefühle aus, Jünglinge fielen den Jungfrauen vor Seligkeit ohnmächtig in den Schoos, Beamte vergassen auf einen Augenblick, dass sie morgen nichts zu thun haben würden, und selbst dem polizeilichen Aufpasser, welcher jeden Abend hinter den Coulissen stehen muss, lies eine Thräne von einem halben Zoll im Durchmesser über die Wange. Ich klatschte wüthend mit, denn ich fürchtete hinausgeworfen zu werden, hätte ich's nicht gethan.

14. VA, P.H. 3557/1828, 'Polizey Rapporte'.

15. Glassbrenner, 43. Den selben Eifer zeigt der Wiener auch im Theater. Der Liebling in der Burg, bei dessen Erscheinen schon Kinder und Greise enthusiastischen Beifall spenden, wird ausgezischt, wenn er sich verspricht; der Sänger im Kärntnerthor, bei dessen Tönen man den Kopf hin und her bewegt, und sich in seinen Melodien zu baden scheint, erhält unzweideutige Beweise des Misfallens, sobald seine Kehle einen Bock schiesst, und der angebetete Komiker an der Wien oder in der Leopoldstadt fällt in momentane Ungnade, überschreitet er mit seinem Spasse die Grenzen, die freilich weit genug ausgedehnt sind.

16. *Meine grosse Reise*. 62. Alle Wiener aber klagen, dass es bei weitem nicht mehr dem frühern Glanze entspreche, den es vor etwa zehn Jahren hatte, wo die grössten

Talente hier vereint waren, wo die LaBlache und Fodor, Ambrogi und der unübertroffene Rubini u. glänzten und das Ballet mit dem Pariser wetteiferte. Jetzt ist die italienische Oper eingegangen, das Ballet nicht ausgezeichnet und die deutsche oper nicht ausserordentlich.

17. Oberhummer, *Polizei*, I, 189. Oberhummer quotes from the Polizey Oberdirections Akten of 1824: ...dass die Aufrechthaltung des Kärntnerthor Theaters aus mehr als einer Polizeyrücksicht sehr wünschenswert ist, indem die Polizeybehörde darauf bedacht seyn muss, die sittlichen Vergnügungen der Einwohner eher zu vermehren, als zu verhindern; um selbe einerseits von anderen, oft die Moralität und die öffentliche Ordnung und Sicherheit gefährdenden Conventikeln... abzuhalten, anderseits in die Tagesgespräche Abwechslungen zu bringen und für selbe einen ebenso reichhaltigen als unschädlichen Stoff zu liefern.

18. HHStA, General Intendanz, Burgtheater, 42 Beilage 1826, 'Vertheilung der mit Sperrssitz und Freybilleten in das k.k. Hoftheater angetragene Personen'.

19. HHStA, General Intendanz, Hofoper, 1823, 'Freyeintrittsbillete'.

20. Hanslick informs that the practice of numbered, reserved seats was not common until the 1830s (I, 96).

21. Dieter Hadamczik, *Friedrich L. Schröder in der Geschichte des Burgtheaters* (Berlin, Selbstverlag der Gesellschaft für Theatergeschichte, 1961) LX, 31.

22. *Sammlung der Gesetze*, 1817, no. 4189, Nieder Oesterreich. Regierungskundmachung vom 1 Feb. 1800, 84. Obschon gestattet ist, jemanden in das Theater zum Platz halten zu schicken, um später nach Bequemlichkeit das Schauspiel besuchen zu können, so wird doch zur Vermeidung alles Unglückes verbothen, Kinder unter 16 Jahren zu diesem Endzweck in das Theater zu schicken.

23. VA, P.H. 366/1820, 'Missbräuche in Theater'.

24. VA, P.H. 1405/1829, 'Neuigkeiten in Wien'.

25. *Sammlung der Gesetze*, 1817, 82–3.

26. See Joseph Richter's *Die Eipeldauer Briefe*, ed. Eugen v. Paunel (Munich, Georg Müller, 1918) Part 14, no. 4, 37–40, for a humorous contemporary reaction to the regulations.

27. Glassbrenner, 213. Und trat nun die Prima Donna Sigr. Strepponi heraus, so klatschte man sich die Hände wund, und kam nun ja die Prima Donna assoluta, Sigra. Schütz-Oldosi, Virtuosa di Camera di S.M. l'Archiduchessa di Parma, oder vollends die andere Prima Donna assoluta, Sigra. Tadolini, so tobte und lärmte und jubelte man, dass die Balken seufzten, rief sie zehn, zwölf bis zwanzig Mal heraus und forderte jede einzelne Nummer da Capo.

4 PUBLIC CONCERTS

1. Hilde Fischbach-Stojan, 'Franz Schubert, sein Weg in die Oeffentlichkeit', Diss. Innsbruck, 1948; Weber, Table 3, 160.

2. The efforts of the Damen Verein eventually led to the founding of the Gesellschaft der Musikfreunde. See Hanslick, I, 179–80 and Pohl, 4. The history of the Damen Verein is traced in a booklet in the VA, P.H. 4148/1836, entitled, *Die Gesellschaft adeliger Frauen zur Beförderung des Guten und Nützlichen in Wien*.

3. Franz I's birthday was on 11 February and his nameday was 3 October. Empress Caroline was honored in the theaters on 3 November and 7 February, according to concert programs housed in the NB, Musiksammlung.

4. GdMf Concert Program, 11 February Geburtsfeier Seiner M. des Kaisers von den Zöglingen der k.k. Theresianischen Ritter-Akademie, 1822. Schubert's contribution was his Op. post. 157.

5. NB, Musiksammlung Concert Program, 1 and 2 May 1826, Kärntnerthor Theater.
6. GdMf, Concert Program, 5 December 1825, Landständischensaal. A special poem, 'Mozarts Todtenfeyer' by A. F. E. Langbein was recited by Anschütz. The proceeds of the concert went to Seyfried. For Beethoven's concerts see Deutsch, *Biography*, 751–2 n.
7. Begun in the eighteenth century, the Augarten concerts once featured Vienna's most promising musicians, including Mozart, who introduced many new works there. Although their popularity waned in the nineteenth century, the May Day concerts continued. Hanslick, 1, 70–5.
8. A vivid description of the festival is provided by Friedrich Reischl in *Wien zur Biedermeierzeit*, 199–207.
9. WStB, Concert Program, 11–12 July 1830, 'Brigittenau Volksfest'.
10. A decree of the Hofkanzlei in January 1820 set aside Normatagen for charity benefits. *Sammlung der Gesetze*, 1820, no. 2, 2.
11. For a more detailed description of the various concert halls in the city, refer to Ullrich, 'Konzertsälen', 108–18, and Rudolf Klein, 'Konzertpflege', 290–9.
12. HHStA, General Intendanz, Hofoper, K. 71 Oper, fo. 167.
13. For example, the fee for a concert by Friedrich Thierfeld was waived on 26 April 1825, possibly because the concert was under the direction of Pieringer and Sonnleithner. *Exhibitions Protocoll der Gesellschaft der Musikfreunde 1812–1829*, no. 402.
14. GdMf Archives: Concert announcement inviting musicians to participate in Louis Spohr's *Das befreyte Deutschland*, 28 November 1819, and Beethoven (MacArdle-Misch), 444.
15. Spohr, *Journeys*, 168; Adam Carse, *The Orchestra from Beethoven to Berlioz* (Cambridge W. Heffer & Sons, Ltd, 1948) 137.
16. GdMf Concert Program: First rehearsal was scheduled for 26 October 1819 and the concert was presented on 28 and 30 November 1819.
17. One exception may have occurred in 1817 when the pianist Kruft performed a *Phantasie und Polonaise*, although the program does not indicate whether the work was improvised.
18. Klein, 29; Ullrich, 112; Biba, 'Abendunterhaltungen', 9–10.
19. Beethoven (Anderson), II, no. 1066, 935. Note: Beethoven plays on Gebauer's name by writing, 'Geh! Bauer' (Go peasant!), just as he interchanges the word Abtrittskarte (lavatory ticket) for Eintrittskarte (admission ticket).
20. The Euryanthe Overture was played at seven concerts and Oberon at eight concerts that year alone according to concert programs in NB, Musiksammlung and Theatersammlung (on microfilm).
21. Blümml and Gugitz, 'Basilius Bohdanowicz und seine musikalische Familie', *Von Leuten und Zeiten*, 238–56.
22. GdMf, Concert Program: 8 November 1828; 23 February 1823.
23. The number was probably the result of his lost income during the country's bankruptcy in 1811, the subsequent devaluation of the florin, and the financial problems of his noble patrons.
24. In 1824 Lent began on 3 March and Easter observances ended on 18 April. Thus, Beethoven had about one month to organize his concert if he wished to present it during the regular concert season.
25. Beethoven (MacArdle and Misch), 44.
26. Thayer, 909, 911; Beethoven (MacArdle and Misch), no. 387, 445–6.
27. Thayer stated that the weather that day was 'delightful', but the diary of Karl Rosenbaum records that the day was 'trüb, kühl, und windig' – even too windy

for him to go into his garden. He attended Beethoven's concert instead and wrote only that David sang the Rossini aria in a mediocre way. If Rosenbaum is correct about the weather (his entries were written daily), Beethoven's second concert can be seen as an even greater failure. Rosenbaum, Sunday 23 May 1824, 13ihr.

28. Angelica Catalani (in 1818) and Rossini (in 1822) had received similar tumultuous receptions before in Vienna.

29. Perth, 6 June 1828. Es hat mich viel Geld gekostet, ich habe mich in Schweiss gebadet, aber ich habe ihn gehört, und um sich eine Begriff von seinen Spiele zu machen, muss' man ihn hören. Die Wirkung, welche seine der Violinentlackten Töne auf jeden Zuhörer mache, lässt sich nicht beschreiben. Wir haben grosse, ausgezeichnete Violinspieler in Wien, Mayseder, Böhm, Clement, Hellmesberger, Lubin, Jansa, Fradl, etc: aber Paganini ist nicht nur der grösste, der erste, er übertrifft nicht nur alle, sondern liefert auch den Beweis, wie weit alle gegen seine erstaunungswürdigen Kunst noch zurück sind. Wenn er uns jetzt dirch die weiche, schmelzenden Töne mächtig ergreift, zur Wehmuth stimmt und uns beinahe Thränen entlackt, so weiss er uns gleich darauf in die fröhlichste Stimmung zu versetzen, kaum glauben wir dieser zu huldigen, so beherrscht er schon wieder durch die Kraft, die ihm zu Geboth steht, einen Tyrannen gleich, sein Instrument auf eine Art, dass man wähnt, er müsse es neu unter seinen Händen zertrümmern... Ich vermag keine Vergleichung zwischen ihn und einen anderen Violinspieler anzustellen, und doch möchte ich dies so gern thun, aber mit wem soll ich ihn vergleichen? Ich möchte sagen: Paganini ist das unter den Violinspieler, was einst in seiner glänzensten Epoche Napoleon unter den Feldherren Europas war.

30. NB, Musiksammlung: Concert Program, 13 May 1828, Hofburg, and 12 June 1828, Kärntnerthor Theater.

31. For a fuller listing of Paganini's concert repertory see Hanson, 'Vienna', Appendix F.

5 MUSIC IN THE SALON

1. Sonnleithner, 737–8. Der heute sogenannte Mittelstand war noch vorzüglich im Allgemeinen [mit] weniger Zeit und Sinn für höhere geistige Genüsse. Seit den letzten Jahrzehnten des achtzehnten Jhs. hat sich aber dieser Zustand nach und nach wesentlich verändert, ja beinahe umgekehrt. Die Regenten als solche betrachten (mit ehrenvollen Ausnahmen) die Unterstützung der Künste beinahe nur, wie eine unvermeidliche Last; die ihnen zunächst stehenden 'grossen' Herrn, haben ihre Prachtbauten, ihre Bildergallerien, ihre Musikkapellen, meistentheils aufgegeben und sich anderen Musen zugewendet...Im neunzehnten Jahrhundert sind die hochgestellten Mäzenaten grössentheils verschwunden, und die Musen haben sich unter den Schutz des bescheidenen Mittelstandes geflüchtet.

2. Glossy, *Studien*, 64. 16 March 1817. Kein Minister macht mehr ein Haus. Vor 30 Jahren war Wien deshalb eine so beliebte Residenz, weil jeden Tag ein Haus für jedermann offenstand, Diners und Assambleer gewesen sind, indessen anno 1816 und 1817 in der Regel alle Häuser geschlossen sind...

3. Thürheim, II, 195. Mehrmals spielte man in diesem Winter bei der Fürstin Lubmoriska und Gräfin Esterhazy, geborene Marquise Roisin. Das Haus der letzteren gehörte zu den angenehmsten Wiens. Niemand besass so sehr das Talent, kleine Feste zu erfinden und zu arrangieren, wie sie und ihr Gatte. Da gab es lebende Marionetten, burleske Maskeraden, lebende Charaden, chinesische Schattenbilder,

Schach – und Whistpartien, deren Figuren von Personen der Gesellschaft dargestellt wurden.

4. Andlaw, I, 168. Soll ich nun kurz Ton und Geist der damaligen Gesellschaft bezeichnen, so möchte ich sie ebenso sein als harmlos nennen; ohne politische Kabale bewegte sich die Unterhaltung in einem ziemlich einförmigen Kreise, an sich unbedeutenden Dingen eine grosse Wichtigkeit beilegend, über die man später selbst oft lächelte. Es galt einen Kampf um den Vorzug in der Eleganz, man stritt sich in allem Ernste um die Frage, wer zur 'Crême' gehöre, und nicht immer bestimmten gerade Schönheit, Reichthum, Verstand, Rang oder Geburt, ob in diesem fashionablen Reiche Bürgerrechte zu erwerben waren, denn launisch wie sie ist, liess seine Regentin, die Mode, nur zu oft den Zufall walten.

5. Tuvora, 96–7. Die Salons der Finanzfamilien, besonders einige derselben, haben sich dadurch, dass sie das Recht, eingeführt zu werden, ausserordentlich leicht machten, eine gewisse Publicität erworben, Fremde strömen dort ab und zu... Vornehme, begüterte, gut gestellte, unterrichtete Männer wird man allerdings herzufinden...

6. See the excellent biography by Hilde Spiel entitled *Fanny von Arnstein oder die Emanzipation.*

7. *Bemerkungen*, 112–13. Von des Mittags um 12 Uhr bis spät Mitternacht trifft man hier die ausgesuchteste Gesellschaft an, zu der man, ohne besondere Einladung, täglich den Zutritt hat. Um unausgesetzt die Honneurs ihres Hauses machen zu können, geht sie nie oder selten aus, wahrlich kein geringes Opfer, dessen Gewicht der Fremde nicht dankbar genug anerkennen kann. Man kommt ohne grosse Ceremonie und geht ohne sich zu beurlauben; verbannt ist jede lästige Etikette der höhern Zirkel; der Geist, entfesselt vom Zwange der Convenienz, athmet hier freyer.

8. *Rahel Varnhagen und Ihre Zeit*, Friedrich Kemp (Munich, Kösel Verlag, 1968), 70–1.

9. *Jahrbuch der Tonkunst* (1797) quoted in Spiel, 331. Frau von Arnstein: die lernhaftesten und schwersten Kompositionen sind ihr Lieblingsspiel. Sie liest sehr gut, hat eine leichte Hand und meisterhaften Anschlag. In Geschwindigkeit exzelliert sie. Es ist zu bedauern, dass sie seit einigen Jahren den Geschmack daran verloren zu haben scheint, denn sie berührt das Fortepiano sehr wenig mehr. Leute von ihrem Vermögen sollten die dürftige Kunst nicht verlassen, welcher es ohnehin je länger je mehr anthäthiger Aufmunterung fehlt. Auch hat sie eine sehr angenehme Stimme und geläufige Kehle. Ihre Tochter verspricht ebenfalls viele Talente für die Musik.

10. Reichardt quoted in Spiel, 327. ...spielte Frau von *Pereira* mit dem Frl. von Kurzbeck eine sehr brillante Doppelsonate von Steibelt recht meisterhaft und dann mit unglaublicher Langmut und Güte viele schöne Walzer, nach welchen sich schöne, junge Welt in dem immer zunehmenden Gewühl lustig umdrehte. Sobald der äusserste Saal zum Souper eröffnet wurde, entfernte ich mich: es war gegen Mitternacht...

11. GdMf, Index der Gesellschaft der Musikfreunde des Öesterreichischen Kaiserstaates von 1812–30, no. 85,3; no. 285.

12. de la Garde quoted in Spiel, 428. Eine ausgezeichnete Musik, wie man sie damals nur in Wien hören konnte, bezauberte des Ohr. Die vornehmste Gesellschaft von Wien drängte sich in den Salon, alle einflussreichen Personen des Kongresses, alle Fremde von Rang, alle Häupter der fürstlichen Häuser waren anwesend. Es fehlten eigentlich nur noch die Souveräne...

Note: The emperor and his family observed strict class separation in social affairs.

13. Gentz, II, 168. Die Gesellschaft in diesen beiden Häusern, so sehr ich auch die beiden

Schwestern ehre, grentzt doch immer gar zu nahe an *mauvaise société*. Nun [muss] ich mich allemal überwinden, dorthin zu gehen; aber es wäre krasse Undankbarkeit, wenn ich sie hernachlässigte...

14. Tuvora. 86. Man begegnet in diesen üppigen Salons häufig Wiener Schöngeistern und Künstlern, selten hingegen den wahrhaft verdienstvollen heimischen Professoren und Gelehrten, nicht als ob diese sich selbst zurückzögen, sondern weil man sich keine Mühe nimmt, sie herbeizuziehen; und das kann wohl bei der Lage der Dinge nicht anders sein. Die Finanzfamilien betrachten die Kunst und die Wissenschaft nicht in ihrer souverainen Herrlichkeit; sie erscheint ihnen lediglich als ein Mittel, das Leben zu schmücken und zu verherrlichen.

15. Weis, lv. Du musst wissen, fuhr ich fort, dass jetzt beinahe ganz Wien musikalisch ist; du wirst selten ein Haus finden, wo nicht ein Fortepiano den übrigen Möbeln beygestellt steht, selbst wenn unter der Familie Niemand musikalisch seyn sollte, so gehört es doch zum *bon ton*, ein solches Instrument zu besitzen.

16. Normann, 43. Ausserdem ist die Zahl der Dilettanten ungeheuer. Fast in jeder Familie von mehreren Mitgliedern ist ein Dilettant. Fortepianos fehlen gewiss nirgends in wohlhabendern Häusern, und in eng gebauten Häusern tritt sehr oft das komische Verhältniss ein, dass sich die Parteien wegen der Stunden, in welchen sie sich zu über denken, Abrede nehmen müssen. Sehr oft hört man in einem Haus, zu ebener Erde Violine spielen, im ersten Stock Fortepiano, im zweiten Flöte, im dritten Gesang und Guitarre, während im Hofe noch obendrein ein blinder Mann sich mit einem Clarinett abmüht.

17. See Cyril Ehrlich, 'Social Emulation and Industrial Progress – The Victorian Piano', Inaugural Lecture, The Queen's University of Belfast, 5 February 1975, 3–4.

18. See the following for a more complete discussion: Hans Worb, 'Salonmusik', (121–30) and Imogen Fellinger, 'Die Begiffe Salon und Salonmusik in der Musikanschauung des 19ten Jahrhunderts', in *Studien zur Trivialmusik des 19ten Jahrhunderts*, ed. Carl Dahlhaus (Regensburg, Bosse Verlag, 1967).

19. *Seufzer*, 112. Ein Musikchor führt unterdessen beliebte Piecen auf, und sind Töchter im Hause, so wird auch wohl ein Tänzchen gemacht. Jedes angesehene Haus hat nicht nur seinen eigenen Musiklehrer, sondern auch einige Bediente, welche zugleich gute Musikanten sind. Die Zimmer sind parketirt und gewischt, und gefirnisst, also zum Tanz jeden Augenblick bereit.

20. Fritz Hartmann kept his diary in French in order to practice using the language.

21. See Deutsch, *Biography*, 784 for the names in the picture; also Maurice Brown's discussion of the work in 'Schwind's Schubert-Abend bei Josef Spaun', in *Essays on Schubert* (London, Macmillan, 1966) 155–68.

22. See her memoirs (vols II and III) for descriptions of her salon between the years 1798 and 1822.

23. The most recent and complete biography of Kiesewetter is written by Herfrid Kier, *G. R. Kiesewetter* (Regensburg, Bosse Verlag, 1968).

24. Herfrid Kier, 'Kiesewetters Historische Hauskonzerte', *Kirchenmusikalisches Jahrbuch*, LII (1968), 95–120.

25. Pölchau quoted in Kier, 'Hauskonzerte', 111. Bitte keine grossen Erwartungen mitzubringen: es ist nur meine kleine Haus–Taschen– und Reise-Kapelle, die sich versammelt, und die Ausführungen aus dem Stehgreif. Wir versammeln uns um halb 7, und treiben Musik bis etwa 10: dann nehmen wir eine kleine Restauration wobei es vielleicht auch nicht ganz ohne Sang ablaufen möchte...

26. Kier, *Kiesewetter*, 65. In der musikalischen Saison lasse ich seit 18 Jahren Musik der alten Meister spielen. Es sind nicht Konzerte nach der Art des Herrn F, der die

Geschichte von Jahrhunderten im Laufe von zwei Stunden [ ], sie sind auch nicht zu vergleichen mit den rein klassischen Produktionen des Herrn Choron. Aber die Personen, die meine Konzerte besuchen, empfangen richtige Eindrücke des Geschichtsablaufes, da es der Gegenstand meines Programmes ist, und ich ganze Stücke spielen lasse oder beachtliche Fragmente aller Arten.

6. MUSICAL INSTITUTIONS: RELIGIOUS AND MILITARY

1. Uniate Greek Catholics recognized the authority of the Pope in Rome, but retained their Slavonic Byzantine liturgy and allowed their clergy to marry. See Leslie Tihany, *A History of Middle Europe* (Rutgers, NJ, Rutgers University Press, 1976), 112.
2. Pezzl, *Beschreibung* (1841), 27. Pezzl presumably did not include secular priests (parish priests) in his survey.
3. Normann, II, 28. Bleib ein ehrlicher Kerl, folg' dein Vatern und glaub' wasd' willst.
4. Glassbrenner, 47. Auch der Pietismus, diese geistige Seuche, welche im Norden unzählige Opfer hinrafft und den Gang der Aufklärung hemmt, findet in Wien keine Anhänger...er [der Wiener] fragt wenig nach Zeremonie und findet überall seinen Gott, wo er Genuss und Schönheit findet. Die Welt schmeckt mir noch, ruft er, warum soll ich verhungern?
5. Normann, II, 47. Das Land seufzt unter einer Menge drückender Klosterherrschaften, welche viel einsaugen, Schätze aufhaufen und dem Volke seine besten Quellen entziehen. Die Unzufriedenheit hierüber ist auch im gemeinen Volke ziemlich allgemein...
6. Nicolai, 81.
7. See Blümml and Gugitz, 'Das Annafest im alten Wien', *Im alten Wien*, 63–86.
8. *Sammlung der Gesetze*, 1826, no. 266, 371, 'Verboth der Verfertigung der Christus und anderer Heiligen Bildern von Pfefferkuchen Teig'.
9. HHStA, Oberkämmeramt, 14/28 (old 84) Resolutions Buch VIII, 1825–8, no. 30, No. 17071/11454, 2 April 1825. Sr. Majestät haben zu Folge eines h. Hofdekreten vom 19/27 d. M. zur Verfindung, dass die Musiker in den Kirchen mehr zur Zerstreuung und Unterhaltung als zur Beförderung der Andacht dienen, zu befehlen geruht, der gesammten Geistlichkeit zur Pflicht zu machen, dass die Kirchenmusiker nirgends Frauenzimmer genommen, oder zugelassen werden, mit alleiniger Ausnahme derjenigen, die vermöge ihres Standes dazu verbunden sind, als die Frauen, Töchter und Schwestern der Corregenten, Schulmeister u. dgl., und dass auch keine solchen Stücke produzirt werden, die mehr für ein Theater zu verfügen. Hindurch erhält der Magistrats Bericht vom 22 v.M. Z. 4555 die Erledigung.
10. A notable exception is Otto Biba's monograph on church music in Vienna around 1783. See Biba, 'Kirchenmusik', 19–51.
11. Schmidl, 213. For a fuller history of the Hofkapelle refer to Ludwig Köchel's *Die kaiserliche Hof-Musikkapelle* (Vienna, Beck'sche Universitäts Buchhandlung, 1899), and Karl Wisokoro-Meytsky's *Die Hofmusikkapelle: The Musical Establishment of the Vienna Court* (Vienna, Hofmusikkapelle, 1965). Some information about the church musicians is available in Adam Carse's *Orchestra*, 252–3.
12. Novello, 178–9. Her mention of the seventeenth-century composers Hasse and Vinci may suggest that the church already had begun to return to the styles advocated by the Cecilian Movement.

13. Pezzl, *Skizze*, 281. Mit der heiligen Messe wurde ebenfalls eine Art von Unordnung getrieben. Man las deren zu gleicher Zeit so viele, dass sie, statt die Andächtigen in einer ruhigen Gemütsversammlung zu halten, dieselben vielmehr [zerstrauten].
14. The practice in the Mass and Office is recorded by Kilian Reinhardt in his book of rubrics entitled, *Rubriche Generali per le Funzioni Ecclesiae Musicali di tutto l'Anno. Con un'Appendice in fine dell'Essenziali ad Usa, e Servizio dell'August, Austriaca ed Imp. le Capella*, 1727.
15. See Alexander Ringer, 'Salomon Sulzer, Joseph Mainzer and the Romantic a cappella Movement', *Studia Musicologica*, XI (1969), 355–70.
16. For a sociological study of class rank of Austria's army officers during the nineteenth century, refer to Nikolaus von Peradovich, *Die Führungsschichten in Oesterreich und Preussen (1804–1918)* (Wiesbaden, Franz Steiner Verlag, 1955).
17. Normann, 100. Wie anders ist dies geworden seit anno 1826. Mit Schrecken hört ein Vater, wenn ihm ein Sohn geboren wird, und ist er herangewachsen, so hat er keine andere Sorge, als ihn bald als möglich aus der Schule zu nehmen und ihn militärfrei zu machen. Arme verstümmeln sich und Reiche zahlen und bestechen, Verbrechen werden ausgeübt und ein schändlicher Handel getrieben von den rekruitirenden Beamten, die die Macht über Leben und Freiheit der Menschen in Händen haben. Tragikomisch ist der Anblick der studirenden Jugend, unter welcher sich die Zahl der Krüppel und Elenden in eben dem Grade vermehrt, in dem sich die Zahl der Gesunden vermindert.
18. Normann, 13. Ein grosser Uebelstand in der oesterreichischen Armee ist die schlechte Behandlung der Soldaten. Die Gemeinen und Unteroffiziere... werden mit Er angesprochen und unterliegen entehrenden köperlichen Strafen, Stockprügeln und Spiessruthen.
19. VA, P.H. 1179/1827, 'Festa di Zara – Il Natalizio di sua Maestra Francesco I'.

7 POPULAR MUSIC

1. Langenschwarz, 23. Der Wiener im Tanzsalon ist völlig ein anderer Mensch. Sein Geist, der vorher schon *schläfrig* ist, geht beim Tanzen in den förmlichsten *Schlaf* und *Starrkrampf* über, während der Körper neu auflebt, und jeder Nerv im 6/8 Takt zittert.
2. Pemmer, 164. Pemmer writes that the impost tax, begun during the reign of Maria Theresia, required nine employees to collect and process (Einnehmer, Kollektanten, Gegenhandler, Journalisten, and 5 Uebernehmer). He surmises therefore that the tax must have been lucrative to have supported so many officials for so many years.
3. *Sammlung der Gesetze*, 1827, 189. A ball organizer's first offense cost between 2 and 50 fl.; a second offense doubled the amount, and a third offense revoked his right to give other balls. Infringements by the host of private balls cost him between 10 and 100 fl.; and for any offending guest 2–10 fl. could be charged. Musicians could expect police arrest for 3 to 24 hours, extending to two or three days if the offense were repeated.
4. In 1825 the archbishop declared that Carnival would last only five weeks that year, since Easter was unusually late (Wilmot, 1–2). The 'Ball Season' is still observed in Vienna today, although the restrictions of Ash Wednesday and Lent are no longer enforced by the state.
5. The dance collections are listed in Deutsch, *Biography*, *passim*.
6. *Characters in the Grand Fancy Ball Given by the British Ambassador*, 2nd edn (London, R. Ackermann, 1828), 10–11.

7. Glassbrenner, 72. In Wien aber ist diese Wuth ausgeartet. Da sieht man wenig Tänzerinnen mehr, sondern lauter Bacchantinnen. Sie zucken schon fieberhaft, sobald der Arm des Mannes sie berührt, dann pressen sie ihre Brust dicht an die seinige, den Kopf an seine Schulter, und nun lassen sie sich herumschleifen, saugen in dieser wollüstigen Lage jede Bewegung des Mannes, jene lüsterne Musik ein; die Unschuld flieht erschreckt aus dem Saale, die Weiblichkeit zerrt sich flehend zu ihren Füssen, und der Tod steht in der Ecke und lacht sich in's Fäustchen.

8. Laube, 257. Nach Metternich ist Sperl der wichtigste Mann in Wien. Jener ist Minister des Auswärtigen dieser Minister des Innern.

9. *Ibid.*, 275. Es versammelt sich dort allerdings keine *haute volée*, es ist eine sehr gemischte Gesellschaft. Aber die Ingredienzen sind nicht zu verachten, und das Gebräu ist klassisch-wienerisch.

10. Stöger, 4 (1897) no. 2, 24; no. 3, 41–5; 61–5.

11. Of the many biographies of the Strauss family, the most useful for this study were the following: Hans Jäger-Sustenau, *Johann Strauss. Der Walzerkönig und seine Dynastie* (Vienna, Verlag für Jugend und Volk, 1965) and Egon Gartenberg, *Johann Strauss. The End of an Era* (University Park, PA, University Press, 1974).

12. *Hans Jörgel*, Part 15, 1833 (?); Weis, liv–lv; Boas, 141.

13. *Meine grosse Reise*, 78. Musikcorps ist sicher und jedes Instrument so eingeübt, dass alles ein Strich, ein Ton, ein Crescendo, ein Fortissimo oder Piano ist. Selten habe ich die Blasinstrumenten so delicat behandeln hören, wie in den zwei Tauben, wo Lanners Bande unter seiner Leitung von 6–11 Uhr Abends spielte.

14. See Ludwig, *Biedermusikanten*, 23; Schmidl, 324.

15. Normann, 36. Die Lieder ohne Text werden in Bierhäusern gewöhnlich von einem Zitherschläger auf dem Instrumente vorgetragen, während die Anwesenden dazu pfeifen und paschen. Manche bringen es auf diesem Instrumente sogar zur Virtuosität, wie der weltberühmte Wiener Bierwirth Heiligschein, der sogar Concerte auf der Zither gab. [The meaning of Bierwirth is unclear. Either he owned the tavern or was the bar tender.]

16. Normann, 38. Es wird in Wien auch ein eigener Handel mit Liedern getrieben und selbst in der Stadt findet man auf offener Strasse ein bedeutendes Waarenlager von 'gans neichen weltlichen Liadern, de mer erst kriagt ham'. Solche Liederver-käuferinnen laufen entweder die Strassen ab oder haben einen eigenen Verkaufplatz, wo geistliche und weltliche Lieder an einer Schnur hängen, mit den Geschichten von den vier Heumanskindern, der Genovesa, der bildlichen Darstellung aller Menschenalter, der verkehrten Welt, des Mannes, der von seiner Frau geprügelt wird, und umgekehrt, eines mikroskopisch vergrösserten Flohs und dergl.

17. Blümml and Gugitz, 'Der Harfendichter Ludwig Bleibtreu', *Im alten Wien*, 273–4.

18. Glassbrenner, 53. Im Wurstelprater und im Lerchenfeld sitzt Vater und Mutter, Sohn und Tochter, und alle lachen herzlich über die giftigen Zoten, die mit artigen Melodieen überzuckert, aus dem Munde der sogennanten Harfenisten ertönen und von höchst characteristischen Mienen und Gesten begleitet werden; um ihren Effekt zu erhöhen...

19. They were alluding perhaps to the July revolution in Paris or the Polish uprising in Warsaw, both in 1830.

20. Weis, lvi. Doch um Musik zu hören, darf man nicht erst eine Schenke besuchen, es ist in der Stadt kein sogenanntes Durchhaus (wo man nämlich durch zwey entgegen gesetzte Thore von einer Gasse in die andere gelangen kann) wo nicht der häusigen Passage wegen, ein Bursche oder ein Mädchen mit Harfe oder Guitarre steht. Diese sind meistens Blinde und halbblöde bedauernswerthe Geschöpfe, welche durch ihr Spiel Lebensunterhalt suchen.

21. Meynert, 234–5....mit seinen verbrauchten Lieder wusste er jederzeit seltsam die rechte Melodie meines Herzens zu accompaniren, auch hielt er stets, sobald er meiner ansichtig ward, besseres Tempo, als dies gewöhnlich bei ihm der Fall war...Sie klingen einfach, so lieblich eintönig an unser Herz, wie eine uralte Volkspoesie, die Jeder verstehen und wiederdichten kann, und die dessen ungeachtet hoch über dem Gewöhnlichen steht.
22. Müller, *Die Winterreise*, trans. by Philip L. Miller, *The Ring of Words* (New York, W. W. Norton & Co., 1973), 258–9.
23. VA, P.H., Ministerium von Innern, Carton 1370 IV-M-7, 1822...Die tägliche Erfahrung lehret, dass derley mit Leyern oder Schaukausten heranziehende Invaliden nicht selten zu den gefährlichen Landstreichern gehören, und dass sie, wenn sie auch nicht Verbrecher sind, es doch nur zu leicht bey dem unordentlich müssigen Lebenswandel, den sie führen, werden können...

SUMMARY – EPILOGUE

1. Henry Schnitzler, '"Gay Vienna" – Myth and Reality', *Journal of the History of Ideas*, 15 (1954), 103.
2. Johann Slokar, *Geschichte der oesterreichischen Industrie* (Vienna, F. Tempsky, 1914), 83–93, 105.
3. Carl August Schimmer, *Geschichte von Wien* (Vienna, I. P. Sollinger, 1844), 297.
4. See the collection of anecdotes from eyewitnesses edited by Johann Vogel, *Aus dem alten Wien* (Vienna, Prondel & Evald, 1865).
5. See the reviews of Op. 159, Fantasy for Violin and Piano, or the reluctance of the publishers to buy the String Quartets in G and D, or the difficulties in performing the Symphony in C (Deutsch, *Biography*, 715–16, 746, 761).
6. David Pinkey, *The French Revolution of 1830* (Princeton, Princeton University Press, 1972), 253–5.
7. Heintl, 124–5. Es herrschte eine Stimmung, jener gleich, wenn man am Horizont ein furchtbares Gewitter heraufziehen sieht, welches ringsherum alles zu verheeren droht. Man sieht es, zittert davor, und muss dennoch den Erfolg abwarten. Die Generalstände waren verheissen, die Nation im Gefühle ihrer, durch die öffentliche Meinung vereinigten Kraft, sah der Erfüllung dieser Verheissung mit Zuverlässigkeit entgegen.
8. Bauernfeld, *Erinnerungen*, 371. Uns übrigen, die wir nach wie vor am Boden kleben geblieben, leuchtete die Juli-Revolution wie ein flammendes Meteor in die kümmerische Finsterniss der blödsinnigen oesterreichischen Nacht. Von da an begannen wir erst fleissig Zeitungen zu lesen und stärkten unsern Mut an Börne und Heines Ergiessungen. Die 'Spaziergang eines Wiener Poeten' nicht zu vergessen.
9. See St Leonard, ed., *Polenlieder, Deutscher Dichtung*. 1, 'Der Novemberaufstand in der Polenlieder', (Krakow, Podogozze, 1911).
10. J. von Hammer, 'Gassbeleuchtung in Wien', *Wiener Zeitung*, 17 April 1828; *Wien Chronik*, ed. Perfahl, 386.
11. Julius Marx, *Die wirtschaftlichen Ursachen der Revolution von 1848 in Oesterreich* (Graz, Hermann Böhlaus, 1965), 94–123.
12. Gutzkow quoted in Bauer, 67. Forscht man nach den Gründen dieser Aenderung, so liegen sie offen zutage. Die Kunst des Daseins ist schwieriger geworden. Das Geld hat einen geringern Wert als sonst. Man braucht mehr zum Ausgeben, und die Einnahmen sind die alten geblieben.

13. Pichler, II, 383. Hierzu kommt noch das stets mehr überhandnehmende Tabak-rauchen, ohne welches der grösste Theil der Männer jetzt nicht mehr leben und das er doch in Gegenwart der Frauen oder in dem unseligen Salon nicht verüben kann: Sowie die zahlosen Kaffee – und Gasthäuser welche Tabakrauchen die angenehmsten Möglichkeiten darbieten, diesem Gelüst nachzuhängen Verbind-lichkeit ledig zu sein.

14. Bauernfeld, *Erinnerungen*, 154. Die 'Concordia' und der 'Hesperus' und andere mehr oder minder literarische Gesellschaften hingen nur lose und äusserlich aneinander, ohne die gemüthlichen und freundschaftlichen Elemente, welche uns damals so traulich vereinigten. Kurz die harmlosen Tagen sind vorüber.

15. Rudolf Hormann, *Der Wiener Männergesangverein. Chronik der Jahren 1843–1893* (Vienna, Verlag des Wiener Männergesangverein, 1893).

16. Bauernfeld, *Tagebücher*, 31 August 1827, 40. Was wird aus uns Allen? Werden wir zusammenhalten?

BIBLIOGRAPHY

ARCHIVAL MATERIALS

The primary sources pertinent to a study of Viennese culture and art are housed in various of the national and municipal archives in Vienna. A brief introduction to these archives explains their individual contribution.

The Haus-, Hof-, und Staatsarchiv (HHStA) contain documents relating to Austria's nobility, court, and highest offices of government. Devoted primarily to political and administrative matters, the records from the court theaters reveal much about court balls, concerts, and musicians' salaries.

The Niederoesterreichisches Landesarchiv (NOeLA) – the archives of the state of Lower Austria – at one time housed records of that state's highest court, tax and business matters. But when the archives were moved to another location in 1850, a portion of the collection was donated to the Court Archives and the rest were discarded or dispersed elsewhere. The archives still own a hand-written index and brief resumé of its former holdings, called the Präsidialindex.

Once housed in the Justizpalast, the Allgemeines Verwaltungs-archiv (VA) contain the records of the former Ministry of Internal Affairs, which included the papers of the Police and Censorship offices. During the bitter political struggles of 1927, however, the Justizpalast was burned to the ground. Only a small fraction of the collection was salvaged, and that is badly damaged. A hand-written Zettelkatalog, arranged alphabetically, and written before the fire, provides access to the collection.

The Archiv der Stadt Wien (WStA) preserves the records of Vienna's municipal government and a special collection pertaining to the city's eminent citizens. Among its sequestration records lies detailed information about the general populace, and its account books record the money spent by the city for music as well as its income from music impost taxes. Also housed in the Rathaus is the Viennese City Library (WStB) which contains many rare manuscripts of music, letters and diaries as well as a large collection of concert programs.

For music, the archives of the Gesellschaft der Musikfreunde (GdMf) are invaluable. There are preserved the internal records of the Friends of Music Society and its conservatory, and the papers and music of many musical personalities.

The National Library (NB), within the divisions of the Musik-, Theater-, and Manuskript Sammlungen, contains many priceless collections of memoirs, concert and theater programs, and music manuscripts.

Bibliography

(HHStA) Haus-, Hof-, und Staatsarchiv

Kabinets Protokoll vols. 124, 134, 161 (1786–1803).
Staat. Wissenschaft und Kunst. Carton 11.
Polizeykorrespondenz, old no. 75 (1812–37).
Staatskanzlei ad Polizei 58–60 (old 77–80) (1740–1848).
Staatskanzlei Nothenwechsel:
  Noten. von Polizei. Cartons 36, 38, 39 (old 45–8) (1819–25)
  Noten. ad Polizei. Cartons 10–14 (old 11–15) (1822–30).
Oberstkämmeramt r4–11 von O.MeA. Rückgest. Akten (1792–1842).
General Intendanz, Burgtheater (1825–6).
General Intendanz, Hofoper (1823–5; 1826–7).
Kammerzahlamts Kassa Hauptbuch (1810–21).

H. Bittner, ed., *Inventare des Wiener Haus-, Hof-, und Staatsarchiv* (Vienna, Adolph Holzbauer, 1940).

Rudolf Till, 'Archivalische Quellen zur Kulturgeschichte Wien', *Verein für Geschichte der Stadt Wien*, xv (1959), 92–106.

(NOeLA) Niederoesterreichisches Landesarchiv

Polizei Indis. Statthalt Arch. NOe. Regierung 20.41051.
Präsidialindex – Noe. Reg. 1820–30.
Helmut Feigl, 'Das Archiv für Niederoesterreich und seine Archivare 1893–1940' (typed manuscript).

(VA) Allgemeines Verwaltungsarchiv

Polizei Hofstelle (P.H.), Zettl (Z): (each folder cited individually in work by Zettl number and title).

Carton 1051 IV-J-NOe. 'Städtische Sachen (1825–6)'.
Carton 1348 IV-M-3 'Anstalten gegen Tumulte zur Entdeckung staatsgefährlicher Gesellschaften (1815–48)'.
Carton 1370 IV-M-7 'Ordnung, Anstand in Schank, Kaffeehäuser, Tanzsäle'.

Inventare oesterreichischer staatlicher Archive (Vienna, k.k. Hof und Staatsdruckerei).
Inventare des Allgemeinen Archiv des Ministerium des Innern (1909).

(WStA) Archiv der Stadt Wien

Gustav Gugitz, 'Auszüge über Persönlichkeiten des Wiener Kulturleben'. HS. B 323 41 exemplar (in the Verlassenschaftsabtheilung of the archive).

Hofkanzlei Zettl Catalog (drawer 158–61).

Merkantil Gericht: Fasc. 3
  A-19, A-90 (Arnstein–Eskeles).
  E-25, E-87 (B. and D. Eskeles).
  G-67, G-173, G-183 (Geymüller).

Oberkämmeramt (11–10) Erträgnisse:
Empfangs Journal, 1819–30.
Geld Ausgabe, 1819–30.
Erforderniss fixierte, 1819–30.

Bibliography

Gustav Gugitz, *Bibliographie zur Geschichte und Stadtkunde von Wien nebst Quellen- und Literaturhinweisen* (Vienna, Touristik-Verlag, 1947), I.

(GdMf) Archive of the Gesellschaft der Musikfreunde-

Concert Programs Collection.
Index der Gesellschaft der Musikfreunde des österreichischen Kaiserstaates von 1812–30.
Exhibitions Protokoll der Gesellschaft der Musikfreunde Gründung, 1812–29.
Exhibitions Protokoll des Committees des Conservatorium, 1827–9.
Geld Rechnungen für das Jahr 1821 and the years 1822–30.

(WStB) Bibliothek der Stadt Wien
Concert Program Collection.
Verzeichnis der von Januar 1798 bis 1802 mit Verbot gelegten Bücher (typed manuscript B 6075).

Portheim Catalogue.

Handschriftabteilung –
Diaries of Franz and Friedrich Hartmann.
Diary of Wenzel Müller.
Diary of Mathias Perth.

(NB) National Bibliothek, Wien
Musiksammlung: Concert Program collection, *c.* 1820–30.
Theatersammlung: Concert and theater programs, *c.* 1820–30.
Handschriftsammlung: Diary of Karl Rosenbaum (1821–9).

EYEWITNESS ACCOUNTS:

Another large component of this study is based upon the experiences of eyewitnesses. Here also a brief introduction to the conventions of the various genres in which they wrote is needed as well as a word of caution about the authors' bias. In general, the literature written by eyewitnesses falls into four types: travel literature; diaries, memoirs and letters; literary portraits; and periodical articles.

Travel Literature – Guide books and travel accounts already were a popular literary genre by the end of the eighteenth century. Guidebooks supplied prospective tourists with practical information about Viennese life as well as its main attractions. The guides tend to be written objectively, with close attention to topography, climate, and statistical information. The works published in Vienna (Jenny, Schmidl, Pezzl, Hebenstreit) presumably were sanctioned by the Austrian government and censors and, as such, are free from derogatory remarks or political speculation.

Travel accounts (journals, letters, literary sketches) reflect a more personal impression. They offer a wide range of subjective responses and experiences. For example, Richard Bright, a physician and medical researcher, looks into Vienna's hospitals and the question of public health; Thomas Dibdin, an English librarian and book collector, describes Viennese libraries and private collections; Edward Holmes, an English organist, comments on musical life; and Frances Trollope, a professional writer of travel literature, caters to her female readers by concentrating on Viennese fashion, etiquette, and activities among the upper classes. As the literary historian, Friedrich Sengle has noted, many writers of travel literature saw themselves as romantic authors and therefore their works sometimes are full of spontaneous, romantic speculation and idealized landscapes (ii, 238–61). Many of their works are largely fiction.

In addition, travel literature was written by middle-class professionals such as journalists, doctors, businessmen and diplomats. Many were ill equipped to observe or impartially judge the actions of either the Viennese nobility or lower class, with whom they had little contact. Some travelers could not speak German and had to depend upon translators (often unreliable) or communicated in another language (often French). Some writers had other handicaps. James Holman, a British naval lieutenant, was blind and totally dependent upon others for visual descriptions of the city. Furthermore, as transient residents, travelers were prone to make judgments on the basis of superficial knowledge and first impressions. Thus, they describe Vienna at a precise moment, often without any historical context.

Diaries, memoirs, and letters – Unlike travel literature, diaries, memoirs, and letters were written by residents who usually concentrated on the people and events of importance in their own lives. The diaries fall between two extremes of simply listing events without any comment (like those of Schreyvogel, Costenoble, and Müller) or purely literary works with little reference to daily events (like those of Bauernfeld, Grillparzer, and Schubert). Letters usually communicate messages, hence they contain the writer's recent thoughts and activities and they may mention current events of interest. For example, the letters of Sophie Schröder, actress at the Burgtheater, relate information about the theater, her contracts, and costumes; while Schubert's letters describe musical activities, and Martha Wilmot writes mostly of domestic affairs with comparisons between life in Vienna and London.

Memoirs and autobiographies also record similar experiences, but usually in retrospect after many years. As a result, the authors may write with an historical perspective, ordering and arranging events as to their eventual importance. The memoirs of Bauernfeld emphasize the events leading to the revolution of 1848, while Caroline Pichler stresses the achievements of her literary salon. However, the memoirs are not always reliable since some authors confuse or incorrectly date past events. For example, the memoirs of Ignaz Castelli, written when he was about eighty years old, not only betray memory lapses, but also are guilty of idealization and exaggeration of his own role in historical events.

Literary Portraits – Literary portraits, or *Sittengemälde*, like travel literature were a popular literary genre from the eighteenth century. The works portray and often criticize Viennese manners and morals by means of satire, comparison, or debate. The works of Richter and Stifter are entertaining, humorous satires while those by Glassbrenner, Hecke, and the anonymous author of *Das constitutionelle Dresden . . .* draw poignant comparisons between life in Vienna and other European cities. The most infamous work in this genre is the portrait from 1828 by Karl Postl under the pseudonym of Charles Sealsfield. His inflammatory denunciation of Viennese rulers led to numerous literary battles and rebuttals, among which were those by Blumenbach in 1837 and the anonymous, presumably English, writer of *Sketches of Germany* in 1836.

Periodical literature – Newspapers, journals, *Taschenbücher* and almanacs supplied information about current events and contained some contemporary reviews of artistic activity in Vienna. But since these works were scrutinized closely by the censors, their reports are often colorless and inoffensive. Some of the musical reviews must be read with caution also because reviewers occasionally reviewed plays and concerts which they did not attend.

Beyond the limitations of these genres, the works of eyewitnesses also reveal particular biases which color their experiences. For example, only a few accounts, such as those by Metternich, Gentz, Thürheim, and Heintl, were written by aristocrats. Hence the majority of the works reflect a middle-class outlook.

A sizable number of the works were written by Englishmen and north Germans and thus contain some national bias as well. The English authors tend to be indignant about the intrusions of Austrian secret police, censors, and travel restrictions into their affairs. Protestant English observers, writing about a Catholic Vienna, also betray many deep-seated, religious prejudices which may account for their deprecating remarks about 'popish' icons and public religious ceremonies. The writers John Russell, Edward Holmes, and Frances Trollope manifest comparatively Puritanical views when they criticize what they perceive to be promiscuous behavior. They are scandalized by the Viennese theater costumes, by the parties during Carnival, and 'shameless' ballroom dancing. Moreover, after the defeat of Napoleon, most English reveled in their victory and displayed great national pride. This pride, together with their greater degree of social mobility, may explain why they tend to make patronizing remarks about the backwardness of Austrian government, or why they criticize the more formal etiquette of Viennese society.

North German writers share many of the religious views of the English, but they also harbor antagonism toward southern-European cultures. They condemn the Viennese for their 'Mediterranean' indolence, and their lack of discipline, self control, and intellectual prowess. However, in questions of literary or musical achievements, they vigorously defend Austrian art against the boasts of superiority made by the French and Italians.

Political beliefs, either monarchist (conservative) or republican (liberal) also divide the writers. Monarchists such as Turnbull, Heintl, Meynert, Normann, and Blumenbach repeatedly extoll the virtues and legitimacy of the Austrian imperial rulers, while warning of the dangers of anarchy and the horrors of revolution should the liberals gain power. But republicans like Postl, Forstmann, and Tuvora constantly point to the corruption and injustice in the Austrian government and press for immediate change and for a constitution.

Bibliography

TRAVEL LITERATURE AND LITERARY PORTRAITS

[Adrian-Werburg, Victor]. *Oesterreich und dessen Zukunft*, Hamburg, Hoffmann & Campe, 1843.

Atterbom, Per Daniel Amadeus. *Reisebilder aus dem romantischen Deutschland (1817–1819)*, Stuttgart, Steingrüben Verlag, 1970.

Bemerkungen oder Briefe über Wien eines jungen Bayern auf einer Reise durch Deutschland an eine Dame vom Stande, Leipzig, Baumgärtnersche Buchhandlung, 1804.

[Blumenbach, Wenzel Karl Wolfgang]. *Austria and the Austrians*, 2 vols, London, Henry Colburn, 1837. This is an English version of *Vertraute Briefe über Oesterreich von einem Diplomaten der ausruht*, Leipzig, Philipp Reclam Jr, 1837.

Boas, Eduard. *Reiseblüthen aus der Oberwelt*, Grimm. J. M. Gebhardt, 1834.

Bright, Richard. *Travels from Vienna through Lower Hungary*, Edinburgh, Archibald Constable & Co., 1818.

Cadet de Gassicourt. *Voyage en Autriche, en Moravie et en Bavière*, Paris, L'Hillier, 1818.

Charles, Jean [Braun von Braunthal]. *Wien und die Wiener im öffentlichen, häuslichen, geistigen und materiellen Leben*, Stuttgart, J. B. Metzler'sche Buchhandlung, 1840.

Das constitutionelle Dresden, das monarchische Wien und München im Jahre 1832 – Abhandlung über Kunst und die Sitten des Tages, Merseburg, Friedrich Weidemann, n.d.

de Bury, Blaze, Baroness. *Germania, its Courts, Camps and People*, London, Henry Colburn, 1850.

de la Garde, Comte. *Gemälde des Wiener Congresses 1814–1815*, Dr Ludwig Eichler (trans.), Leipzig, Friedrich Fleischer, 1844.

Dibdin, Thomas F. *A Bibliographical Antiquarian and Picturesque Tour in France and Germany*, London, Robert Jennings, 1829.

Empfindsame Reise eines expatrierten Schwärmers durch Teutschland, Böhmen, Oesterreich, Italien, Ungarn u. die Türkei, Leipzig, A. Fest'scher Verlag, 1836.

Forstmann, Eduard [Carl Georg Herloss]. *Wien wie es ist. Forsetzung der Sitten und Charaktergemälde von London und Madrid*, Leipzig, Magazine für Industrie und Literatur, 1827.

Fürst, Nicolay. *Vermischte Schriften*, Vienna, Carl Armbruster, 1823.

[Glassbrenner, Adolph]. *Bilder und Träume aus Wien*, Leipzig, Fried. Wolkman Verlag, 1836.

Gräffer, Franz. *Kleine Memoiren und Wiener Dosenstücke*, Anton Schlosser and Gustav Gugitz (eds.), Munich, Georg Müller, 1918.

[Hebenstreit, Wilhelm]. *Der Fremde in Wien und der Wiener in der Heimat*, Vienna, Carl Armbruster, 1829.

Hecke, Johann Valentin. *Wiens Kunst, Natur u. Menschen. In Vergleichen der Betrachtung mit Berlin, London u. Nordamerika*, Berlin, E.H.G. Christiani, 1826.

Heintl, Franz Ritter von. *Bemerkungen auf einer Reise von Wien nach Paris im Jahre 1831*, Vienna, Auf kosten des Verfassers, 1832.

Hermann, Georg [Georg Hermann Borchardt]. *Das Biedermeier. Im Spiegel seiner Zeit*, Hamburg, Gerhard Stalling Verlag, 1965.

Holman, James. *Travels through Russia, Siberia, Poland, Austria, Saxony, Prussia, Hanover during the years 1822, 1823, 1824*, London, Simpkin & Marshall, 1826.

[Holmes, Edward]. *A Ramble among the Musicians of Germany*, New York, Da Capo Press, 1969 (reprint of London, Hunt and Clark, 1828 edition).

Horn, Wilhelm. *Reise durch Deutschland, Ungarn, Holland, Italien, Frankreich, Grossbritanien und Irland*, Berlin, T.C.F. Enslin, 1831.

Hurter, Friedrich. *Ausflug nach Wien und Pressburg im Sommer 1839*, 2 vols., Schaffhausen, Hurt'sche Buchhandlung, 1840.

Bibliography

Jäck, Heinrich Joachim, and Joseph Heller. *Reise nach Wien, Triest, Venedig, Verona und Innsbruck*, Weimar, Landes Industrie – Comptori, 1822.

Jenny, Rudolph E. von. *Handbuch für Reisende in dem oesterreichischen Kaiserstaate*, Vienna, Anton Doll, 1822.

Klingemann, August. *Kunst und Natur – Blätter aus meinem Reisebuch*, 2 vols., Braunschweig, G.C. Meyer Verlag, 1821.

Kohl, J. G. *Austria, Vienna, Prague, Hungary, Bohemia, and the Danube*, London, Chapman & Hall, 1844.

[Langenschwarz]. *Europäische Geheimnisse eines Mediatisierten. Metternich und Europa. Wien und Oesterreich*. Hamburg, Georg Boormann, 1836.

Laube, Heinrich. *Reise durch das Biedermeier*, Vienna, Wilhelm Andermann Verlag, 1946.

Meine grosse Reise von Leipzig nach Oesterreich, Leipzig, A. Fest'schen Buchhandlung, 1835.

Menzel, Wolfgang. *Reise nach Oesterreich im Sommer 1831*, Stuttgart, Cotta'sche Buchhandlung, 1832.

Meynert, Hermann. *Herbstblüthen aus Wien*, Leipzig, C.H.F. Hartmann, 1830.

Nicolai, Friedrich, *Reise durch Deutschland, 1781*, Paul Wertheimer (ed.), Vienna, Leonhardt Verlag, 1921.

Normann, Hans [Anton J. Gross-Hoffinger]. *Wien wie es ist*, II, Leipzig and Löwenberg, Eschrich & Co., 1833.

Novello, Mary and Vincent. *A Mozart Pilgrimage being the Travel Diaries of Vincent and Mary Novello in the Year 1829*, Rosemary Hughes (ed.), Nerina Medici di Marignano (trans.), London, Novello & Co., Ltd, 1955.

Oesterreichische Zustände von einem beschaulichen Reisenden. Cassel and Leipzig, J.C. Krieger'sche Buchhandlung, 1838.

Pezzl, Johann. *Skizze von Wien: Ein Kultur- und Sittenbild aus der josefinischen Zeit*, Gustav Gugitz and Anton Schlossar (eds.), Graz, Leykam Verlag, 1923 (reprinted from 1786–90).

Beschreibung von Wien, edns 5 and 7, Vienna, Carl Armbruster. *c*. 1820 and 1826; edn 8, Vienna, Rudolf Sammer, 1841.

Pietznigg, Franz (ed.) *Mittheilungen aus Wien. Zeitgemälde des Neuesten u. Wissenwürdigsten*, Vienna, J. P. Sollinger, 1832.

Planche, J. R. *Descent of the Danube from Ratisbon to Vienna during the Autumn of 1827*, London, James Duncan, 1828.

Realis [Gerhard R. W. von Coeckelberghe zu Dützele], *Curiositäten und Memorabilien – Lexicon von Wien*, Vienna, n.p., 1846.

Reeve, Henry. *A Journal of a Residence at Vienna and Berlin 1805–1806*, London, Longman, Green & Co., 1877.

Reichardt, Johann Friedrich. *Vertraute Briefe geschrieben auf einer Reise nach Wien und den oesterreichischen Staaten zu Ende des Jahre 1808 und zu Anfang 1809*, Gustav Gugitz (ed.), Munich, Georg Müller, 1915.

'Briefe geschrieben auf einer Reise nach Wien', in *Source Readings in Music History*, ed. Oliver Strunk, New York, W. W. Norton Co., Inc., 1950, 728–40.

[Richter, Joseph]. *Das alte und neue Wien oder Es ist nicht mehr wie eh' – Ein styrische Gemälde entworfen von einem alten Laternputzer*, Vienna, Christoph Rehm, 1800.

Russell, John. *Reise durch Deutschland und einige südlich Provinzen Oestreichs in den Jahren 1820, 1821 und 1822*, Leipzig, A.G. Liebeskind, 1825.

Schaden, Adolf von. *Meister Fuchs oder humoristischer Spaziergang von Prag über Wien und Linz nach Passau*, Dessau, c. Schlieder, (*c*. 1822).

Bibliography

Schmidl, Adolf. *Wien wie es ist. Die Kaiserstadt und ihre nächsten Umgebung nach authentischen Quellen, mit besonderer Berücksichtung wissenschaflichter Anstalten und Sammlungen, und einem Anhange: 8 Tage in Wien*, Vienna, Carl Gerold, 1837.

Scalsfield, Charles [Karl Anton Postl]. *Austria as it is, or Sketches of Continental Courts by an Eyewitness.* London, Hurst, Chance and Co., 1828.

Oesterreich wie es ist, Victor Klarwill (ed. and trans.), Vienna, Kunstverlag Anton Schroll & Co., 1919.

Seufzer aus Oesterreich, Leipzig, Literarisches Museum, 1834.

[Sherer, Moyle]. *Notes and Reflections during a Ramble in Germany*, London, Longman, Ries, Orne, Brown and Green, 1827.

Sketches of Germany and the Germans, 2 vols., London, Whittaker & Co., 1836.

Slade, Adolphus. *Travels in Germany and Russia*, London, 1840.

Smart, Sir George. *Leaves from the Journals of Sir George Smart*, H. Bertram Cox (ed.), New York, Longman, Green & Co., 1907.

Spohr, Louis. *The Musical Journeys of Louis Spohr*, Henry Pleasants (ed. and trans), Norman, University of Oklahoma Press, 1961.

Stael, Madame de. *Deutschland und Frankreich*. A. E. Brinkmann (ed.), Hamburg, Hoffmann und Campe Verlag, 1941.

Stifter, Adalbert. *Aus dem alten Wien*, Gustav Wilhelm (ed.), Vienna, Oesterreichischer Bundesverlag, 1926.

Strang, John. *Germany in MDCCCXXXI*, London, John Macrone, 1836.

Strombeck, Friedrich, *Darstellungen aus einer Reise von Niedersachsen nach Wien*, Braunschweig, Vieweg und Sohn, 1839.

Trollope, Frances. *Vienna and the Austrians; some Account of a Journey through Swabia, Bavaria, the Tyrol, and Salzburg*, London, Richard Bentley, 1838.

Turnbull, Peter E. *Oesterreichs soziale und politische Zustände*, E. A. Moriarty (ed.), Leipzig, J. J. Weber, 1840.

[Tuvora, Joseph]. *Briefe aus Wien von einem Eingeborenen*, Hamburg, Hoffman und Campe, 1844.

Vertraute Briefe aus Wien, Leipzig, Theodor Thomas, 1850.

Vertraute Briefe zur Charakteristik von Wien, Görlitz, Hermsdorf und Anton, 1793.

Vogl, Johann Nepomuk. *Aus dem alten Wien*, Vienna, Prandel und Ewald, 1865.

Weber, Carl Julius. *Deutschland oder Briefe eines in Deutschland reisenden Deutschen*, Stuttgart, Hallberg'scher Verlag, 1834.

Weis, J. B. *Wien's Merwürdigkeiten mit ihrem geschichtlichen Erinnerungen. Ein Wegweiser für Fremde und Einheimische*. Vienna. In Commission bei Franz Wimmer, 1834.

Wien Chronik, Jost Perfahl (ed.), Salzburg, Bergland Buch Verlag, 1969.

MEMOIRS, DIARIES, LETTERS, PERSONAL WRITINGS

Andlaw-Birseck, Franz Xavier. *Mein Tagebuch aus Aufschreibungen der Jahre 1811–1861*, Frankfurt am Main, J. D. Säuerlanders Verlag, 1862.

Anschütz, Heinrich. *Erinnerungen aus dessen Leben und Wirken*, Vienna, Leopold Sommer, 1866.

Bauer, Wilhelm (ed.), *Briefe aus Wien*, Leipzig, Insel Verlag, n.d.

Bauernfeld, Eduard. *Gesammelte Schriften*, XII: *Aus alt und neu-Wien*, Vienna, Wilhelm Braunmüller, 1873.

Aus Bauernfelds Tagebüchern, Carl Glossy (ed.), I, Vienna, Verlag von Carl Konegen, 1895.

Bibliography

Erinnerungen aus Alt-Wien. Josef Bindtner (ed.), Vienna, Wiener Druck, 1923.

Wiener Biedermeier: Begegnungen und Erlebnisse, Oesterreich-Reihe, CVI–CVIII, Vienna, Bergland Verlag, 1960.

Beethoven, Ludwig van. *New Beethoven Letters*, Donald MacArdle and Ludwig Misch (eds.), Norman, University of Oklahoma Press, 1957.

Letters of Beethoven, Emily Anderson (ed. and trans.), New York, St Martin's Press, Inc., 1961.

Konversationshefte, IV (Aug. 1823) and v (1823–4), Karl-Heinz Köhler and Grita Herre (eds.), Leipzig, Deutscher Verlag für Musik, 1968 and 1970.

Bruchmann, Franz. *Franz Bruchmann der Freund J. Chr. Senns und des Grafen August v. Platen*, Moriz Enzinger (ed.), Innsbruck, Universitäts Verlag, 1930.

Castelli, Ignaz. *Memoiren meines Lebens*, Josef Bindtner (ed.), Munich, Georg Müller, 1913.

Memoiren meines Lebens (abridged version), Munich, Winkler Verlag, 1969.

Chezy, Helmina von. *Unvergessenes. Denkwürdigkeiten aus dem Leben Helmina von Chezy*, II, Leipzig, F. A. Brockhaus, 1858.

Costenoble, Carl Ludwig. *Aus dem Burgtheater 1818–1837. Tageblätter*, Vienna, Carl Konegen Verlag, 1889.

Deutsch, Otto Erich. *Schubert. Memoirs by his Friends*, London, Adam and Charles Black, 1958.

Schubert. A Documentary Biography, New York, Da Capo Press, 1977.

Ditters von Dittersdorf, Karl. *Lebensbeschreibung*, Norbert Miller (ed.), Munich, Kösel-Verlag, 1967.

Fareanu, A. (ed.). 'Leopold Sonnleithners Erinnerungen an Franz Schubert', *Zeitschrift für Musikwissenschaft*, I (April 1919), Part 7, 466–83.

Frankl, Ludwig August. *Erinnerungen von Ludwig August Frankl*, Stephan Bock (ed.), Prague, J. G. Calveische k.k. Hof und Universitäts Buchhandlung, 1910.

Gentz, Friedrich. *Ungedrückte Denkschriften, Tagebücher und Briefe von Friedrich von Gentz*, Gustav Schlesier (ed.), 2 vols, Mannheim, Heinrich Hoff Verlag, 1840.

Briefe von und an Friedrich von Gentz, Friedrich Carl Wittichen (ed.), Munich, Verlag R. Oldenburg, 1910.

Grillparzer, Franz. *Briefe und Tagebücher*, Carl Glossy and August Sauer (eds.), Stuttgart and Berlin, J. G. Cotta'sche Buchhandlung, n.d.

Tagebücher und Literarische Skizzenhefte (Zweiter Teil 1822 – Mitte 1830), Vienna, Anton Schroll, 1909.

Prosaschriften, Part I, XIV, Vienna, Anton Schroll & Co., 1925.

Grillparzers Selbstbiographie und Tagebücher, Vienna, A. J. Walter Verlag, 1946.

Grün, Anastasius [Anton Auersperg] *Spaziergänge eines Wiener Poeten*, Hamburg, Hoffmann & Campe, 1832.

Gyrowetz, Adalbert. *Biographie des Adalbert Gyrowetz*, Vienna, Mechitharisten-Buchdruckerei, 1848.

Hartmann, Franz. 'Hartmannische Familien Chronik'. WStB, Ja 73234.

'Tagebuch (1825–1831)'. WStB, Ja 73235.

Hartmann, Friedrich. 'Journal', WStB, Ja 73235.

Holtei, Karl von. *Vierzig Jahre*, Berlin, Berliner Lesecabinet, 1843.

Hormayr, Joseph Friedrich. *Anemonen – aus dem Tagebuch eines alten Pilgermannes*, Jena, Friederich Fromann, 1845–7.

Kübeck von Kübau, Karl. *Tagebücher*, Vienna, Gerold & Co., 1909.

Kupelwieser, Leopold. *Leopold Kupelwieser – Erinnerungen seiner Tochter*, Vienna, Jos. Roth'sche Verlagsbuchhandlung, 1902.

Bibliography

Laube, Heinrich. *Gesammelte Schriften*. I. *Erinnerungen 1810–1840*, Vienna, Wilhelm Braunmüller, 1875.

Lewald, August. *Aus Wien*, Vienna, Hirschfeld Verlag (c. 1848).

Loewe, Carl. Dr *Carl Loewes Selbstbiographie*, C. H. Bittner (ed.), Berlin, Wilhelm Müller Verlag, 1870.

Metternich, Prince Richard (ed.), *Memoirs of Prince Metternich 1815–1829*, Mrs Alexander Napier (trans.), IV, New York, Charles Scribner's Sons, 1881.

Moscheles, Charlotte. *Life of Moscheles*, A. D. Coleridge (trans.), I, London, Hurst & Blackettl, 1873.

Müller, Wenzel, 'Tagebucher', WStB, Jb 51926.

Oehlenschläger, Adam. *Briefe in die Heimat*, George Lotz (trans.), Altona, I. F. Hammerich, 1820.

Perth, Matthias. 'Tagebuch'. WStB. Parts 1 and 2.

Pichler, Caroline. *Denkwürdigkeiten aus meinem Leben*. Karl Blümml (ed.), 2 vols., Munich, Georg Müller, 1914.

Prokesch-Osten, Anton, Graf. *Briefwechsel mit Herrn von Gentz und Fürst Metternich*, Vienna, Carl Gerolds Sohn Verlag, 1881.

Aus dem Tagebüchern des Grafen Prokesch von Osten: 1830–1834, Vienna, Verlag von Christoph Reissers Söhne, 1909.

Rosenbaum, Josef Karl. 'Tagebücher 1821–1829'. NB, Manuscript Sammlung, Sn 203–4.

Die Tagebücher von Joseph Carl Rosenbaum 1770–1829, Else Radant (ed.), *Haydn Jahrbuch*, v, Vienna, Theodor Presser, 1968.

Saphir, Moritz Gottlieb. *Humoristiche Schriften*. I: *Meine Memoiren*. Karl Meyerstein (ed.), Berlin, Th. Knaur Nachf., 1889.

Schreyvogel, Josef. *Josef Schreyvogels Tagebücher 1810–1823*, Karl Glossy (ed.), II and III, Berlin, Verlag der Gesellschaft für Theatergeschichte, 1903.

Schröder, Sophie. *Briefe von Sophie Schröder*, Heinrich Stümcke (ed.), Berlin, Selbstverlag der Gesellschaft für Theatergeschichte, 1910.

Schubert, Franz. *Franz Schubert's Letters and Other Writings*, Otto Erich Deutsch (ed.), New York, Alfred Knopf, 1928.

Schwind, Moritz von. *Moritz von Schwinds Briefe*, Otto Stoessl (ed.), Leipzig, Bibliographische Institut, n.d.

Sonneck, O. (ed.) *Beethoven. Impressions by his Contemporaries*, New York, Dover Publishing, 1954.

Sonnleithner, Leopold von. 'Musikalische Skizzen aus Alt-Wien', *Recensionen und Mittheilungen über Theater und Musik*, VII, Vienna, 1861, 737–47, 753–78.

Spaun, Joseph. 'Aus den Lebenserinnerungen Joseph Spauns', Karl Glossy (ed.), *Jahrbuch der Grillparzer Gesellschaft*, VIII (1898), 275–303.

Spohr, Louis. *Lebenserinnerungen*, Foler Göthel (ed.), Tutzing, Hans Schneider, 1968.

Thürheim, Lulu von, Gräfin. *Mein Leben – Erinnerungen aus Oesterreichs Grosser Welt*, Rene van Rhyn (trans.), 4 vols., Munich, Georg Müller Verlag, 1913.

Ticknor, George. *Life, Letters and Journals of George Ticknor*, New York, Houghton, Mifflin & Co., 1909.

Varnhagen, Rahel. *Rahel Varnhagen und ihre Zeit* (Briefe 1800–33), Friedrich Kemp (ed.), Munich, Kösel Verlag, 1968.

Weckbecker, Hugo, Freiherr von. *Von Maria Theresia zu Franz Joseph – Zwei Lebensbilder aus dem alten Oesterreich*, Wilhelm Weckbecker (ed.), Part 2, Berlin, Verlag für Kultur-politik, 1929.

Bibliography

Wilmot, Martha. *More Letters from Martha Wilmot: Impressions of Vienna 1819–1829*. Introduction by Marchioness of Londonderry and H. M. Hyde, London, Macmillan & Co., Ltd, 1935.

SECONDARY SOURCES

Banik-Schweitzer, Renate and Wolfgang Pircher. 'Zur Wohnsituation des Massen im Wien des Vormärz', *Forschungen und Beiträge zur Wiener Stadtgeschichte*, VIII, (1980), 133–74.

Bäuerle, Adolf, ed., *Was verdankt Oesterreich der beglückenden Regierung Sr. Majestät Kaiser Franz I?*, Vienna, Anton v. Haykul, 1834.

Beidtel, Ignaz. *Geschichte der Oesterreichischen Staatsverwaltung 1740–1848*, Frankfurt a.M, Sauer & Auvermann, 1968.

Biba, Otto. 'Die Wiener Kirchenmusik um 1783', *Beiträge zur Musikgeschichte des 18. Jahrhunderts*, I (1971), 7–67.

Franz Schubert in den musikalischen Abendunterhaltungen der Gesellschaft der Musikfreunde', *Schubert Studien*, 19 (1978), 7–31.

'Franz Schubert und die Gesellschaft der Musikfreunde in Wien', *Bericht Schubert Kongress Wien 1978*, Graz, Akademische Druck und Verlagsanstalt, 1978.

Bibl, Viktor. *Die Niederoesterreichischen Stände im Vormärz*, Vienna, Gerlach & Weidling, 1911.

Die Wiener Polizei: Eine kulturische Studie, Vienna and Leipzig, Stein Verlag, 1927.

Bietack, Wilhelm. *Das Lebensgefühl des 'Biedermeier' in der oesterreichischen Dichtung*, Vienna, Wilhelm Braunmüller, 1931.

Bittner, Ludwig, ed., 'Chronologisches Verzeichnis der oesterreichischen Staatsverträge', *Kommission für neuere Geschichte Oesterreichs*, VIII (1909).

Blümml, Emil and Gustav Gugitz. *Von Leuten und Zeiten im alten Wien*, Vienna, Gerlach & Wiedling, 1922.

Boehn, Max von. *Biedermeier. Deutschland von 1815–1847*, Berlin, Bruno Cassierer, n.d.

Brion, Marcel. *Daily Life in the Vienna of Mozart and Schubert*, Jean Stewart (trans.), New York, Macmillan, 1962.

Brown, Maurice J. E. *Schubert – A Critical Biography*, London, Macmillan & Co., 1958.

Essays on Schubert, New York, St Martin's Press, 1966.

Brunner, Otto. 'Staat und Gesellschaft im vormärzlichen Oesterreich im Speigel von I. Beidtels Geschichte der oesterreichischen Staatsverwaltung 1740–1848', *Staat und Gesellschaft im deutschen Vormärz 1815–1848, Industrielle Welt*, I (1962).

Carner, Mosco. *The Waltz*. Sir George Franckenstein and Otto E. Deutsch (eds.), London, Max Parrish & Co. Ltd, 1948.

Cooper, Martin. *Beethoven – The Last Decade 1817–1827*, London, Oxford University Press, 1970.

Deutsch, Otto Erich. 'Schubert's Income', *Music and Letters*, XXXVI (1955) 165–6.

Schubert Thematic Catalogue of all his works, New York, W. W. Norton & Co., 1950.

Doblinger, Max, 'Der Burschenschaftliche Gedanke auf Oesterreichs Hochschulen vor 1859', *Quellen und Darstellungen zur Geschichte der Burschenschaft und der deutschen Einheitsbewegung*, VIII (1966) 31–150.

Farmer, Henry G. *The Rise and Development of Military Music*, London, W. Reeves, 1912.

Fesl, Maria, 'Die Städte um Wien und ihre Rolle im Wandel der Zeit', *Forschungen zur deutschen Landeskunde*, CLI, Bad Godesberg, Selbstverlag der Bundesanstalt für Landeskunde & Raumforschung, 1968.

Bibliography

Fournier, August. *Die Geheimpolizei auf die Wiener Congress*, Vienna, F. Tempsky, 1913.

Gartenburg, Egon. *Johann Strauss: The End of an Era*, University Park, Pennsylvania State University Press, 1974.

Gesetzbuch über Verbrechen und schwere Polizey-Uebertretungen, Vienna, k.k. Hof & Staats Druckerey, 1814–15.

Gesetze und Anordnungen für die deutsche Oper der k.k. Hoftheater, Vienna, Degen'schen Buchhandlung, 1807.

Glossy, Carl, 'Grillparzer und die Ludlamshöhle', *Jahrbuch der Grillparzer Gesellschaft* VIII (1895), 251–5.

Wiener Studien und Dokumente, Vienna, Steyermühl Verlag, 1933.

'Zur Geschichte der Theater Wiens II (1821–1830)', *Jahrbuch der Grillparzer Gesellschaft*, XXV (1920), vi–xxiii; 1–150.

Gotwals, Vernon, 'Joseph Haydn's Last Will and Testament', *The Musical Quarterly*, XLVII (1961), 334–7.

Hanslick, Eduard. *Geschichte des Concertwesens in Wien*, 2 vols., Vienna, Wilhelm Braunmüller, 1869.

Helfert, Freiherr A. von. *Aloys Fischer – Leben und Charakterbild*, Innsbruck, Vereinsbuchhandlung, 1885.

Hickmann, E. *Wien im XIX Jahrhundert*, Vienna, Alfred Holder, 1903.

Houben, H. *Das gefesselte Biedermeier – Literatur, Kultur, Zensur in der guten alten Zeit*, Leipzig, Hässel Verlag, 1924.

Jahrbuch der Tonkunst von Wien und Prag, Vienna, Schönfelder Verlag, 1796.

Janik, Allan, and Stephen Toulmin. *Wittgenstein's Vienna*, New York, Simon & Schuster, 1973.

Kalischer, Peter. *Beethoven und seine Zeitgenossen*, Berlin, Simon und Loeffler, IV, 1908.

Kann, Robert A. *A Study in Austrian Intellectual History*, New York, Frederick A. Praeger, 1960.

Kier, Herfrid. *Raphael Georg Kiesewetter (1773–1850)*. XIII, *Studien zur Musikgeschichte des 19. Jahrhunderts*, Regensburg, Bosse Verlag, 1968.

Kinsky, Georg. *Das Werk Beethovens – thematisch bibliographisch Verzeichniss*. Munich, G. Henle Verlag, 1955.

Kirchenordnung-Erklärendes Handbuch der musikalischen Gottesdienste für Kapellmeister, Regenschori, Sänger, Tonkünstler, Vienna, J. B. Wallishauser, 1828.

Kissinger, Henry A. *A World Restored*. Boston, Houghton, Mifflin, n.d.

Klein, Rudolf. 'Traditionsstätten der Wiener Konzertpflege', *Oesterreichische Musikzeitschrift*, XXV, Part 5 (1970), 290–9.

Knessl, Lothar, *Musik im Biedermeier*, Linz, Oesterreichische Stickstoffwerke, AG, 1968.

Kobald, Karl. *Beethoven – seine Beziehung zu Wiens Kunst und Kultur, Gesellschaft und Landschaft*, Vienna, Amalthea Verlag, 1964.

Lach, Robert. *Geschichte der Staatsakademie und Hochschule für Musik und Darstellende Kunst in Wien*, Vienna, E. Strache, 1927.

Leitich, Ann Tizia. *Wiener Biedermeier*, Bielefeld, Helhage & Klasing, 1941.

Lennhoff, Eugen. *Politische Geheimbünde*, Munich and Vienna, Georg Müller, 1968.

Liechtenstern, Josef M. *Grundlinien einer Statistik des oesterreichischen Kaiserthums nach dessen gegenwärtigen Verhältnissen*, Vienna, Carl Gerold, 1817.

Loesser, Arthur. *Men, Women and Pianos. A Social History*, New York, Simon & Schuster, 1954.

Ludwig, O. Vincenz. *Altwiener Biedermeiermusikanten*, Vienna, Verlag der Bukem, 1924.

Bibliography

Mandell, Eric. *The Jews of Austria*, Josèf Fraenkel (ed.), London, Vallentine, Mitchell & Co., Ltd, 1967.

Marek, George R. *Beethoven. Biography of a Genius*, New York, Thomas Y. Crowell Co., 1969.

Marx, Julius. *Die oesterreichische Zensur im Vormärz*, Munich, R. Oldenbourg, 1959.
  'Polizei und Studenten. Ein Beitrag zur Vorgeschichte des 13. März 1848 in Wien', *Jahrbuch des Vereins für Geschichte der Stadt Wien*, XIX–XX (1963–4), 218–50.

Mayer, Franz, Raimund F. Kaindl and Hans Pirchegger. *Geschichte und Kulturleben Oesterreichs, Von 1792 bis zum Staatsvertrag von 1955*, III, Vienna, Wilhelm Braunmüller, 1965.

Mayr, Josef Karl. *Wien im Zeitalter Napoleons-Staatfinanzen, Lebensverhältnisse, Beamte, und Militär*, Vienna, Verlag Gottlieb & Cie, 1940.

Meisl, Carl (ed.). *Taschenbuch des kaiser-königlichen privil. Leopoldstädter Theaters für das Jahr 1820, 1821–23*, Vienna, 1820–3.

Memoirs of the Secret Societies of the South of Italy Particularly the Carbonari, London, John Murray, 1821.

Mirow, Franz. *Zwischenaktsmusik und Bühnenmusik des deutschen Theaters in der klassischen Zeit*, Berlin, Selbstverlag der Gesellschaft fur Theatergeschichte, XXXVII (1927).

Naumann, Hans, 'Studien über den Bänkelgesang', *Primitive Gemeinschaftskultur, Beiträge zur Volkskunde und Mythologie*, Jena (1921), 168–90.

Oberhummer, Hermann. *Dienstlaufbahn der Leiter und Stellvertreter der Wiener Polizeibehörden seit der Umwandlung des Theresianischen Polizeiamtes in die Polizeioberdirektion*, Vienna, Polizeidirektion, 1929.
  Die Wiener Polizei, 2 vols., Vienna, Gerold & Cox, 1937.

Pemmer, Hans. 'Alt Wiener Gast und Vergnügens Stätten', (typed manuscript in WStB).

Perger, Richard and Robert Hirschfeld. *Geschichte der k.k. Gesellschaft der Musikfreunde in Wien*, Vienna, 1912.

Pohl, C. F. *Die Gesellschaft der Musikfreunde des oesterreichischen Kaiserstaates und ihr Conservatorium*, Vienna, Wilhelm Braunmüller, 1871.

Politzer, Hans, 'Alt Wiener Theaterlieder', *Das Schweigen der Sirenen; Studien zur deutschen und oesterreichischen Literatur*, Stuttgart, J. B. Metzlersche Verlagsbuchhandlung, 1968, 160–84.

Prohaska, Dorothy. *Raimund and Vienna*, Cambridge, Cambridge University Press, 1970.

Rameis, Emil. *Die oesterreichische Militärmusik von ihrem Anfänge bis zum Jahre 1918*, Eugen Brixel (ed.), Tutzing, Hans Schneider, 1976.

Rebiczek, Franz. *Der Wiener Volks- und Bänkelgesang in den Jahren 1800–1848*, Vienna, Gerlach & Weidling, n.d.

Reed, Schubert. *Schubert. The Final Years*, New York, St Martin's Press, 1972.

Reischl, Friedrich, *Wien zur Biedermeierzeit*, Vienna, Gerlach & Weidling, 1921.

Rieder, Heinz. *Wiener Vormärz: das Theater, das literarische Leben, die Zensur. Oesterreich-Reihe*, LXVIII, Vienna, Bergland Verlag, 1959.

Rommel, Otto (ed.). *Der oesterreichische Vormärz*, Leipzig, Philipp Reclam, 1931.
  Die Alt Wiener Volkskomödie, Vienna, Anton Schroll & Co., 1953.

Sammlung der Gesetze für das Erzherzogthum Oesterreich unter der Enns, Vienna, k.k. Hof und Staat Aerial Drückerey, 1815–35.

Sandgruber, Roman, 'Indikatoren des Lebensstandards in Wien in der ersten Hälfte des 19. Jahrhunderts', *Forschungen und Beiträge zur Wiener Stadtgeschichte*, VIII (1980), 57–74.

Bibliography

Sauer, August. *Aus dem alten Oesterreich. Kleine Beiträge zur Lebensgeschichte Grillparzers und zur Charakteristik seiner Zeit*, Prague, 1895.

Schaffran, Emerich. *Vormärzliches Wien*, Vienna, Adolf Leiser Verlag, 1939.

Schenk, E., 'Der Langaus', *Studia musicologia*, III (1962) 310–16.

Schindler, Anton Felix. *Beethoven as I knew him*. Donald MacArdle (ed.), Chapel Hill, University of North Carolina Press, 1966.

Schliemann, Hans. *Wiener Schattenbilder*, Ed. Poetzl (ed.), Vienna, Robert Mohr, n.d.

Schlögl, Friedrich. *Wiener Blut*, Vienna, L. Rosner, 1875.

Schmidt, August. *Denksteine*, Vienna, Mechitharisten – Congregation, 1848.

Schönholtz, Friedrich Anton von. *Traditionen zur Charakteristik Oesterreichs seines Staats-und Volksleben unter Franz I*, Gustav Gugitz (ed.), Munich, Georg Müller, 1914.

Sengle, Friedrich. *Biedermeier*, Stuttgart, J. B. Metzler, 1972.

Slokar, Johann. *Geschichte der oesterreichischen Industrie und ihrer Förderung unter Kaiser Franz I.*, Vienna. F. Tempsky, 1914.

Smekal, Richard (ed.). *Altwiener Theaterlieder von Hanswürst bis Nestroy*, Vienna, Wiener Literarische Anstalt, 1920.

Solomon, Maynard, *Beethoven*, New York, Schirmer Books, 1977.

Spiel, Hilde. *Fanny von Arnstein oder die Emanzipation*, Frankfurt a.M., S. Fischer Verlag, 1962.

Spohr, Louis, 'Aufruf an deutsche Komponisten', *Allgemeine musikalische Zeitung*, XXIX (1823), columns 457–64.

Stekl, Hannes. *Oesterreichs Aristokratie im Vormärz*, Munich, R. Oldenbourg Verlag, 1973.

Stöger, Viktor, 'Der Apollo Saal', *Alt Wien Monatsschrift für Wiener Art und Sprache*, IV (1897), no. 2, 24; no. 3, 41–5; no. 4, 61–5.

Stubenrauch, Moritz. *Statistische Darstellung des Vereinswesens im Kaiserthume Oesterreich*. Vienna, k.k. Hof & Staats Druckerey, 1857.

Thayer, Alexander Wheelock. *Life of Beethoven*, Elliot Forbes (ed.), Princeton, Princeton University Press, 1964.

Tietze, Hans (ed.), *Das vormärzliche Wien in Wort und Bild*, Vienna, Anton Schroll & Co., 1925.

Till, Rudolf. *Geschichte der Wiener Stadtverwaltung in den letzten zweihundert Jahren*, Vienna, Verlag für Jugend und Volk, 1957.

Ullrich, Hermann, 'Aus vormärzlichen Konzertsälen Wiens', *Jahrbuch des Verein für Geschichte der Stadt Wien*, XXVIII (1972), 106–30.

Weber, William. *Music and the Middle Class*, New York, Holmes and Meier Publishers, Inc., 1975.

Werner, Oskar (ed.). *Arien und Bänkel aus Alt Wien*, Leipzig, Insel Verlag, 1914.

Wierzynski, Casimir. *The Life and Death of Chopin*. Norbert Guterman (trans.), New York, Simon & Schuster, 1949.

Wiesner, Adolph. *Denkwürdigkeiten der Oesterreichischen Zensur vom Zeitalter der Reformation bis auf die Gegenwart*, Stuttgart, Adolph Krabbe, 1847.

Witzmann, Richard. *Der Ländler in Wien*, Vienna, Arbeitstelle für dem Volkskundeatlas in Oesterreich, 1976.

Wolf, Gerson. *Geschichte der Juden in Wien (1156–1876)*, Vienna, Geyer Edition, 1974.

Zausmer, Otto. 'Der Ludlamshöhle Glück und Ende', *Jahrbuch der Grillparzer Gesellschaft*, XXXIII (1932–3), 86–112.

Lebendes, Schaffendes Biedermeier, Vienna, Wiener Urania, 1936.

Zenker, Ernest. *Geschichte des Wiener Journalismus*, Vienna, Braunmüller, 1892.

Bibliography

Zoder, Elisabeth, 'Vom Tanz im Alten Wien', *Oesterreichische Musikzeitschrift*, XXIII (1968), 479–94.

DISSERTATIONS

Aspöck, Ruth, 'Beitrag zu einer Theorie der Unterhaltung dargestellt an Wiener Vergnügen im 19. Jahrhundert', Vienna, 1972.

Bammer, Winfried. 'Beiträge zur Sozialstruktur der Bevölkerung Wiens (auf Grund der Verlassenschaftakten des Jahres 1830)', Vienna, 1968.

Fahrnberger, Wilma. 'Die Wiener Jahrbücher der Literatur und ihre Einflussnahme auf die Gestaltung der öffentlichen Meinung', Vienna, 1950.

Frieben, Birgit. 'Die Sozialstruktur Wiens am Anfang des Vormärz', Vienna, 1966.

Hanson, Alice M. 'The Social and Economic Context of Music in Vienna from 1815 to 1830', Urbana, Illinois, 1980.

Jäger-Sustenau, Hans. 'Die geadelten Judenfamilien im vormärzlichen Wien', Vienna, 1950.

Obrovski, Herta. 'Die Wiener Vereinswesen im Vormärz', Vienna, 1970.

Ullrich, Anton. 'Die Musik im Wiener Almanachen von 1777–1817', Vienna, 1953.

INDEX

Index

Index

Index

Vienna (*cont.*)
207 n3; society 18–19, 70ff, 154ff,
169, 191, 193; Viennese character and
reputation 11, 13–14, 52, 129, 163,
178–9, 217 n4
Vogel, Michael 11, 120, 124, 125, 186,
206

waltz 150, 162–3, 168
Weber, Carl Maria von 57, 58, 82, 202;
performance of works 62, 64, 65–6,
74, 99, 213 n20

Weigl, Josef 95, 132, 136, 188, 201
Wiener Währung (WW) 3
Winter Riding School
(Winterreitschule) 93, 160
Witticzek, Josef 119–20, 205
Wranitsky [Anton Sr] 8

Zedlitz, Josef 75, 193
zither players 169, 172
Zizius, Johann 121–2
Zögling concerts *see* conservatory